WINTHROP FOUNDATIONS OF PUBLIC MANAGE

D0447757

Toward a Functioning Federalism

David B. Walker

Assistant Director,
Advisory Commission on Intergovernmental Relations

Winthrop Publishers, Inc.

Cambridge, Massachusetts

Library of Congress Cataloging in Publication Data

Walker, David Bradstreet, 1927–
  Toward a functioning federalism.

  (Foundations of public management series)
  Includes index.
  1. Federal government—United States—History.
  2. Intergovernmental fiscal relations—United States—
  History. I. Title. II. Series.
  JK311.W18   321.02'0973   81-2123
  ISBN 0-87626-894-7   AACR2
  ISBN 0-87626-893-9 (pbk.)

Design by David Ford

Winthrop Foundations of Public Management Series

© 1981 by Winthrop Publishers, Inc.
  17 Dunster Street, Cambridge, Massachusetts 02138

Printed in the United States of America

10 9 8 7 6 5 4 3 2 1

To Melissa, Stephen, and Justin

Contents

Foreword by Charles H. Levine   xi

Preface   xiii

PART I: AN OVERVIEW OF THE CURRENT CONDITION

1. Signs of the System's Overload   3

The Muncie Story/ Twelve Dimensions of the Dramatic
Change/ Conclusion/ Notes to Chapter 1

PART II: EIGHTEEN SCORE YEARS OF EVOLUTION
AND ADAPTATION

2. The Beginnings of American Federalism and
Its Intergovernmental Relations, 1620-1789   19

Introduction/ How It Began/ The Constitutional
Convention: Creativity Under Difficult Circumstances/
Notes to Chapter 2

3. From Dual to Cooperative Federalism, 1790-1960 46

Introduction/ The Dual Federalism of the Rural Republic
(1789-1860)/ The Second Era: Dual Federalism, with
Differences (1861-1930)/ The Rise and Maturation of
Cooperative Federalism (1930-1960)/ Notes to Chapter 3

Foreword to the Winthrop Foundations of Public Management Series

Over the past several years growing interest and concern about the management of government have paralleled the growth of government itself. As a result, the study of public administration has been infused with new ideas and new approaches, giving it a new intellectual vitality and excitement. This has spread to those who must grapple with public problems as well as to those who study, teach, and conduct research about the public sector.

The books in the Winthrop Foundations of Public Management Series are intended to convey the new dynamism of public management. Each is intended to analyze a major aspect of public management—for example, intergovernmental relations, budgeting, human resources, decision making, organization behavior, and program management—by examining closely the blend of administrative, legal, political, and economic factors involved in producing government structures, processes, and outputs. The authors have approached their task by integrating the latest theoretical thinking with their empirical research to account for the behavior of public managers and organizations and the role of goals, functions, and norms in ongoing organizational arrangements. In every case the authors have stepped beyond the boundaries of a single discipline to search widely for perspectives, approaches, and research that might improve our understanding of public sector operations and enhance governmental performance.

The readers of this series—be they students taking an undergraduate course in public administration, those enrolled in a professional master's degree program, or people employed full time as public managers—should find the books uniformly readable, insightful, and useful. Readers should come to better understand and more fully appreciate the distinctive features of public management and organizations, and the difficulties involved in improving governmental performance in a democratic system that values accountability, equity, and rationality.

Charles H. Levine

Preface

Over the past decade and a half, a new system of domestic government has emerged in the United States—one whose degree of
complexity and interdependency, extent of interlevel contacts
and constraints, and vastly expanded scope of intergovernmental
financing and servicing arrangements are in marked contrast to
the simpler, more separated features of its predecessor patterns of
the nineteen-fifties and certainly of the twenties. The broad outlines of these dramatic recent developments are set forth in the
first chapter of this book.

To place the current system in its proper historical perspective, the intent of the Founding Fathers is probed and the first
three eras of American intergovernmental history (1790-1860,
1860-1930, and 1930-1960) are examined briefly in the next
two chapters. Against this historical backdrop, the "newness" of
today's pattern of intergovernmental relations stands out clearly.
The system, after all, was intended originally to function chiefly
with minimal intergovernmental interaction and little "sharing"
of functional responsibilities, and during the fourteen decades
from 1790 to 1930 this was the dominant practice. Moreover,
while the New Deal and its aftermath generated a somewhat
greater federal-state-local collaboration in the provision of services,
the fairly limited scope of the intergovernmental relationships of
this period only underscores the dramatic changes that have occurred since 1960.

This present system, then, represents a definite break with the past. It was and is shaped primarily by a welter of dynamic forces—judicial, fiscal, servicing, attitudinal, social, political, and representational—that were unleashed primarily in the mid-sixties. These were strengthened in the seventies, and are analyzed at some length in chapters 4 through 8. This recent trend toward thrusting nearly every facet of domestic American policy into the intergovernmental arena—from national concerns (like income maintenance programs) to clearly local ones (like bikeways, noise pollution, and rat control)—has created major problems in the areas of finances, administration, and official accountability. After pondering the operations and outputs of this heavily overloaded system, many observers, including the author, question the functional capability of contemporary American federalism, and some even weigh seriously alternative proposals for drastic reform.

This volume traces the evolution of American federalism from its beginnings to the present. By detailing the judicial, financial, servicing, and political developments that comprise this chronicle, the dramatic differences and the increasing dysfunctionality that characterize contemporary American federalism and its maze of intergovernmental relationships are highlighted.

What emerges from this analysis may provide fresh insights to political scientists, public administrators, policy analysts, and even practicing politicians. Above all, however, it is intended to give to students of American government a clearer understanding of our federalist tradition, of the intricate workings of our contemporary domestic government process, and of the forces that helped shape them.

A study of this kind inevitably involves others, though all who have helped shape it cannot possibly be cited. Special mention, however, should be accorded to those who reviewed the manuscript during its evolution: David R. Beam, Cynthia Cates Colella, Bruce D. McDowell, Carol J. Monical, Albert J. Richter, and Mavis Mann Reeves. Samuel Beer and Charles Levine were invaluable in their review and critique of the final work, and without the typing assistance of Linda S. Silberg and Lynn Cara Schwalje, and the copyediting skills of Anne Lunt, few of the deadlines would have been met. Full responsibility for the content of the interpretations in this study, of course, rests with the author.

TOWARD A
FUNCTIONING
FEDERALISM

PART

An Overview of the Current Condition

1

Signs
of the
System's
Overload

THE MUNCIE STORY

Muncie, Indiana (pop. 83,000) has been cited and studied as the typical American city. Ever since the nineteen twenties, when Robert S. and Helen Merrell Lynd exhaustively examined it for their sociological classics (*Middletown* [1929] and its sequel *Middletown in Transition* [1937]), this flat midwestern town has served as a microcosm of the nation's attitudes and beliefs. According to recent reports, Muncie is mad at, but dependent on, the system.[1]

"In 1924, the federal government was symbolized by the post office and the American flag," explains sociologist Theodore Caplow. "Today, two-thirds of the households in Muncie depend on federal funds, to some extent."[2]

According to Penelope Austin, Caplow's research colleague, between 1968 and 1977 $679,357,000 in federal aid and direct payments flowed into Muncie from twenty-nine agencies through 976 programs—a dollar figure four times what the local leadership thought it was.

Despite its size, Muncie faces many of the challenges confronting many older cities: the disappearance of manufacturing jobs (some five thousand since 1970), the trek of the affluent to the suburbs, a loss of retail trade to suburban malls, an overbuilt school system now facing the need to close some facilities, an inadequate bus system, a merit-based but unionized municipal

bureaucracy that seems less productive and vastly more costly than its patronage-dominated predecessor, a declining local revenue base, and a state-imposed property-tax lid since 1974.

Some, but not all, of these local conditions help explain why social security benefits to Muncie residents now come to about $30 million annually; why welfare aid comes to $10 million; why $10 million in federal aid helped build the new sanitary system; why the public schools got $1 million in 1978 from a range of federal grants; why the bus system was supported with $500,000 in mass transit funds; why Ball State University, the biggest employer in the city, was allotted $11 million in scholarship funds in 1978 and $3 million more for research efforts; and why 38 percent of Ball Memorial Hospital's patients relied on Medicare and Medicaid to pay their bills last year. These figures only begin to chronicle Muncie's reliance on federal aid and to hint at the degree of federal involvement today in the family and community life of its citizens.

What is the response to this exploding federal presence from Munsonians? Contemporary researchers find them almost as ambivalent about contemporary federal activism as their parents and grandparents were to the efforts of the New Deal in the Depression-ridden thirties. Both cases reveal an inability to reconcile the traditional feeling of self-reliance with seeking and receiving greater help from Washington. As Austin explains it: "The ideology is still independence at the same time that anybody in government who knows anything about finance has his hand stretched out. 'Throw the feds out,' is still the rallying cry, but that's not a viable option because the local property taxes won't support the local programs."[3]

When a pair of newspaper reporters quizzed Munsonians on their attitudes toward the federal government and its aid programs early this year, "nary a friend of federalism (i.e., the federal government) could be found, from the Workingman's Donut Shop to the Delaware Country Club."[4] Criticism was as strong in blue-collar neighborhoods as among the more well-to-do. And this in a community that still matches the nation's average family size (3.9 members), its income ($16,000), median age (29.4), and politics (2-1 Democratic registration, a 51-49 percent vote for Carter in 1976 and a 55 percent vote for Reagan in 1980's three-

way contest). If Muncie is the nation's microcosm, the "mutinous" mood of its citizenry says a great deal about the condition of contemporary federalism, the labyrinth of intergovernmental relations that underlies it, and the public philosophy that once sustained it.

How Typical Is Muncie?

Muncie clearly has experienced a fundamental change in its relations with the federal government since the thirties (as well as with its state government, though this was not highlighted in the above case study). And the ever-increasing number, variety, fiscal significance, and administrative complexity of these vastly expanded contacts with the federal government suggest a basically transformed rather than a merely adapting pattern of intergovernmental relations. Moreover, the local reactions to these seemingly disconnected but dramatic federal program developments underscore one of the fundamental difficulties of a system wherein the gap between revenue raising and service provision is growing wider and wider.

But are these dimensions of change as seen from and reflected in Muncie true of the nation as a whole? And what of the states, the presumed legal parents of the localities, in this time of transformation? From a system-wide vantage point, one stark generalization can be made: never have the funding, functioning, administration, and staffing of so wide a range of state and especially local services been as "intergovernmentalized" as they are today. The Muncie story, then, is characteristic. If anything, it understates the complexity and breadth of the cities' intergovernmental links and their constraining influence, since it did not cover a range of other federal-aid-related and recent state developments.

Two principal reasons for this increasing and incessant intergovernmentalization of the system are the phenomenal recent expansion of the federal assistance system, along with a range of closely related regulatory developments, and marked changes in the states' fiscal and regulatory policies toward their localities since the mid-sixties. In combination, these have produced a multiplying of—not a mere adding to—federal-state, federal-multistate, federal-state-local, federal-local, federal-state-regional-local, federal-multilocal, and even federal-quasi-private linkages and interdependencies (if not dependencies) that characterize the present system (nonsystem) of American intergovernmental relations. Hence the adjective *overloaded.*

TWELVE DIMENSIONS OF THE DRAMATIC CHANGE

What are some of the specifics of the system's overload? Turning first to the prime conditioner of the current system, federal assistance programs, the following merit attention:[5]

1. *The deluge of federal-aid dollars,* involving more than a quadrupling of the outlays to state and local governments between 1968 and 1979 (reaching an estimated $82.1 billion in 1979; see table 1-1), which even in terms of constant dollars amounted to almost a doubling of the 1968 total.

2. *A steady proliferation in the number of programs,* with a more than 50 percent hike in the separately authorized and funded grants during the same period (reaching the 500 mark at the end of 1978), and this despite the constraining efforts of two conservative presidents.

3. *A near perfecting of the Johnsonian theory of panoramic partnership,* with those now directly eligible for one or more federal aids including all of those of the Creative Federalism period—all of the states, some special districts, some urban cities and counties, some school districts, and some nonprofit units—as well as a whole range of new ones: all other local general governments, including towns and townships, almost all school districts, additional special districts and authorities, and more than 1800 substate regional bodies (encouraged largely by some thirty federal programs). And all this the result of the continuation of most of the Great Society programs and, more significantly, the enactment of new ones in the seventies—such as general revenue sharing (GRS, 1972), the Comprehensive Employment and Training Act (CETA, 1973), the community development block grant (CDBG, 1974), and three counter-cyclical programs (1975-77) whose eligibility and entitlement provisions converted a host of local governments into new direct recipients of federal assistance.

4. *A shift in the power position of these various "partners,"*

Table 1-1   Federal Grants-in-Aid as a Percentage of State-Local Receipts from Own Sources, 1960–1980 (dollar amounts in billions)

Fiscal year[1]	Federal grants		State-local receipts from own sources[2]		Federal grants as a percent of state-local receipts from own sources
	Amount	Percent increase	Amount	Percent increase	
1960	$ 7.0	7.7%	$ 41.6	10.1%	16.8%
1961	7.1	1.4	44.9	7.9	15.8
1962	7.9	11.3	48.7	8.5	16.2
1963	8.6	8.9	52.2	7.2	16.5
1964	10.1	17.4	56.5	8.2	17.9
1965	10.9	7.9	61.6	9.0	17.7
1966	13.0	19.3	67.0	8.8	19.3
1967	15.2	16.9	73.9	10.3	20.6
1968	18.6	22.4	82.9	12.2	22.4
1969	20.3	9.1	93.9	13.3	21.6
1970	24.0	18.2	105.0	11.8	22.9
1971	28.1	17.1	116.6	11.0	24.1
1972	34.4	22.4	131.6	12.9	26.1
1973	41.8	21.5	146.9	11.6	28.5
1974	43.4	3.8	158.9	8.2	27.3
1975	49.8	14.7	171.4	7.9	29.1
1976	59.1	18.7	190.2	11.0	31.1
1977	68.4	15.7	221.0	16.2	31.0
1978	77.9	13.9	245.4	11.0	31.7
1979	82.9	6.4	268.6	9.5	30.9
1980 est.	89.8	8.3	294.5	9.6	30.15

1. Data for 1960 through 1976 are for fiscal years ending June 30; for 1977 through 1980, for fiscal years ending September 30.
2. As defined in the national income accounts.
Source: ACIR, News Release, 24 March 1980, Washington, D.C.

with the states occupying a lesser yet still powerful recipient position, receiving about 75 percent of all federal aid to states and localities. Cities, counties, and school districts assumed a more significant role than ever before. Direct assistance to the localities rose from 10 percent of the total of federal aid in 1965 to 25 percent in 1977 (see table 1-2), thanks largely to the new pro-

Table 1-2   Federal Grants That Went Directly and (with a Few Exceptions) Exclusively[1] to Local Governments: FYs 1968 and 1977 (estimated)

	1968	1977
General revenue sharing	. . . . .	$4436[1]
General support aid	. . . . .	1133[1]
Block grants		
CETA—Title I	. . . . .	1083[1]
Community development	. . . . .	2089
Categorical grants		
Local public works	. . . . .	577
CETA—Titles II and VI	. . . . .	2467-3242[1]
Other	$2318	4634
	$2318	$16,419-$17,194
Percentage of total federal grants	12.5%	24.0-25.1%

1. Four items listed here did not go exclusively to local governments but it was possible to separate out the local portion (estimated), which is shown here. The four are general revenue sharing, general support aid (ARFA), CETA—Title I, and CETA—Titles II and VI. GRS and ARFA were split 2/3 local, 1/3 state.

grams cited above, all of which either bypassed the states or left them in a minor role. Random impressions suggest that this shift in influence is partly reflected in the relationship among the various public interest groups representing the states, counties, and cities in Washington. Meanwhile the federal government still plays a senior partner role fiscally, but its administrative capacity, collaborative intentions, and program purposes now are being questioned by the states and localities with considerable vigor.

5. *More grant dollars* (about 75 percent) now flow pursuant to congressionally mandated formulas than was the case a decade ago, thanks to the fact that GRS, most of the funds under all of the block grants, and all of the aid from formula-based and open-ended categoricals are in this group. A major factor in this development was the designing in the seventies of substate allocational formulas for the newer forms of aid going directly to units of local general government, and this, in turn, has prompted a new style of "grantsmanship," wherein energetic efforts are mounted

to help Congress fashion the formulas and to affect the eligibility provisions.

6. *Ever-expanding program thrusts* in broad as well as increasingly more narrow functional areas, with all of the major endeavors of intergovernmental and national significance (such as welfare, health, hospitals, transportation, and education) being assisted by federal grants, and people-related programs experiencing the greatest dollar and proportionate gains since 1965; along with the enactment of an array of grants for activities that a short time ago would have been considered as state or local responsibilities (like rural fire protection, car-pool demonstration projects, jellyfish control, estuarine sanctuaries, juvenile justice, libraries, and solid-waste disposal). In some cases, federal grants have stimulated wholly new servicing roles among some recipient governments, especially local governments, as with community development and manpower for certain cities and urban counties. The only opposite trend to this growing servicing marbleization was the federal takeover of the adult welfare categories in 1972; but even this move was not total, since state "add-ons" were permitted.

7. *A major expansion since 1966 in the forms of federal aid* (i.e., the manner in which the funds are distributed and administered), with all the traditional types of categorical grants (see table 1-3) still in heavy use, along with the newer "fewer strings" programs like GRS and at least five block grants. Categoricals still accounted for 80 percent of the 1977 federal-aid package, while block grants represented only 12 percent and GRS 8 percent. In dollar terms, local governments, especially cities and counties, have benefited more from the emergence of GRS, two of the block grants, and the countercyclical programs, only one of which was really categorical in character (see table 1-2). The states, on the other hand, are involved more with the categoricals, though they also share in some of the newer forms of aid.

8. *Some broadening of recipient discretion,* with general revenue sharing providing greater flexibility than the other types of aid, and block grants providing somewhat greater leniency when they are broad in functional scope and funded adequately than the categoricals. Of special significance, however, is the servicing and fiscal discretion that results from receiving a large mix of

Table 1-3   Types of Categorical Grants

	1975		1978	
Formula-based	*Number*	*Percent*	*Number*	*Percent*
Allotted formula	96	21.7%	106	21.5%
Project grants subject to formula distribution	35	7.9	47	9.6
Open-end reimbursement	15	3.4	17	3.5
Total formula-based	146	33.0	170	34.6
Project	296	67.0	322	65.4
Total	442	100.0%	492	100.0%

Source: ACIR, *A Catalog of Federal Grant-In-Aid Programs to State and Local Governments: Grants Funded FY 1978* (Washington, D.C.: U.S. Government Printing Office, February 1979), p. 1.

federal aid—categoricals, block grants, and GRS; and, if the proportion is heavily weighted in favor of GRS and block grants, as it is with larger cities and counties, then random evidence suggests that even greater discretion is, in fact, acquired.

9. *A creeping conditionalism.* Conditions now come with all forms of federal aid, despite the earlier claims that GRS and block grants are essentially "no strings" and "few strings" assistance programs. The procedural strings (civil rights, citizen participation, and auditing requirements) that were added to GRS in 1976 and the tendency of most of the block grants to pick up program and other constraints over time have brought this about. Moreover, an array of national-purpose, across-the-board requirements in the equal rights, equal access, environmental, handicapped, historic preservation, and personnel areas (to mention only the more obvious of the sixty-odd that now apply) are attached to practically all federal assistance, giving rise to a new and controversial era of federal regulatory activity. These conditions are much more intricate, more intrusive, and more pervasive than the largely programmatic strings of the sixties. They have been especially burdensome for smaller local jurisdictions, and have produced nearly as much litigation as actual implementation.

10. *More elusive fiscal effects.* Gauging the financial impact

of federal aid is much more difficult now than it used to be. Earlier studies tended to agree that federal aid stimulated greater state and/or local outlays, either in the aided program area or overall. Recent analyses, though less than comprehensive, are not so certain, and some indicate that the impact is merely additive or even substitutive—especially with the newer forms of aid and for larger jurisdictions involved with several federal aid programs. The general tendency over the past decade and a half to enact more grants having low or no recipient matching requirements and the uncertain effect of alternative "maintenance of effort" provisions clearly are factors in this. The degree to which federal aid to localities is "targeted" to jurisdictions with greater "need" is yet another aspect of the fiscal impact issue. Studies by the Advisory Commission on Intergovernmental Relations show that the countercyclical programs with their stress on "unemployment" had produced—in conjunction with GRS, CDBG, CETA, and the categoricals—a situation where distressed cities indeed received more on a per capita basis than healthier local jurisdictions, to the point where federal aid for some was equal to half what they raised from their own revenue sources (see table 1-4).

11. *Strengthened generalists?* A clear attempt has been made for over a decade now to favor general governments and generalists in federal aid programs. State executive branches generally have been strengthened greatly since the early sixties, but direct links between this development and the growth of federal aid during the same period are tenuous. Moreover, a countertrend emerged in the seventies in the form of detailed congressional prescriptions regarding program administration at the recipient level which have undercut gubernatorial authority. Recent efforts on the part of the state legislatures to strengthen their position regarding aid expenditures by state agencies, however, do relate to the rapid growth in federal aid and to their belief that executive branches have been bolstered by it at the local level. Many of the newer federal programs of direct aid, particularly community development, have emphasized the role of elected officials and a concerted approach to program implementation, but only meager evidence can be obtained that suggests that this has generated many basic management changes within recipient local jurisdictions.

Table 1–4   Direct Federal Aid as a Percent of Own-Source General Revenue, Selected Cities and Fiscal Years 1957–78

	Fiscal years				Exhibit: per capita federal aid[3]	
	1957	1967	1976	1978 Est.	1976	1978 Est.
St. Louis	0.6%	1.0%	23.6%	56.1%	$ 86	$228
Newark	0.2	1.7	11.4	64.2	47	291
Buffalo	1.3	2.1	55.6	75.9	163	239
Cleveland	2.0	8.3	22.8	60.3	65	190
Boston	.[1]	10.0	31.5	30.2	204	219
Unweighted Averages	0.8	4.6	29.0	57.3	113	233
Baltimore	1.7	3.8	38.9	46.4	167	225
Philadelphia	0.4	8.8	37.7	53.8	129	204
Detroit	1.3	13.1	50.2	76.8	161	274
Chicago	1.4	10.9	19.2[2]	42.1	47	117
Atlanta	4.3	2.0	15.1	40.0	52	167
Unweighted Averages	1.8	7.7	32.2	51.8	111	197
Denver	0.6	1.2	21.2	25.9	90	150
Los Angeles	0.7	0.7	19.3	39.8	54	134
Dallas	0	•	20.0	17.8	51	54
Houston	0.2	3.1	19.4	23.8	44	71
Phoenix	1.1	10.6	35.0	58.7	57	117
Unweighted Averages	0.5	3.1	23.0	33.2	61	105
Unweighted Average of 15 Cities	1.1	5.2	28.1	47.5	95	179

1. Less than .05%.
2. Percentage based on federal aid excluding general revenue sharing. Funds withheld pending judicial determination.
3. Based on 1975 population.
Source: ACIR staff computations based on U.S. Bureau of the Census, *City Government Finances in 1957, 1967, and 1976.* Estimated city own-source general revenue for 1978 based on annual average increase between 1971 and 1976. Direct federal grants to each city for fiscal 1978 based on (a) ACIR staff estimates of the federal stimulus programs for 1978 and (b) Richard Nathan's estimates for all other federal aid in fiscal 1978 as set forth in his testimony before the Joint Economic Committee on 28 July 1977.

12. *Using grant conditions as a means of creating new quasi-governmental institutions.* Witness the more than thirty federal-aid programs, enacted largely since 1965, that have encouraged the establishment of more than 1800 single-purpose, multicounty planning bodies. Though multipurpose, generalist-dominated regional units (usually councils of government) have benefited from the A-95 review and comment process, these bodies have not been designated, at least half the time, to carry out the functions of the other federal regional programs. The busy substate regional scene, then, is primarily a product of procedural and institutional strings attached to federal aid programs enacted over the past fifteen years. Yet the institutions produced by these programs, whether generalist or specialist dominated, are not authoritative, legally or politically.

With these twelve broad brushstrokes, which will be treated in greater detail in later chapters, an intricate, almost incomprehensible national picture of current intergovernmental relations (admittedly from a Washington vantage point) emerges that clearly complements most of the Muncie story, save for the fact that the Indiana community is not involved with all of the myriad federally mounted intergovernmental initiatives. Moreover, like Muncie's, the national story suggests a basic break with the not-so-distant past. Ponder the many highlighted contrasts between the early sixties and now. Put yourself back into the Eisenhower years and remember the near glacial annual growth in federal grant outlays; the minuscule extent of bypassing of state governments; the narrow range of localities that were recipients of direct federal assistance; the relatively weak "representational" efforts of cities, counties, and school districts; the narrow program range of federal assistance; the monolithic reliance on the categorical grant type; the near total absence of across-the-board national requirements for national social and environmental purposes; the clearly stimulative purposes of nearly all federal grants; the more obvious attempt, though on a very limited scale, to structure chiefly state governmental arrangements through single state agency, merit system, and antipatronage requirements; and the total lack of any federal attempt to build new institutional bodies and procedures at the substate level. Drastic change in the form of far greater federal interventionism into nearly every program area and every subnational jurisdiction and an overloading of the system—such are the hallmarks of these twelve recent develop-ments in intergovernmental relations as initiated from Washington.

But what of the states during this same period? Have they been as passive as the above chronicle would suggest?

The states *have contributed to this emerging pattern of the system's overload* in the past decade and a half, though Washing-ton has rarely acknowledged or understood this quiet, yet nearly equally significant development. During this period, the bulk of the states have[6]

——provided more financial aid to their localities, but still largely in traditionally assisted program areas, especially education, and without a distinct city focus as such;

——given much more recognition that in fiscal terms, at least, income, sales, and property taxes are but three angles of one revenue triangle and that the property-tax angle had been much too large;

——reflected much more of a tendency to assume directly the performance of new responsibilities and to mandate a shift upward of certain local functions, but with most of these actions being carried out in an ad hoc fashion and with no attempt to formulate an overall servicing assignment policy;

——exhibited a growing practice to mandate service levels, condi-tions of employment, and sometimes functions, with "fiscal note" warnings to legislators and to localities more often than not lacking;[7]

——granted much more local discretion to enable cities and coun-ties to adopt alternative forms of government, to enter into interlocal contracts and agreements, and, to a lesser degree, to transfer functions, though complex procedural require-ments and limited structural options often impede their use;

——permitted only modest shifts in granting all cities and coun-ties all functional powers not denied by state constitutions or by state laws, in liberalizing annexation laws, in discourag-ing special district formations, and in giving their substate districts greater authority;

——indicated no real change, essentially, from the traditional state policy of leaving basic local and regional restructuring issues to permissive legislation and to hard-to-achieve local initiatives and referenda; and

——made no real effort to link systematically the fiscal and functional challenges to both state and local governments, despite numerous study commissions of late, with the local institutional (and jurisdictional) issue.

In short, most of the states, like the federal government, have scrapped any pretence of adhering to the conventional dual-federalism concept (e.g., the compartmental or layer-cake theory[8]) of intergovernmental relations in their own relations with their localities. Now, some would say that this is but a logical derivative in the present era of the constitutional tenet that the states are the legal parents (and source of all the legal, functional, structural, and fiscal powers) of their localities. Yet historically, as we shall see, the states have played the "neglectful" parent almost as frequently as the attentive one. But no longer.

Today, their practice generally bears little resemblance to that of the fifties or even the early sixties. Through a broad combination of inducements (i.e., conditional financial aid and permissive authorizing legislation), mandates, and statutory constraints and limits, they have conditioned heavily the finances, functions, forms, and generally fragmented jurisdictional character of their local governments. Despite some efforts to sort out functions by devolution or by state assumption and despite the expansion of local structural discretion, the dominant state theme seems to be one of a growing role in local finance (including management), service standards, and personnel. And this applies as much to cities, despite their lesser position in the state-aid picture, as it does to school districts and counties, which traditionally have had much more of a state agency character to them. In a way, then, that combines—to a much greater degree than the federal government's approach—intergovernmental fiscal transfers, conditions, mandates, and direct statutory constraints as well as inducements, the states have fashioned their own heavily collaborative, if not intrusive, intergovernmental relations.

CONCLUSION

These recent federal- and state-initiated intergovernmental developments combine to indicate basic systemic change. This seems to be seen most clearly at the local level. Witness the saga of Muncie.

To contend that these trends are merely logical extensions of the intergovernmental pattern of the New Deal is to ignore the stark contrasts between the simpler, more sorted-out, less expensive features of the earlier one and the widely pervasive, highly intrusive, hyperintensive traits of today's.

Cooperative federalism, then, and its comparatively simple "marble cake" metaphor no longer captures the reality of intergovernmental practice. The scale of interaction and of conflict is simply too great and the orbit of intergovernmental relations now encompasses the bulk of American governmental operations and programs. Today's is an overloaded, cooptive system, whose evolution, dynamics, and many subtle manifestations have profound implications for the functioning of American federalism, now and in the future.

NOTES TO CHAPTER 1

1. Saul Friedman and Frank Greve, "Taking the Pulse of 'Middletown,'" *Boston Globe,* 18 March 1979, p. A-1.
2. Quoted in ibid.
3. Quoted in ibid.
4. Ibid.
5. See Advisory Commission on Intergovernmental Relations, *Summary and Concluding Observations* (A-62) (Washington, D.C.: U.S. Government Printing Office, June 1978), pp. 65–78.
6. See David B. Walker, "Localities Under the New Intergovernmental System," *Fiscal Crisis in American Cities, The Federal Response,* L. Kenneth Hubbell, ed. (Cambridge, MA: Ballinger Publishing Company, 1979), pp. 33–42 and 48–50.
7. "Fiscal notes" usually require that cost of proposed legislation and/or administrative rules and regulations to affected local governments be estimated prior to their enactment or promulgation.
8. See chapter 3 for a detailed analysis of the dual-federalism concept.

PART

Eighteen
Score
Years
of Evolution
and Adaptation

2

The Beginnings of American Federalism and Its Intergovernmental Relations, 1620-1789

INTRODUCTION

Theories of federalism and of intergovernmental relations are interdependent, not mutually exclusive. "Federalism—old style" may be "dead," as one authority puts it, but, to revise the other half of his thesis, intergovernmental relations—old style—also is dead.[1] Put differently, the historic theories of federalism not only describe and sometimes prescribe a legal concept, they also infer or explicitly depict patterns of fiscal, administrative, and pragmatic relationships among governmental levels. In short, theories of federalism and intergovernmental relations are inseparable. What differences there are arise largely from the fact that the two appear to manifest themselves in different areas of governmental operations. Federalism appears to be largely a judicial issue and the concern of constitutional lawyers and historians, while intergovernmental relations ostensibly serves as a dynamic description of the web of interlevel linkages that have arisen (largely over the past fifty years) in the interdependent areas of public finance, public services, and public administration. Yet attempts to separate the two by assigning them to differing functional areas and to differing sets of experts ignore the interrelatedness of these areas. The continuing vitality of the concept and practice of judicial review in this country assures this.

Why, then, is there a need to use different terms at all? The concept of federalism, if not the term itself,[2] has been a perennial point of political and constitutional controversy, accommodation, and debate for nearly two centuries of American history. The term *intergovernmental relations,* on the other hand, is hardly a half-century old. Its origins, as Wright points out, still are obscure, though professors Clyde F. Snider and William G. Anderson were among the first to use it in describing the drastic changes in the administrative, programmatic, and funding relations between and among the federal government, the states, and their localities that had emerged in the Depression years.[3] Today, of course, it is a commonplace term in political science, public administration, public policy, and public finance, if not in politics itself.

Yet there always have been intergovernmental relations in large governmental systems, since interactions among governments always exist in such systems. There are intergovernmental relations in unitary systems, despite the fact that a central government therein possesses primary and undisputed legal authority over the structure, powers, finances, and servicing efforts of the subnational governmental units. There are even intergovernmental relations in authoritarian or totalitarian regimes, despite their centralization of all political and governmental powers at the center. Moreover, there are intergovernmental relations in a federal system whose public functions and finances are fairly clearly separated by governmental level. Interlevel contact, after all, occurs in any governmental system where there are subnational or constituent governmental units. The only real issues to be determined are their scope in terms of the kinds of activities and the degree to which they reflect a hierarchic or non–superior-subordinate interrelationship, and the extent to which they are based on collaboration rather than conflict. The history of American federalism and of American intergovernmental relations, then, hinges primarily on these questions of the extent, variety, basic motives, and significance of the interlevel contacts that have occurred in our federal system since 1787. As seen in this and in subsequent chapters, these have shifted significantly over the past two centuries.

HOW IT BEGAN

In comparative governmental terminology, the First American Republic (the Articles of Confederation) was the almost inevitable, historically logical outgrowth of over 150 years of colonial rule and of the dozen years' debate with the mother country that preceded the Declaration of Independence. The Second Republic, established by the Constitution of 1787, was, on the other hand, far less a matter of predetermined development. Human ingenuity, as much as the legacy of the past and the impact of recent events, was crucial in shaping a new federative regime less than a dozen years after the signing of the Declaration. But why the seeming inevitability of the First Republic as contrasted with the creative statecraft features of the great charter that established the Second?

The Articles of Confederation, which were drafted in 1776 and finally adopted in 1781, formalized the de facto institutional arrangements that had evolved during the First and Second Continental Congresses. These, of course, involved a unicameral deliberative body at the national level based on equal representation of the states, with basic powers to act in the fields of defense and foreign relations, but not in the areas of taxation and the regulation of commerce. In the latter as well as in other crucial areas, the states were authoritative. A confederal formula—albeit a strong one compared to other such arrangements—evolved during the Revolution and was formally adopted in the year of Yorktown, and this was inevitable!

The Colonial Conditioning

The more than a century and a half of British rule had produced a strong pattern of local self-government (with colonial towns and the colonies being "virtually synonymous" at the outset, as Leach notes),[4] and a high degree of partial autonomy and authentic assertiveness on the part of the colonial assemblies. These developments were due to the sustained strength of transplanted English local governmental customs; the distance from the mother country; and the long period of "salutary neglect," as historians have described it, on the part of Great Britain. Moreover, they evolved despite the powerful formal role of the royal governors in eleven of the thirteen colonies during the greater part of three score and ten years prior to independence.

Reinforcing the separateness of the thirteen colonies' evolution was the fact that to the extent that formal contacts (intergovernmental relations[5]) were had with London, the relationships were bilateral, between a single colony and the pertinent imperial agency or official. In short, there was a distance between and among the colonies, as well as between each of them and Westminster.

The Pre-Revolutionary Debate

This separateness was further reflected in the arguments developed by the colonial spokesmen in their off-again-on-again debate with London over the various imperial policies enacted by Parliament during the period 1764–75. During the first phase of this controversy, certain powers of Parliament were questioned. Whether it was a matter of taxing internally (the Sugar and Stamp Acts) or of taxing externally for revenue purposes (the Townsend Acts), the contending colonial leaders relied heavily on the rights of Englishmen, especially the right to direct representation (clearly feasible in their separate colonial assemblies, but rejected by most as impossible in Parliament), and the compact as well as the rights-guaranteeing character of their various charters from the Crown as major argumentative weapons. Some of the colonial leaders, like Governor Stephen Hopkins of Rhode Island and John Dickinson of Pennsylvania, developed a clear-cut *federative theory* of the British Empire based on a division of legislative powers, with the power to tax in any form rejected and Parliament's power to regulate trade acknowledged.

Following a four-year calm triggered by Parliament's repeal in 1769 of all the duties on colonial imports (save for tea), a measure to shore up the sagging fortunes of the East India Company was enacted. This produced a major crisis in 1774, including a Tea Party in Boston Harbor. The subsequent passage of four punitive parliamentary acts at the behest of the ministry of Lord North brought the colonists to the point of forming for the first time instruments of extralegal government—the "committees of correspondence" and provincial congresses, as well as the First Continental Congress. These so-called Intolerable Acts also prompted an outburst of renewed colonial pamphleteering—with Sam Adams, the youthful Hamilton, James Wilson, and John Adams rejecting the power of Parliament to enact any laws (including those regulating commerce) that are binding on the American colonies. With the latter three, a definite *dominion theory of empire* was developed, wherein the level of the colonial assemblies was raised to that of Parliament and the Crown served as the imperial link. John Adams explained it thus:

I contend that our provincial legislatures are the only supreme authorities in our colonies. Parliament, notwithstanding this, may be allowed an authority supreme and sovereign over the ocean . . . ; our charters give us no authority over the high seas. Parliament has our consent to assume a jurisdiction over them. . . . Our allegiance to his majesty is not due by virtue of any act of a British parliament, but by our own charter and province laws. . . . It follows from thence, that he appears king of Massachusetts, king of Rhode Island, king of Connecticut, etc.[6]

By the time of Lexington and Concord, then, the insurgent colonial leaders had developed the idea of dominion status for each of the thirteen provinces, with a concept of empire that forecast clearly the confederation of sovereign states that now comprises the (British) Commonwealth of Nations.[7] The earlier idea of a federative system based on a division of legislative powers had been scrapped for a futuristic concept that was totally rejected by the loyalists on this side of the water and by the dominant body of leadership on the other. After all, it conflicted head on with the "king-in-parliament is supreme" doctrine that had emerged as the dominant British constitutional principle from the "Glorious Revolution of 1689."

The Impact of Independence

Against this intellectual background and a series of acts taken in London to crush the rebellion that began in the "spring of '75," Tom Paine's Common Sense can be better understood. Published in January of 1776, it became an instant success. Two themes dominated the tract: a scathing attack on the institution of the British monarchy and a dramatic call for immediate severance of all political, governmental, and emotional ties with the mother country. Parliament was for the most part ignored. That link, after all, already had been cut in the dominion theory of John Adams, James Wilson, and Alexander Hamilton.

The political mind and spirit of America was being prepared for the high drama of June and July of 1776, and the introduction by Robert Henry Lee of Virginia on June 7 of a resolution in the

Second Continental Congress declaring that "these United Colonies are, and of a right ought to be, free and independent States." From the committee of five to which the resolution was referred came the Declaration (largely from the pen of Thomas Jefferson, with minor modifications made by Benjamin Franklin and John Adams). In it, and following the eloquent appeal to world opinion and the superlative statement of fundamental American political principles (the concepts of natural law and natural rights, the compact basis of the state, the doctrine of popular sovereignty, and the right under certain circumstances to revolution) in the first two paragraphs, there appears a lengthy indictment of George III, largely unfamiliar to contemporary readers.

Though most of the "long train of abuses" listed flowed from acts of Parliament, the monarch was singled out as the source of despotic government, reflecting Jefferson's and the Congress's acceptance of the recently developed dominion theory of colonial status within the empire. Since the Crown was the only imperial link under this theory, the Crown itself became the focal point of the grievances cited in the Declaration, and it was the authoritative institution with which "the political bands" were severed. The Declaration, then, ended the transatlantic debate over theories of empire, theories that constituted varying approaches to organizing the intergovernmental relations between Great Britain and its thirteen American colonies. With the severance of the political ties, the Continental Congress and the States assumed the authority of the Crown (and Parliament) and, in effect, a new debate began—but this time it was wholly an intra-American affair.

The First Republic: A Confederacy

Initially, however, there was little controversy, in that the confederative formula was almost universally accepted as the proper one for structuring the relations between the states and the new nation, underscoring the continuing strength of their sense of separateness and the continuing appeal of the dominion theory of empire. Only now it was an American empire and an American pattern of intergovernmental relations that were being constructed.

John Dickinson's June 7 resolution was accompanied by a companion measure calling on Congress to establish a committee to draft a constitution for the "United Colonies."[8] With the adoption of the resolution, Dickinson was appointed to head the committee, and a draft plan for a confederation was reported eight days following the signing of the Declaration. The only real points in controversy were the provisions that apportioned the expenses of the new central government among the states on a basis of population and that gave Congress the authority to adjudicate state boundary controversies. Some signs of later big-state, nationalist versus small-state, noncentralist divisions emerged in the ensuing debate, but the latter group carried the day when it secured enactment of a clause guaranteeing to each state "sovereignty, freedom and independence."

In essence, the final document allotted to Congress those powers that it already had been utilizing (to wage war and make peace, to enter into treaties and alliances, to dispatch and receive ambassadors, to regulate Indian affairs, and to establish a postal system) and that had been exercised by the Crown and Parliament in the old days of "benign neglect" prior to 1763.[9] The key powers denied to the Congress (regulation of trade and taxation) were those that had triggered the colonial dispute with and ultimate departure from the British system. It was around these two powers, of course, that the earlier federative and dominion theories of empire were fashioned. In denying both, the framers of the Articles adhered primarily, but not wholly, to the dominion theory.

A "confederacy," then, was established and was so designated in Article I, wherein "each State . . . retains every power, jurisdiction and right not expressly granted to the United States, in Congress assembled." The weaknesses of this arrangement, of course, soon became manifest both at home and abroad. The difficulties in collecting state revenue allotments, in paying war veterans, in meeting loan payments, in properly garrisoning the western territories, and in having to depend on the states for its revenues were but some of the more obvious signs of the fiscal disability of the Congress under the First Republic, thanks largely to the lack of a direct taxing power. The inability to enter into commercial treaties (because Congress could not guarantee state compliance), to retaliate against discriminatory foreign trade policies, to curb "trade wars" among the states, and to enforce provisions of existing treaties revealed the new regime's frailties abroad. This, of course, stemmed from the lack of effective national authority in interstate and foreign commerce, and from Congress's inability to gain acceptance even in those few areas where Congress was supposedly authoritative. All this suggests a state-centered variety of inter-governmental relations, arising from the need of the central government to rely on the states as its primary implementing agents and to achieve state cooperation if almost any of its functions were to be discharged successfully.

Nonetheless, not all of the postwar difficulties can be attributed to the deficiencies in the confederal formula and the state-centered intergovernmental relations that flowed from it. The economic dislocations caused by the War and by being outside the British imperial system and the resulting postwar depression would have occurred regardless of the nature of the new regime.

The drive for constitutional change derived impetus from all these developments, as well as from Congress's inability to prevent states from issuing their own paper money. Conflicts between hard and paper currency factions sprang up in several states, and led to Shays' Rebellion in Massachusetts. By 1787, nearly all of the new nation's leading statesmen had come to recognize the defects in the design of the first constitution, and the drive for reform became irresistible. At the same time, as we shall see, not all of the provisions of the old charter were scrapped and the experience under it was a critical factor in helping to reformulate a more balanced federative principle.

THE CONSTITUTIONAL CONVENTION: CREATIVITY UNDER DIFFICULT CIRCUMSTANCES

Shortly before the fifty-five delegates convened in Philadelphia, Madison formulated the essential task of the Convention: constructing a new type of polity, which was neither a wholly centralized one nor merely a confederation or a league.[10] This was the question that Parliament under the old pre-1763 empire answered by allowing a significant gap to arise between the theory of the indivisibility of Parliamentary sovereignty and the practice of significant colonial autonomy. This was the prime assignment (as Edmund Burke so eloquently framed it) that Parliament had been unable to discharge during the dozen years prior to independence. It was the basic issue that prompted the development of federative, then dominion, theories of empire by colonial spokesmen during this same period. And it was the polar points of tension in this required geographic division of governmental powers that the Articles of Confederation had failed to reconcile.

The Framers, then, came to their task with the old imperial practices and their experiences during the pre- and actual Revolutionary period, as well as under the Articles, clearly in mind. They had witnessed and written about a range of alternative patterns of intergovernmental relations: superior-subordinate, independent versus mutually interdependent, conflicting versus complementary, heavily compartmentalized versus heavily commingled, center-oriented versus constituent unit-based. The question of allocating powers was not as difficult as the one of how to formulate, establish, and maintain the principle of union. The former, after all, had a fairly lengthy historical record to fall back on, while the latter was still a matter of conflicting theories and interpretations. It would require some superlative statecraft to solve satisfactorily this question of imperial order, but America had sent her best to Philadelphia, and the fifty-five men who actually attended proved fit for this transcendent task.

Would It Be a Government?

The Randolph (or Virginia) plan, which was first introduced and soon used as the basis of the Convention's work, provided the main nationalist option. A bicameral Congress both of whose chambers were to be based on population, direct election of the lower house and selection of the upper by the lower, the assigning to it of all powers of the Continental Congress as well as the power to "legislate in all cases in which the separate States are incompetent, or in which the harmony of the United States may be interrupted by the exercise of individual Legislation," and the congressional power to disallow state enactments that constrained "the Articles of Union" suggest the degree of change from the Articles. Moreover, the proposed authority of the national Congress "to call forth the force of the Union" against recalcitrant states suggests an enforcement device that would have been unimaginable in the old confederacy, though the plan's overall pro-legislative features were less exceptional.

Subsequently, the Convention went into a Committee of the

Whole, wherein Randolph immediately moved, at the urging of Gouverneur Morris of Pennsylvania, the temporary setting aside of the first item in his plan in order to present a new resolution. Its purpose was to establish the basic intention of the Convention and to do this in strongly nationalistic terms. It declared that no "Union of the States merely federal" or any "treaty or treaties among the whole or part of the States would be adequate," and concluded "that a national government ought to be established consisting of a supreme Legislature, Executive, and Judiciary." The first two principles were accepted with practically no debate. The final proposition did generate a debate over the meaning of a "federal" (confederal) as against a "national, supreme Government." Yet it was adopted only six days after the Convention was organized, with Connecticut alone dissenting. This was an early and remarkable victory for the nationalist viewpoint and, in some respects, the first and most significant Convention decision relating to the nature of the system they would devise. Despite a subsequent resurgence of small-state and anticentralist strength, the question of whether it was a government or a strengthened league that they were formulating was answered by this vote. It was to be a government that would interact directly with the citizenry.

But how was it to be composed? With what powers and what kind of separation of powers? With what relationship to the states and to the citizenry? With what form of mediation, if any, between the levels? All these issues were yet to be settled, and the drama of the Convention from then on turned on the delegates' proposals, reactions, and compromises on the vital questions that flowed from the pivotal decision of May 30. Four other major decisions subsequently were made that critically conditioned the design of the new system and combined to establish what later authorities would classify as a modern federal system.

The Four Decisions

1. "The Great Compromise"

Following the May 30 vote, attention shifted back to the Randolph plan and the issue of Congress's composition immediately dominated the discussion. Both the method of election and mode of apportioning representatives were in controversy. The bicameral principle itself was not an issue, reflecting the defensiveness of the small state-confederationist members at this point. They advanced no real opposition to the Randolph proposal that the lower house be popularly elected, and this resolution was approved. But most nationalists and the antinationalists rejected the plan's call for election of the upper by the lower chamber.

A week later, John Dickinson moved that the Senate be elected by the state legislatures, with nationalists like Madison and Wilson urging popular election and small-state leaders like Roger Sherman arguing for representation of the states as such. The Dickinson resolution finally was adopted unanimously.

The even greater difficulty of apportionment remained, however. Should representation in the two houses be based on population or on state parity? The nationalists defended the proportionate principle largely in terms of popular representation and contended that citizens of small states would have an equal voice with those of the larger ones. But the opposition countered with heated arguments against proportionate representation and its undercutting of state sovereignty.

Sherman offered a compromise that called for such representation in the lower house and state equality in the upper, but the nationalists successfully vetoed it. Rufus King then moved that the lower house be based on "some equitable ratio of representation." That motion carried, whereon Sherman moved that each state should have one vote in the Senate, but this was rejected. A bare majority then sanctioned a resolution stipulating that the upper house adhere to the same rule of representation as the lower, and that resolution was approved. The nationalists had carried the day, but the drama was far from over.

With the arrival of additional delegates from small states and a growing awareness of their embattled position, the antinationalists launched a skillful and partially effective counterattack with the so-called Patterson (or New Jersey) plan. In this "now or never" situation, Patterson advanced a scheme that was "purely federal" (confederal, in today's terms). Basically, it called for a revamped Continental Congress with added powers (taxation and commerce regulation), an executive selected by it, the authority to coerce recalcitrant states, and legal supremacy accorded to all treaties and congressional acts. However, it provided for no change in the state equality precept in its basis of representation.

A near nasty debate on the defects of the Articles ensued and the nationalists succeeded in defeating the proposal. The amended Virginia plan subsequently was reported from the Committee of the Whole, but the battle was not over, for the state parity principle was by no means dead. For two days Luther Martin of Maryland argued the inseparability of state equality and the "federal idea," while Madison observed that the small states had nothing to fear from the larger since the individual interests of the latter differed greatly. Franklin urged the institution of daily prayer to help avoid the impending impasse.

After nearly a week and a half of diligent and disputatious debate, the Convention again sanctioned proportionate representation for the lower house. Three days of protracted debate followed in which moderates urged the need for a compromise and for a recognition that "we are partly federal, partly national," as Connecticut's Oliver Ellsworth put it. When it ended, the antinationalists succeeded in achieving a tie vote on a resolve placing the upper house on a proportionate representational basis. At this point, the moderate nationalists, at the urging of C. C. Pinckney of South Carolina, suggested establishment of a committee to devise a compromise.

The resulting recommendations called for a lower house based on population with one member for every forty thousand inhabitants, the origin of all appropriation measures in this chamber, and equal state representation in the upper house. With the amendment that members of the Senate vote as individuals instead of as a state delegation, the Convention accepted the committee's report with no other major changes, and the "Great Compromise" was achieved.

Though later events proved the accuracy of Madison's forecast of large-state differences and the false assumptions in Martin's analysis, the composition question was real and more than just a minor difficulty for the Convention. Without this compromise, impasse would have been reached and a breakup of the assemblage would probably have resulted. The partial recognition of state sovereignty in the structure of the central government inflamed the more ardent nationalists, and some of their warnings were prophetic of events that transpired in the Senate from the early 1830s to the outbreak of the Civil War. Nevertheless, without it, no plan for a "more perfect Union" or any national, though limited, government would have been possible.

2. The Division of Powers

Another basic Convention decision related to the powers of the proposed new government. Unlike the congressional composition issue, this question was settled largely in committee and with only minor debate. Nonetheless, it was a major decision. The Virginia plan, after all, left to the Congress a vague, almost plenary authority to "legislate in all cases in which the separate States are incompetent," and only a handful of delegates questioned the scope of this authority.

Yet the Committee on Detail, when it produced a constitutional draft in early August, set forth a series of specific delegated powers, including, of course, those of taxation and of regulating commerce, which even the New Jersey plan had sanctioned. The reasons for this committee action are still obscure. Some members had complained of the indefinite nature of congressional authority under the Randolph proposal, but the issue sparked no discussions comparable to those relating to the method of electing and apportioning the members of Congress.

Some authorities have conjectured that the moderate cast of the committee's membership may explain their action here.[11] The supremacy of national acts would have been more difficult to sustain in state courts if Congress's powers were only broadly bounded, and enumeration of its powers could be used in arguments favoring the Constitution's ratification. Memories of having to contend with a deliberative body that claimed the whole orbit of legislative authority must also have played a role. In any event, the listing was quickly accepted.

Though this decision was a relatively easy one, and clearly rooted in tradition, it had immense implications for the future.[12] The lengthy, later political and judicial debates over the nature of the expressed and especially the implied powers assigned to the national government would have assumed a very different character had the Randolph approach been adopted. Moreover, the evolution of intergovernmental relations doubtlessly would have been quite different, more direct perhaps, and less devious at times had the national government's power been as broadly encompassing as the Virginia plan contemplated.

3. Choosing the Chief Magistrate

A third fundamental decision (post-May 30), critical to the future of American federalism, was the compromise on the method of electing the president. The executive office, though given less attention than the Congress, produced its share of long discussions and delayed decisions. As much of the foregoing has suggested, the overwhelming majority of the convention delegates—nationalists and state-sovereignty men alike—were prolegislative in their institutional bias, reflecting their revolutionary heritage. Yet confidence in legislative bodies was beginning to erode and all were advocates of separation of powers, though like their state counterparts, they were not sure how to incorporate institutionally the principle.

At first glance, the question appears to be a horizontal one—of assuring the independence of the executive, especially vis-à-vis the Congress—but it had vertical implications as well. The evolution of a separate presidency armed with adequate executive powers was a "torturous" one, indeed.[13] Both the Virginia and New Jersey plans, after all, called for congressional election, and the Convention sanctioned this method on five different occasions.[14] Yet a tiny minority, led by Wilson, Morris, and Madison, persisted in its push for a strong, separate chief magistracy.

Both Wilson and Morris argued initially for popular election, only to be countered successfully by the legislative defenders. The Committee on Detail, as it turned out, dealt with this most important unresolved "detail" in a lengthy paragraph that set forth a compromise version of the electoral college concept.

Each state was accorded the same number of electors as its total of congressional members and was to choose them "in such manner as its legislature may direct," thus recognizing the states, the possibility of popular election at the discretion of the states, and the mixed, partly "federal," partly "national" basis of congressional representation. The electors were to ballot for two persons, with the man having the greatest number of votes gaining the presidency, provided the vote constituted an absolute majority of all electors. This feature of the Constitution, most authorities on political parties agree, was and is a critical one in explaining the coalition-building efforts of the major parties prior to the actual balloting for the office. Finally, the committee stipulated that if no candidate gained the required majority, the Senate would choose a president from the five men receiving the most number of votes, thus recognizing the legislature and the state parity principle.

Before the Convention, many delegates expressed the view that cases where a candidate gained the necessary majority, would be rare, hence legislative selection would be a common occurrence. Strong executive proponents agreed and fought the proposal, but it was sufficiently attractive to win over legislative selection adherents to the electoral-college concept.

The only basic change in the committee's proposal was adoption of a Sherman resolution calling for the House, not the Senate, to elect in instances of a no-absolute-majority winner. To assure that no combination of two or three states would dominate the process, it also stipulated that each state delegation would vote as a unit and that a majority of state votes would be required to elect. Here, an effort to favor the more "democratic" of the two chambers was made, but the bias in favor of legislative selection remained along with the principle of parity of the states. This feature of the electoral college remains unchanged to this day and is one of the key features of the formal presidential election process that has been singled out for criticism and reform.

This complicated compromise, on a quick examination, appears to be no compromise at all, but rather a surrender to the legislative-ascendancy advocates and to the state-sovereignty proponents. In truth, and with the benefit of nearly two hundred years of hindsight, it was a victory for the separation-of-powers principle, for a separately constituted and independent chief magistrate, and for nationalism and democracy, as well as for the states. Within a generation, presidential electors were popularly elected, and even earlier (thanks to the emergence of parties) they had been reduced to the status of party rubber stamps, thus rendering the electoral college a triumph for those who argued for a separate, popular, and national constituency for the office. At the same time, the need to run in each of the states, not the nation as a whole, and to acquire an adequate territorial spread of one's electoral votes—

along with the later state-imposed "winner-take-all" requirement—has been felt by many to have exerted a moderating influence on presidential politics, to have strengthened the state basis of the two-party system, and to have buttressed the federal system. Contemporary proponents of direct election of the presidency, of course, would and do reject all of these arguments.

4. Who Arbitrates and by What Process?

The final Convention decision of critical import for the future of the new system dealt with a question that all federal polities must confront: Who is to judge in cases of disputes between the central and constituent governments, and by what means? Both the Randolph and Patterson plans answered it by empowering the Congress to coerce states that violated the treaties or duly enacted laws of the United States. The former, of course, also included the prior right of Congress to disallow contravening state enactments.

As the Convention progressed, it became increasingly apparent to the nationalists, if not their opponents, that coercion was more in harmony with the idea of a league, not a government—hence the provision for it in the New Jersey plan. Many delegates also began to recognize that a national government in many of its most essential actions would be operating directly with individuals.[15] But who was to define and maintain the respective spheres of national and state powers? Both camps had great fears on this score, with the nationalists troubled by the prospect of state erosion of national authority and the antinationalists anxious over the potential reduction of the states to the status of "mere corporations."

The scope of the national and state areas of authority also entered into this debate. The enumeration of Congress's powers, as we have seen, meant a rejection of the broad empowering approach, and the proposed disallowance authority was subject to increasing criticism from a few nationalists and many moderate and state-oriented spokesmen. Sherman, speaking for the latter, argued that the device of the congressional negative was the wrong approach, since every state law not negated would remain in effect even though it was contrary to the fundamentals of the Constitution. Hence, he contended, Congress would have to assess every state law to determine its compatibility with federal acts and the Constitution—a practical impossibility.

Gouverneur Morris, a nationalist, also condemned the approach as "terrible to the States" and as being essentially unnecessary, since a law that contravened the Constitution would not be upheld by the courts, thus raising for the first time the possibility of a judicial alternative.[16] Despite Madison's strong defense of disallowance, the Convention scrapped the proposal. At that point, Luther Martin of Maryland resurrected the largely overlooked supremacy provision of the New Jersey plan. After minor changes, it was adopted. By making the treaties enacted under the "Authority of the United States" (so phrased to cover those concluded under the Articles), the Constitution, and laws "made in pursuance thereof" the "supreme law of the Land" and thus binding on state judges, the federal judiciary as arbiter of interlevel conflict became a growing possibility.

Leading nationalists fought the idea and James Wilson led a last-ditch defense of congressional disallowance. Yet the Martin resolution was approved. But why would small state defenders advance this resolution and regard its adoption as a kind of victory? The answer, of course, is that it eliminated the powers of congressional disallowance and coercion and state courts would have the lion's share of the burden in the adjudicative process. What is more, the establishment of inferior federal courts had been rejected by the Convention, apparently because of moderate and small-state fears that a lower federal judiciary would assume direct jurisdiction in certain classes of cases, thus causing a loss in state court status.

Subsequently, Madison and Wilson did succeed in getting Convention adoption of a resolution permitting the national Congress, at its discretion, to establish such tribunals. The right of appeals from state tribunals to the Federal Supreme Court already had been accepted by some delegates, though some authorities believe that the convention "did not regard the right of appeals as establishing a general power in the federal judiciary to interpret the extent of state authority under the Constitution."[17] Nonetheless, the supremacy of national Constitution and laws, when linked with the establishment of a Supreme Court and the right of appeals from state courts (clearly detailed in the Judiciary Act of 1789, along with the establishment of lesser federal courts by that Act), laid the foundation of the Supreme Court's ultimate right to define the nature and extent of state and national authority. Ironically, the adoption of the New Jersey plan's "supreme Law of the Land" provision achieved the goal that Madison and Wilson sought, but by means that few in the Convention clearly understood. It was a crucial Convention decision that most of the nationalists opposed, but one that ultimately helped assure the legal supremacy of the national government.

What Manner of System?

The Constitution was the crowning achievement in statecraft of that extraordinary first generation of Americans. In contrast to its predecessor, many of its basic features were not predictable or inevitable, but instead a product of inventiveness. It also represented a clear break with the past, in that it established a system unknown to political theorists and unlike any other in previously recorded history. Its distinctive blend of certain familiar principles drawn from "the science of politics," as Hamilton phrased it, and from American experience with wholly novel concepts and procedures engendered by the delegates' own creativity and compromises, in effect, established a "unified, internally coherent and highly original model of a new kind of government."[18]

The one overarching goal of the Convention that all the delegates shared and that was the ultimate conditioner of most of the compromises was "to form a more perfect Union." The imperfections of the old Union, both in its external (foreign policy, trade, and defense) affairs and in its internal operations, were acknowledged by all. The antinationalists, after all, were as bent on reform as the nationalists. Their New Jersey plan by no stretch of the imagination can be described as a simple continuation of the status quo of the old regime.

The confederation's frailties in foreign relations were the easiest to document, the easiest to resolve, and the easiest to dramatize in the later struggle for ratification. One authority has gone so far as to contend that foreign policy and military motives, not domestic concerns, were the primary ones in the convening of the Convention as well as the drafting and ratification of the Constitution.[19]

The domestic disabilities of the old Union, however, obviously were of deep concern to the delegates, and this concern extended to the states as well as to the Continental Congress. The Convention's common objective here was the preservation of "republican liberty," that is, certain personal rights like freedom of conscience, protection of one's property, and political liberty, as well as the right to government "by consent of the governed."[20] Their fundamental differences were over the implementing principles and procedures. In essence, the nationalist versus antinationalist divisions were rooted in wholly opposite views on the appropriate governmental arrangements for preserving this legacy of the Revolution.

Roger Sherman and other like-minded antinationalist delegates as well as various antifederalists later opposed what they felt were the predominantly, if not wholly, nationalist features of the proposed Constitution because they viewed these as a basic menace to "republican liberty." This interpretation, as Diamond explains it, "rested on two considerations. First, it argued that only small countries can possess republican governments. Second, it argued that, when such small republics seek the advantages of greater size, they can preserve their republicanism by uniting only in a federal (confederal) way."[21] Madison, of course, turned this "small republic" argument on its head both at the Convention and in *The Federalist*. Republicanism and the liberty it protects are menaced in small jurisdictions, he contended. Only a large country could counteract the destabilizing, antilibertarian tendencies of factions in small republics and secure "private rights and the steady dispensation of Justice."[22] More pointedly, he warned his fellow delegates: "Was it to be supposed that republican liberty could long exist under the abuses of it practised in some of the States?"[23]

In Federalist 10 he went into a deeper analysis of how the factional (interest-group) dangers to republican liberty would be checked in a vast "compound republic." The great diversity of interests in such a large system would preclude the emergence of an arbitrary majority at the national level and the existence of a stable, balanced government of the Union would serve as a positive force in respecting "the rights of every class of citizens" and in protecting the rights of local minorities against local majorities.[24] Hence, Madison wrote: "In the extent and proper structure of the Union, . . . we behold a republican remedy for the disease incident to republican government."[25]

For the nationalists, then, a full-fledged national government was needed to correct the defects of the old confederacy in both

foreign policy and domestic matters. Madison's skillful undermining of the basic premises supporting the small-republic thesis of Sherman and the other antinationalists (not to mention
Montesquieu) and his powerful libertarian argument for a great
republic combined to place a heavy burden of proof on the state-
sovereignty men. His analysis also served as the major intellectual
rationale for the May 30 decision to establish a central government,
not a reconstituted League.

If a government was to be constructed to preserve "republican
liberty," what should be its design? Here, the Framers had little
difficulty in agreeing on several essential features, for political
theory and the long course of American governmental experience
joined in suggesting certain basic principles that ought to be institutionalized. The concepts of a written constitution, separation of
powers, checks and balances (or as one authority phrased it, a
"balance of checks"), bicameralism, representation, and the ultimate sovereignty of the people were viewed as fundamental features of any genuinely republican frame of government.

These precepts of the "new science of politics" were dominated by the overriding concern of many eighteenth-century political thinkers: how to achieve and preserve a free government.
Based on a measured degree of distrust in human nature, a design
was advanced that sought to protect liberty by dividing and balancing power and authority within a polity.[26] In this way, man's
love for power and tendency to abuse it would be restrained by
barring "any monopoly of the instruments of power."[27] Hence the
need for the devices cited above, so that these instruments would
be appropriately divided and balanced.

Yet these principles had only been "tested" in a relatively
small (and unitary) governmental context of the states, and the
heavy weight of Montesquieu's counsel was that they could only
be applied directly in a small country where the commonweal is
"more obvious, better understood, and more within the reach of
every citizen."[28] While the French theorist did develop the concept of a "confederate republic," it far more resembled the outline
of the Articles of Confederation than the design of the Constitution of 1787.

With the exception of David Hume, who in his "Idea of a Perfect Commonwealth" (1752) favored and developed a scheme for

a large representative republic, the teachings of the most influential "republican" theorists led to the small-polity model. Colonial experience and the revolutionary debate were less clear on this point, as we have seen. A de facto division of powers within a large system had been achieved under the old, pre–Sugar Act Empire and Dickinson and Hopkins sought to formalize this in their later federative theory. Yet in neither case were all the features of a free system dealt with satisfactorily (i.e., popular consent, representation, a neutral arbiter, etc.). Moreover, Adams's dominion theory, the imperial organizational premise of the Declaration—not to mention the Articles themselves—led to the small-republic governmental model and only a confederative arrangement at the central level.

Against this background, the dramatically different design of the Constitution can be more clearly understood. What the Framers did, of course, was to substitute a large-scale unitary model (the Virginia plan) for the confederative one (the Articles), and this in a formal sense at least incorporated most of the techniques for dividing and balancing the instruments of power that were found in or thought to be necessary for the small republic. But, thanks to the "small-republic" men (led largely by Sherman), as well as to certain individual nationalists (Morris, Wilson, and Madison) who disliked some of the specifics in the Randolph outline, a series of modifications was made in the unitary draft. The cumulative effect of these changes was to establish neither a national nor confederal system but a federal one, in the modern sense of that term.[29]

What is more, this new federal formula gave Madison, not to mention Hamilton, a far better basis for arguing persuasively for ratification of the Constitution than would have been the case had the Randolph draft of even some of Madison's own nationalist positions prevailed on the Convention floor. The amendments to the Virginia plan, after all, could be and were described as additional, if not new, means of balancing power—not only at the center but between the center and the periphery. Madison's great-republic cure for the ills of factionalism was strengthened considerably by the "federalist" engraftings on the unitary body of the nationalists' initial plan.

Remember Madison's able exposition of the virtues of a "compound republic": "In the compound republic of America, the power surrendered by the people is first divided between two distinct governments, and then the portion allotted to each subdivided among distinct and separate departments. Hence, a double security arises to the rights of the people."[30] How effective, how convincing would this have been had the national Congress of that republic been assigned the broad and ill-defined powers, the authority to coerce states and select presidents, and the solely numerical representational base that the Randolph draft would have accorded it?

Madison's skillful detailing of the "national" and "federal" (confederal) features of the new basic frame in Federalist 39 would have been far less balanced and far more removed from the equilibrium ideal that late-eighteenth-century sophisticates so strongly favored had the dual representational formula for Congress (by territorial units and by the number of people), the clear division of powers by governmental level, and the extraordinary high-wire performance of the electoral college been missing. The Virginian also was able to argue that the functional division and dual-level representational features of the "compound republic" provided a greater protection of "republican liberty" while also affording the people an unusual opportunity to play the role of ultimate balancer in the system.[31]

All this does not mean that the Framers were wholly clear about all of their actions or necessarily thought in terms of abstract political models. Still, the two opposing groups at the Convention had contrasting views of the best means of preserving republican liberty and both adhered to quasi-unitary formulas: with one operating at the center and the other at periphery. Thanks to the "compromises," a halfway house was found and the modern concept of federalism involving "the division of powers between distinct and coordinate governments" was born.[32]

No great debate, however, occurred in the Convention on the nature of federalism. How could it? The bundle of critical decisions that established federalism were made in an ad hoc fashion and their overall significance probably was not appreciated until much later, though Madison's expositions in The Federalist, and to a lesser extent Hamilton's, reveal considerable awareness of what had been wrought in Philadelphia.

Understandably, then, certain crucial questions relating to the essential nature of the Union, to nation-state relationships, and above all to sovereignty, were left unanswered by the manner in which the unique federative, compound republican formula evolved. Even in *The Federalist,* different answers to some of them emerged. Hamilton viewed the new system as a "consolidated" one, while Madison, as we have seen, found it partly federal and partly national. On the question of the scope and significance of the powers assigned to the national Congress, the New Yorker wrote of "an entire change in the first principles of the system," but the Virginian soothingly claimed that they were less a matter of an "addition of New Powers, than the invigoration of its Original Powers."[33] Hamilton saw the delegated powers in the aggregate along with the "elastic clause" as adequate to meet the greatest and widest "variety of national exigencies," while Madison found the powers "few and defined" and chiefly important in times of "war and danger."[34] The seeds of future political antagonisms were already planted!

Little overt attention was given to intergovernmental relations as such either in the Convention debates or *The Federalist.* Yet modern-day authorities find entirely different meanings in their readings of both. Grodzins and Elazar contend that "the Constitution did not set up rigidly independent administrative establishments in both national and state governments. On the contrary, cooperation between the national government and the states was assured from the very first."[35] At the opposite end of the interpretative spectrum stands Scheiber, who concludes that "the Framers conceived of the central government and the states operating in different spheres."[36]

Neither view would appear to be wholly correct. On the one hand, the Convention delegates, or at least the majority of them, sought to extricate the new national government from having to rely on the states for administering its basic functions. The Continental Congress's disastrous dependence on the states in so many areas was a vivid reminder of a pattern of intergovernmental relations that they abhorred; hence their focus on a national government that had different powers and purposes from those of the states.[37] Moreover, the limited scope of national authority assured that "its jurisdiction is limited to certain enumerated objects, which concern all the members of the republic, but which are not to be attained by the separate provisions of any."[38] The assigning of "clearly-stated and clearly-recognizable powers," as an authority of an earlier generation phrased it, was not only necessary to the viable, separate existence of the national government, but also to avoid "friction between governments."[39] These ideas of the Founders, then, support the later theory of "dual federalism," a concept of separate state and federal governments that operate in distinct areas with little major overlap in the sharing of authority and functions.

Despite the foregoing, the Grodzins-Elazar assessment is not totally inaccurate. Several interlevel relationships and interdependences were debated, recognized, or simply assumed by the Founders. The senatorial, judicial, and presidential selection connections with the states already have been noted and all three arose from small-state-engendered "compromises." Yet there were others: suffrage requirements, the elections process and machinery, and the amending process were all constitutionally stipulated functions requiring state collaboration. In addition, the concurrent authority of both levels in the taxing area at least hinted at a future field of both intergovernmental conflict and "mutual forebearance," as Madison phrased it, and the militia was to be jointly administered.

In essence, some of the cooperative but far more of the dual federal theory can find support in the Convention debates and in the Constitution. The Framers, then, crafted an entirely new governmental model, known to later generations as a federal system. Its evolution during the course of the Convention began with the introduction of a basically national, quasi-unitary draft for fundamental constitutional reform which then was subjected to a series of chiefly small-state-led modifications. The result was a system that was neither a unitary regime nor a confederation, but a federal system. A wholly novel governmental arrangement thus was launched and America's greatest contribution to "the science of politics" was rendered.

The fundamental purposes of this new order were to gain respect and authority in foreign relations and at home to promote social and governmental stability, protect "republican liberty," and defend the people's ultimate authority as master of all governments.

Certain key questions regarding the operations of this great republic were not addressed or answered clearly during the Convention's fashioning of the federal formula. The resolution of these questions and the new regime's record in achieving its great goals over the next two centuries will be dealt with in the chapter that follows.

Other key questions were clearly addressed by the Founders, especially by Madison. From a contemporary perspective, however, it would appear that both the questions and the formulated answers to them have been ignored. The recent record, as chapter 8 chronicles it, suggests that contemporary Americans find Madison's warnings regarding the dangers of factions (interest groups) to individual liberty to be merely the alarmist admonitions of a late-eighteenth-century conservative. Moreover, the behavior of today's national policymakers, again as chapter 8 highlights, indicates a widespread forgetfulness regarding the fundamental domestic role the Founders assigned to the national government: the regulation of factions. The failure on the part of the citizenry and the system to honor these early and elemental themes of our political tradition in no small measure explains why contemporary American federalism is not only untraditional, but dysfunctional.

NOTES TO CHAPTER 2

1. Michael Reagan, *The New Federalism* (New York: Oxford University Press, 1972), p. 3.

2. The Founding Fathers used it as current-day students of government would use the term "confederal"; i.e., a system wherein nearly all basic governmental powers rest with constituent units, thus comprising a league whose basis is a treaty or compact among equals and whose purposes are largely restricted to military and foreign-policy concerns—hence Madison's description of the proposed new system in his 39th Federalist paper as being neither wholly national nor wholly federal. In laying claim to the "federalist" designation, the supporters of the new frame, as Deil Wright points out, used a term that the politically knowledgeable of that day understood to be the least centralized of the alternative ways of organizing central government—constituent unit relationships.

3. Deil S. Wright, *Understanding Intergovernmental Relations* (North Scituate, MA: Duxbury Press, 1978), p. 6.

4. Richard II. Leach, *American Federalism* (New York: W. W. Norton & Co., 1976), p. 3.

5. These included contact with the committee on appeals of the Privy Council in cases of judicial appeal; with the Board of Trade on legislative review and disallowance matters; with the treasury and customs commissioners regarding the colonial customs service; with the High Court of Admiralty on marine and violation of trade act cases; and with the Secretary of State for the Southern Department on military, foreign policy, and royal gubernatorial matters.

6. Quoted in Alpheus T. Mason, *Free Government in the Making, Readings in American Political Thought* (New York: Oxford University Press, 1949), pp. 130–31.

7. Alfred H. Kelly and Winfred A. Harbison, *The American Constitution, Its Origins and Development* (New York: W. W. Norton & Co., 1976), p. 75.

8. Kelly and Harbison, op. cit., p. 95.

9. Ibid., pp. 95–96.

10. See Andrew C. McLaughlin, *A Constitutional History of the United States* (New York: Appleton, 1935), p. 54.

11. Kelly and Harbison, op. cit., pp. 133–34.

12. See McLaughlin, op. cit., p. 186.

13. See Clinton Rossiter, *The American Presidency* (New York: Harcourt, Brace & World, 1959), p. 76 ff.

14. Ibid., p. 77.

15. See Kelly and Harbison, op. cit., p. 128; also note that various of the Constitution's provisions explicitly or implicitly assume a reliance by the national government on the states to carry out other of its functions.

16. See McLaughlin, op. cit., p. 184.

17. Kelly and Harbison, op. cit., p. 140.

18. Samuel H. Beer, "Federalism, Nationalism and Democracy in America," *American Political Science Review* 72, no. 1 (March 1978): 14.

19. William H. Riker, *Federalism: Origin, Operation, Significance* (Boston: Little, Brown & Co., 1964), pp. 19–25.

20. Beer, op. cit., p. 10.

21. Martin Diamond, "What the Framers Meant by Federalism," appearing in *A Nation of States*, Robert A. Goldwin, ed. (Chicago: Rand McNally & Co., 1964), p. 35.

22. See ibid., p. 37.

23. Cf. ibid.

24. See Beer, op. cit., pp. 14 and 15; and Diamond, op. cit., p. 37.

25. Federalist 10, p. 62; all references are to the Modern Library edition, edited by E. M. Earle (New York: The Modern Library, 1977).

26. See Beer, op. cit., pp. 12–13.

27. Ibid.

28. Quoted in ibid., p. 13.

29. Riker, op. cit., pp. 20–25.

30. Federalist 51, p. 339.

31. Federalist 46, pp. 304–5.

32. K. C. Wheare, *Federal Government* (New York: Oxford University Press, 1964), p. 2.

33. Federalist 45, p. 303.

34. Federalist 23 and 45, pp. 442 and 303 respectively.

35. Martin Grodzins, *The American System*, Daniel J. Elazar, ed. (Chicago: Rand McNally & Co., 1966), p. 24.

36. Harry N. Scheiber, "American Federalism and the Diffusion of Power: Historical and Contemporary Perspectives," *The University of Toledo Law Review* 9, no. 4 (Summer 1978): 627.

37. Federalist 46, pp. 304-5.

38. Federalist 14, p. 82.

39. McLaughlin, op. cit., p. 180.

3

From
Dual
to
Cooperative
Federalism,
1790-1960

INTRODUCTION

The evolution of American federalism and its resulting intergovernmental relations (IGR) falls into four historical phases: the pre-Civil War period (1789-1860); from the firing on Fort Sumter to the advent of the Great Depression (1861-1930); the age of Roosevelt and its consolidation under Eisenhower (1930-60); and the current era, which began with the election of John F. Kennedy (1960-present). The first three will be treated briefly in this chapter, the last in the five succeeding ones. Other historians have blocked out these periods differently. Yet there is a cohesion to the dominant themes of each of these periods, even though each exhibited its own share of conflicting, centralizing, and decentralizing tendencies as well as strong links to the past.

To fathom the character of each era, its constitutional, fiscal, servicing, and administrative features must be probed. These, after all, are the chief conditioners of the evolving course of American federalism. When combined, they provide the basis for determining the general intergovernmental character of each period.

THE DUAL FEDERALISM OF THE
RURAL REPUBLIC (1789-1860)

The concept of dual federalism, as developed by Corwin, included these four postulates: "(1) The national government is one of enumerated powers only; (2) Also, the purposes which it may constitutionally promote are few; (3) Within their respective spheres the two centers of government are 'sovereign' and hence 'equal'; (4) The relation of the two centers with each other is one of tension rather than collaboration."[1] The period from 1789 to 1860, for the most part, reflected an adherence to these dual-federal themes—constitutionally, politically, and operationally. Madison's compartmentalized "compound republic," in short, was largely realized in the first seventy years under the Constitution.

Other Contending Concepts

During the entire period, of course, nation-centered and state-centered theories of federalism contended with one another.[2] From Hamilton as the first Secretary of the Treasury to John Marshall as Chief Justice of the Supreme Court (1800-35), and thence to Daniel Webster in the Senate in the 1830s and 1840s, a nationalist theory of Union was enunciated. The Constitution was interpreted by them as the people's great charter. It was supreme as law, and created a national government whose enumerated powers were buttressed by a broad reserve of implied powers. In combination, these powers were adequate to meet the most diverse demands placed on the Union government.[3]

The state-centered counterpoint theory was formulated early on by Madison and Jefferson in their Virginia and Kentucky Resolutions (1798), which were drawn up in opposition to the Alien and Sedition Acts. It was partially taken up by Bay State and Connecticut leaders in their vehement opposition to Jefferson's Embargo Act (1807), and was drastically refashioned by various Southern spokesmen, most notably and skillfully by John C. Calhoun, as they sought to counter growing Northern mercantilism, antislavery activity, and, above all, numbers. The two resolutions embodied three concepts:

The Constitution was a compact in that "each State acceded as a State," implying that ultimate sovereignty still resided with the latter.

The powers of the national government were to be bound by "the plain sense and implication" of the Constitution and were not to be construed broadly.

The national government had no exclusive right to judge the scope
of its powers, while the states had an obligation to "interpose"
in any unconstitutional efforts to extend federal authority.[4]

The South Carolinian went much further in his effort to protect the growing Southern minority against the emerging Northern
majority and to curb what he took to be the centralizing impulse
of that wholly new phenomenon: the mass political party. As he
viewed it, all the Madisonian separations and checks were still in
place, but over time a sustained popular majority could and would
reduce them to shallow formalities. Hence, building on Jefferson's theory of the origin of the Constitution, he proclaimed full
state sovereignty and the states' capacity to exercise ultimate
authority to interpret the basic charter. The latter involved a
three-stage process. First, when a state found a congressional
enactment to be in violation of the Constitution it could nullify
it, thus making the law inoperative within its borders. Second, if
the national government persisted in its claim to the power, a
federal constitutional convention or a constitutional amendment would be required to sanction the power. Third, if three-
quarters of the states ratified (creating a concurrent, rather than a
mere numerical majority) the empowering amendment, then the
nullifying state could either acquiesce or assert the ultimate prerogative of its sovereignty: the right to secede peaceably from the
Union.

Calhoun obviously went far beyond the Jefferson and Madison
resolutions, and in this he rejected Madison's interpretation in *The
Federalist*. Regardless of its weak historical foundations, his
state-centered theory of federalism provided the South with its
basic intellectual weaponry in the fratricidal debates that occurred
during the three decades prior to Fort Sumter. As constitutional
theory, it died at Appomattox, but informally applied his concurrent majority doctrine enjoyed a long later life, serving as the master explanation of American politics (see chapter 8).

Judicial Dual Federalism

Despite the conflicts between these two schools of thought, most
of the developments of this period reveal much more of an adherence to the dual-federal doctrine, both in theory and practice. At

the constitutional and judicial levels, and despite some conflicting crosscurrents, this certainly was the case. On the one hand, the Bill of Rights (1791) and the Eleventh Amendment (1798) (which barred access to federal courts in cases where a citizen of one state sues another state, thus overturning the 1793 Supreme Court decision in *Chisholm* v. *Georgia*) could be viewed as restricting national authority, since both placed curbs on it. On the other hand, Madison piloted the Judiciary Act of 1789 through the House, a federal circuit court first declared a state law as unconstitutional in 1791, and John Marshall fourteen years later successfully asserted the power of the Supreme Court to negate an act of Congress. All of these combined to establish the federal judiciary as the ultimate interpreter of the Constitution and the arbiter of conflicts between the states and the nation.

The decisions of the Marshall Court clearly were crucial in establishing the controlling significance of the supremacy, commerce, and contract clauses of the Constitution in cases where national and state powers came into conflict. These decisions, along with *McCulloch* v. *Maryland* (1819), which sanctioned a broad Hamiltonian view of implied powers, laid the basis for applying the "nationalist" label to this Court.

At the same time, the Court recognized an array of legitimate commerce-related actions under the states' police power that were beyond national authority. It also developed the doctrine that a state could regulate commerce and navigation in the absence of congressional legislation, ruled that the Bill of Rights did not apply to state actions, upheld state bankruptcy laws, and denied that a state's tax power could be presumed to have been surrendered by the granting of a corporate charter.[5]

Clearly, the Marshall Court was protective of its own institutional independence, assertive of its authority to render ultimate judgment regarding unconstitutional actions of the nation's political branches and of the states, and selectively protective of Congress's powers under the Constitution. But, just as clearly, it also was mindful that the national government's powers were by no means plenary; that the states are "for some purposes sovereign, and for some purposes subordinate," as Marshall phrased it in one of his most nationalist decisions;[6] and that the relationship between the two levels was essentially one of tension. This last proposition was rooted in the fact that during Marshall's tenure, the Court had declared unconstitutional some acts of half the states. State resentment to these individual decisions and to the Court's general arbitrating role was strong and fairly sustained.[7]

With the successor Taney Court (1835-63), adherence to the postulates of dual federalism was even more pronounced. In a string of commerce-clause cases, it developed the concept of "concurrent powers"—only hinted at in the Marshall decisions. In *Briscoe* v. *Bank of the Commonwealth of Kentucky* (1837), it sanctioned establishment of a state-owned and -controlled bank that was authorized to issue notes for public circulation.[8] Moreover, a broad interpretation of the states' police power emerged from a cluster of other cases. The famous *Charles River Bridge* case (1837) provided Taney with the opportunity to define it as "the powers necessary to accomplish the ends of its [the state's] creation."[9] In other decisions, Taney described it as the power of the states to "provide for the public health, safety, and good order," which was reserved to them by the Tenth Amendment as one of their "sovereign powers . . . complete, unqualified, and exclusive."[10] The combined result of these cases, of course, was to modify considerably the sanctity of contracts, to foster economic competition by ending monopolies, and to stimulate a rash of state banking enterprises.

Corwin felt that the Taney Court's decisions in the areas of commerce and state police powers were a basic threat to the supremacy clause.[11] Others have contended that the Taney Court was no "radical champion of state sovereignty," but rather the developer of "the doctrine of selective exclusiveness—of a limited concurrent state power over commerce" which was both popular and realistic, since most aspects of commerce then still were more within the powers of state, rather than of national regulation.[12] The broad dictum laid down by Marshall in *Gibbons* v. *Ogden* was never overthrown or even challenged, and the Court's right to control state judiciaries in matters of constitutional interpretation was vigorously upheld.[13] The Taney Court, then, gave the principles of dual federalism a somewhat more powerful enunciation than did its predecessor, though not to the detriment of national supremacy in its own limited sphere or of the Court's fundamental role as final judge of what is constitutionally permissible within the states' sphere of action.

Operational Dual Federalism

How did these constitutional and judicial doctrines of dual federalism correspond with operating practice? For the most part, there was a close correspondence. Administratively, a small but separate federal bureaucracy came into being with the establishment of the national government, and so it remained throughout these early dual-federal years. The fact that a separate national administration was established was a foregone conclusion, given the heavily nationalist tenor of the First Congress. Any lingering thoughts (and a few expressed them in the Congress) that the new government would utilize only state agencies to discharge some of its basic functions (tax collection and the post office were cited) were put to rest by the establishment of the departments of State, the Treasury, and War in 1789 and the Navy in 1798. The post of attorney general was created by the Judiciary Act of 1789, but it did not assume cabinet rank until 1870. The post office was given permanent standing in 1794, but again cabinet rank was not accorded until later (1829). The only other department to be formed in this antebellum period was Interior (1849).

Their functions for the most part clearly related to expressly delegated national powers and, in all but two instances (the attorney general and Interior), continued departments that had emerged under the Articles. Their administrative size was small, starting at approximately 1000 civilian employees (and 1300 military) in the Washington administration to 7000 under Monroe, to over 11,000 in the middle of the Jackson administration, to a little over three times that figure during Buchanan's last year in office. While accurate counterpart figures for the states and their localities are unavailable, there is no doubt that the bulk of public administrators—to the extent that there were public functions to be administered—was at these levels.

In terms of finances, a clear division also emerged, with the national government relying heavily on customs and receipts from the sale of western lands and the states on excise taxes.[14] The national government assisted the states under four largely ad hoc actions during this period:

——the cession of portions of the federal land in western public-
    land states for support of common schools as each such state

was admitted into the Union (first enacted by the Continental Congress);[15]

——federal assumption of state revolutionary war debts (1790);

——congressional enactment in 1818 of a measure stipulating that 5 percent of the proceeds from the sale of remaining national lands within a state should go to that state's treasury; and

——the "no strings" distribution of the Treasury surplus in 1837 (before the "Panic" of that year wiped out the surplus).

Efforts to allocate federal funds to states for internal improvements or for other specific purposes were consistently rejected throughout this era. In those few instances where Congress was able to put together the necessary coalition, a presidential veto was inevitably forthcoming. In 1854, for example, an act, sponsored by Dorothea Dix, was passed to provide federal aid to the states for the indigent insane. President Franklin Pierce vetoed it, contending that if "Congress is to make provision for [paupers], the fountains of charity will be dried up at home, and the several States, instead of bestowing their own means on the social wants of their people, may themselves, through the strong temptations, which appears to States as individuals, become humble suppliants for the bounty of the Federal Government, reversing their true relation to this Union."[16]

In terms of governmental functions and services, the states exercised an almost exclusive role (sometimes shared with their localities) in the areas of elections and apportionment, civil and property rights, education, family and criminal law, business organization, local governmental organization and powers, as well as labor and race relations (including slavery).[17] During the last three decades of this period, the states also dominated banking and, as was noted earlier, shared in making national monetary and commercial regulatory policies.

National functions, on the other hand, were still relatively few, and became fewer as the decades passed. Witness the undermining of the second U.S. Bank by Jackson (1832) and the unsuccessful Whig efforts to resurrect it later (1842); the strict constructionist (and vetoing) approach toward "internal improvements" and toward aid for specific program areas on the part of nearly all of the presidents after 1800 (save notably for John Quincy Adams);

and the growing disinclination of Congress to use the powers it possessed, especially under the commerce clause.

How Much Cooperative Federalism?

Where, then, does this leave the germinating seeds of "cooperative federalism" during this period? It leaves them in very barren soil with only isolated cases of collaboration springing up—more at the beginning than at the end. How could it have been anything else? Domestic federal program activities, after all, were few (in manpower terms, chiefly involving the postal service, customs collections, and Corps of Engineers, as well as organizing and providing for territorial governments). And, while there obviously was a necessary interaction between the levels, especially in the judicial, militia, elections machinery, commercial regulatory, and Indian affairs areas, conflict was as much a part of these intergovernmental relationships as cooperation.

The Period in Perspective

A range of legal, economic, social, and political developments during the first seventy-year period—all heavily conditioned by the dominant egalitarian and localistic cultural norms—combined to sustain an operational adherence to Madison's "compound republic" and its implied dual federalism intergovernmental features. The national role was minimal (still restricted largely to "war and danger" and some limited "pork barreling"); its few policies fell under various "distributional" headings; and its expenditures and personnel were consistently meager. The states, on the other hand, were the prime focal points of economic development, political and governmental reform, and party organization. Their economic and social activism was in marked contrast to the laissez-faire policy generally adhered to by the national government.

Clearly, there were in this era two separate spheres of power, each roughly supreme in its own area of authority, with minimal overlap in the exercise of these two sets of authority and with conflict—far more than collaboration—characterizing the interrelationship where overlaps did exist. It was, then, a predominantly dual-federal system, but with some questions arising in the era's later years as to whether the balance of power between the two levels, contemplated by the Founders, was being sustained, given the growing strength of the states (and of sectionalism). These growing doubts set the stage for a bloody fratricidal contest over whether a nation-centered or state-centered theory of federalism would prevail. Yet, as we shall see, dual federalism was not obliterated by the outcome.

THE SECOND ERA: DUAL FEDERALISM, WITH DIFFERENCES (1861-1930)

The second major evolutionary period in the history of American federalism and its intergovernmental relations also lasted for approximately seventy years (1861-1930). It, too, had a dominant political and economic theme—"to perfect the free economy."[18] Moreover, and despite dramatic social, economic, and governmental changes over the period, the dominant theory and practice of federalism throughout still warrant the dual-federalism designation. This second era, however, produced some very different interpretations and applications of the doctrine, as well as a few departures from it. And this sets the period apart from both the era that preceded it and the one that followed.

Constitutional and Judicial Shifts

The Civil War settled several of the questions left unanswered by the Framers and *The Federalist*. It destroyed the doctrine that the Constitution was a compact among sovereign states, each with the right to interpose or nullify an act of Congress, and each with the ultimate right to secede legally from the Union.[19] The Supreme Court scuttled this state-centered concept in *Texas* v. *White* (1869), with a dual-federal theory of perpetual Union articulated by Chief Justice Salmon P. Chase:

The perpetuity and indissolvability of the Union, by no means implies the loss of distinct and individual existence, or of the right of self-government by the States. Under the Articles of Confederation, each State retained its sovereignty, freedom, and independence, and each power, jurisdiction, and right not expressly delegated to the United States. Under the Constitution, though the powers of the States were much restricted, still all the powers not delegated to the United States, nor prohibited to the States, are reserved to the States, respectively, or to the people. . . . Not only . . . can there be no loss of separate and independent autonomy to the States, through their union under the Constitution, but it may be not unreasonably said that the preservation of the States, and the maintenance of their governments, are as much within the design and care of the Constitution as the preservation of the Union and the maintenance of the National Government. The Constitution, in all its provisions, looks to an indestructible Union, composed of indestructible States.[20]

A partly national, partly federal decision, this one. The nationalist view of the Constitution as supreme law and as emanating from the people, and of the Union as being perpetual, clearly are accepted. Yet, so were the earlier dual-federal concepts of divided powers, of two separate spheres of governmental authority and autonomous activity, and of the constitutional guarantee of state autonomy.

Implicitly, Chase here accepts the Marshall-Taney view that the Supreme Court ultimately would serve as the valid interpreter of what were constitutionally permissible actions by either the political branches of the national government or by the states. And in the long period of judicial activism that extended throughout the rest of this period, this view had major implications for both the theory and practice of federalism. Between 1789 and 1860, only two acts of Congress and some sixty state enactments had been declared void by the Court, while from 1874 to 1898, twelve congressional and 125 state acts were vetoed, and from 1898 to 1937, fifty federal and four hundred state laws were found unconstitutional.[21]

The Civil War and its aftermath also produced three constitutional amendments (the thirteenth, fourteenth, and fifteenth), a cluster of civil-rights acts, and a highly intrusive, congressionally dictated approach to reconstruction in the Southern states—all signs of an extraordinary assertion of national legal authority. Yet the Supreme Court itself ultimately put the brakes on drastic constitutional change in this area,[22] the net effect of which was to leave civil and voting rights matters pretty much to the states until the nineteen-fifties and sixties.[23]

The main arena in which judicial conflict arose in this period was the scope of the states' police power as it affected commerce, manufacturing, labor relations, and social welfare—all areas that came to the forefront as ever-advancing urbanization and industrialization transformed the American landscape and political agenda during this era.

By the end of this era (and it did not really end for the federal judiciary until 1937), the Supreme Court had built a half-century record of aggressively acting as the ultimate interpreter of the constitutionality of state laws enacted pursuant to their police power as well as federal statutes passed in furtherance of its commerce or taxing powers. From the late eighties on, the doctrine of substantive due process and a constrained concept of "commerce in commerce" were applied to a range of cases involving state and federal statutes—admittedly with somewhat moderating tests of reasonableness emerging in both by the second decade of this century.

The general effect was to enthrone the federal judiciary and to sanction state actions in some areas, but not in others, as well as to sanction federal laws in some areas, but again not in others. Over time, Congress's regulatory authority (relying primarily on the commerce, but occasionally the tax power) came out somewhat ahead of the states' police power. Yet the latter was upheld ultimately in a range of social and economic areas that would have been unthinkable in the eighties or nineties. Moreover, the states continued to exercise a near-exclusive authority, with little to no federal judicial or other intervention, in the areas of family and criminal law, elections, control over local government, and commercial law.[24] In addition, civil rights, following the 1896 *Plessy* "separate but equal" doctrine, pretty much fell wholly under state jurisdiction, for better or worse, while criminal justice and civil liberties, and state enactments relating thereto, did not become a due-process concern of the Supreme Court until the twenties. A major extension of federal judicial power and some expansion of congressional authority but not always at the expense of the states[25]—these were the main constitutional developments of this second era of American federalism.

At first glance, they would not appear to support fully the dual-federalism designation assigned to it at the outset. But other facets of the intergovernmental relations of the period must be probed before a final judgment is rendered on this issue.

Finances and Functions: Still Divided, but with a Few Signs of Sharing

As Riker points out, sole reliance on formal constitutional analyses of federalism can provide a highly distorted picture of the real relationship between the nation and the states.[26] An examination of the funding and servicing patterns of this era will help serve as a corrective to any distortions that the foregoing judicial analysis may have produced.

Basic changes occurred in the realm of public finance, but not to the point of overturning the older compartmentalized approach to revenue raising, nor of generating any major fiscal imbalances between and among the governmental levels.

Nationally, the prime shift was away from tariff and sales receipts from western land to the income tax—a shift that took two Supreme Court decisions, a constitutional amendment, and more than a quarter of a decade of political pressuring to bring it about in 1913. During the Civil War, a national income tax of sorts had been levied to help finance the Union effort, and it was not challenged in the courts. After more than a decade of agitation by agrarian radicals and eastern liberals, the Congress in considering the Wilson-Gorman tariff (1894) accepted over considerable opposition an income-tax provision sponsored by William Jennings Bryan. It was immediately challenged in federal courts, with some of the ablest legal talent of the day serving as the plaintiffs' lawyers.[27]

By some artful reasoning and ignoring of several federal taxing precedents, the Court's majority concluded in the second Pollack case (the first had produced a 4-4 tie vote) that the tax, in essence, was direct, hence unconstitutional.[28] Apportionment in accordance with state population would, of course, violate the entire thrust of an income tax and the amendment approach ultimately was used, though it took another fourteen years and a progressive congressional coalition to force it.

Some have explained the entire later course of American fed-

Table 3-1 Federal Tax Collections by Type of Tax

(Selected years)
(In millions of dollars)

Year	Income	Consumption	Other	Total
1902	. . .	487	26	513
1927	2,138	1,088	138	3,364

Source: U.S. Bureau of the Census, Historical Statistics, Governmental Finances in 1963 (Washington, D.C.: U.S. Government Printing Office), p. 22.

eralism in terms of this amendment and its assignment to the federal government of the most lucrative of all public-revenue sources. Yet, in terms of the period under analysis here, the rates were quite moderate and the receipts relatively modest. Nonetheless, the income tax heralded a new era in federal finance, becoming the most important single source of federal revenue (from nothing in 1902 to more than three-fifths of the 1927 total) and shifting the bulk of federal financing more onto the shoulders of the wealthier, a goal of the Populists, and later Progressives, who advanced it as a means of redistributing the wealth.

At the state and local levels, less drastic shifts occurred, but shifts there were. The key ones were a growing overall role of the

Table 3-2 State and Local Tax Collections by Type of Tax

(Selected years)
(In millions of dollars)

Year	Income	Consumption	Property	Other	Total
State 1902	. . .	28	82	46	156
1927	162	445	370	631	1,608
Local 1902	. . .	. . .	624	80	704
1927	. . .	25	4,360	94	4,479

Source: U.S. Bureau of the Census Historical Statistics (Washington, D.C.: U.S. Government Printing Office, 1960), pp. 722-24.

Table 3-3   State Intergovernmental Expenditures by Function, 1902 and 1927

(In millions of dollars)

	1902		1927	
Function	*Dollars*	*Percent*	*Dollars*	*Percent*
Education	45	86	292	49
Highways	2	4	197	33
Public welfare	. . .	. . .	6	1
Other	5	10	101	17
Total	52	100	596	100

Source: U.S. Bureau of the Census, *Census of Governments, 1957*, vol. 4, no. 2, *State Payments to Local Governments* (Washington, D.C.: U.S. Government Printing Office, 1959), p. 100.

states, the beginning of their own reliance on an income tax, and a slight hike in local governments' dependence on the property tax (see table 3-2).

Overall, state revenues rose from roughly 18 percent of the 1902 combined total to over one-quarter of the 1927 figure. A modest hike, perhaps, but still a contrast with the earlier period when the local tax effort nearly eclipsed that of the states. This growing state role is explained by fifteen states (and one territory —Hawaii) enacting personal income taxes between 1901 and 1930, by sixteen (and again, Hawaii) adopting corporate income taxes during the same period, by forty-eight levying gasoline taxes, by twenty-seven moving on the cigarette excise front, by all but one charging for automobile registration, and by twenty-two joining the twenty-three that had enacted death duties in the nineteenth century.[29] The mix of taxes in any one package varied considerably from state to state, reflecting a continuance of at least one facet of the previous era's mercantilist practices. General sales, gift, and distilled-liquor taxes, it should be noted, were part of none of the states' tax packages prior to 1930. The overall trend, then, was of gradual diversification with a major reliance on individual excise levies, both new and old. Then, as now, the property tax was the chief local source of revenue (from own sources), accounting for 92 percent of the total in 1890 and rising to 97 percent in 1927. Despite the emergence of some modest tax overlaps among the levels (personal and corporate income and a few excise taxes for some states and the federal government and between some states and their localities with the property tax), clearly the broad picture still was one of a basic separation of revenue sources by governmental level.

Growth of Grants

By way of contrast, intergovernmental fiscal transfers on a continuing basis emerged as a significantly new development chiefly during the last three decades of this period. This represented a different kind of revenue source for recipient governments and suggests the real beginnings of a cooperative federal theme countering the dominant dual-federal principle. State aid to their localities rose from a mere $52 million in 1902 to $596 million by 1927, accounting for a little over 6 percent of local general revenue in the earlier and 10 percent in the latter.[30] The functional areas aided are highlighted in table 3–3. Four generalizations emerge regarding this first phase in the history of state aid:

1. The amounts in absolute and relative terms were small and not all states were involved;
2. The areas aided were the same ones that dominated state efforts in the modern period;
3. School districts and counties inferentially, except in New England, were the prime local governmental recipients;
4. Above all, the paramount responsibility for funding the aided and all other local governmental functions rested with the localities themselves and their property tax.

The emergence of federal cash aid to the states, of course, constituted an equally dramatic break with the previous era, though again, the scale of federal assistance was quite modest. A kind of prelude to this, of course, was the signing by President Lincoln in 1862 of the Morrill Act (an earlier bill had been vetoed by Buchanan), opening the public lands to all the states for support of such agricultural colleges as they wished to establish.[31] The Hatch Act of 1887 supplemented this earlier program by providing for the establishment of experimental stations at the agricultural colleges, but this time, the funding was in the form of a cash grant. The first such program was the textbooks-for-the-blind enactment (1879), but this involved a grant to a nonprofit body (American Printing House for the Blind). By 1900, five cash grant programs were in operation (for textbooks for the blind, 1879; agricultural experiment stations, 1887; state soldiers' homes, 1888; resident instruction in land-grant colleges, 1890; and irrigation, 1894). During the second decade of this century, six more were enacted:

——assistance to state marine schools (1911), which was the first open-ended matching grant;

——state and private forestry cooperation (Weeks Act of 1911) that required the formal submission of a state plan and established minimum performance standards;

——agricultural extension service (Smith-Lever Act of 1914), which stipulated a dollar-for-dollar match;

—— highway construction (1916), which also stipulated a fifty-fifty match as well as planning and state administrative requirements, and contained a complicated three-factor allocational formula;

——vocational education (Smith-Hughes Act of 1917), that permitted the funding of teachers' salaries; and

——vocational rehabilitation (the Fess-Kenyon Act of 1920), a fifty-fifty matching program for disabled veterans.[32]

Most of the six, the 1920 enactment excepted, enjoyed strong state support, additional revenues being their prime concern. Conditions, as has been noted, began to become more detailed. Each again, save for the last, used the grant device as a means of supplementing national efforts and of avoiding the constitutionally doubtful direct-expenditure route.[33] And three of the six (not to mention three of the earlier five) had a clear rural bias.

In the early twenties, two new enactments generated considerable state opposition. The 1921 amendments to the Federal Road Aid Act of 1916 called for a periodic national evaluation of state highway departments to determine if they were able and empowered to coordinate and administer the grant to the satisfaction of the secretary of the Department of Agriculture.[34] This was deemed a national intrusion by the states, though they wanted the added funding. With the maternity and infancy health program (the Sheppard-Tanner Act of 1921), a range of state and professional groups rose in opposition, questioning the need for the program, the degree of national intervention, and the extent to which it reflected national goals and priorities, not those of the states. Soon it was before the federal courts, and in two cases, one initiated by the Commonwealth of Massachusetts and the other by a private taxpayer, the Supreme Court decided on its constitutionality. In *Massachusetts* v. *Mellon,* it held that no violation or attack on state sovereignty was involved in the enactment, in that the grant-in-aid was merely an inducement and a state could (as some did) refuse to participate in it.[35] In *Frothingham* v. *Mellon,* it decided that an individual had no standing in court in such a case, since "after funds have been brought into the Treasury and mingled with other funds there placed, Congress has sweeping power to dispose of these funds."[36] These decisions were crucial in the later evolution of federal grants, though the Sheppard-Tanner Act itself expired by 1929, under opposition from President Coolidge.

By 1930, fifteen grant programs were operating, with highway aid predominant (as table 3-4 shows). With rising state tax receipts in the 1920s, the 1927 federal aid total represented only about 2 percent of all state revenues for the year, hardly a significant sign of major efforts in cooperative federalism. Moreover, the aggregate of state aid to localities for the same years was nearly five times the federal.

Table 3-4   Federal Intergovernmental Transfers by Broad Functional Category for Selected Years (1902-27)

(In millions of dollars)

Year	Total	Education	Highways	Welfare	Other
1902	7	1	. . .	1	5
1913	12	3	. . .	2	7
1922	118	7	92	1	18
1927	123	10	83	1	29

Source: U.S. Bureau of the Census, *Statistical History of the U.S.* (Stamford, Conn.: Fairfield Publications, 1965), pp. 484-516.

Functional Assignments

As much of the foregoing fiscal and judicial analyses have suggested, fairly significant shifts in servicing responsibilities occurred during this seventy-year period. The national government, over time and not easily, acquired a functional role that was in marked contrast to the one it held in 1860 or would hold in 1960. The most obvious functional development, of course, was the significant growth in national authority, activities, policies, and programs. The dominance of the national government in the military, foreign policy, monetary, and banking areas was established. Moreover, a new role was gradually carved out—of the national government serving as positive (not passive, as was the case formerly) regulator (and even reformer) of the economic system, subject of course to the curbs provided by the Supreme Court. The antitrust, fair-trade practices, various interstate commerce prohibitions, and direct regulation of railroads and radio communications efforts combine to suggest a major departure from the dominantly negative or neutral role the national government assumed in such matters during most of the pre–Civil War era. And the new promotional efforts in economic development, natural resources conservation, and social welfare and education—generally by direct action, but sometimes by grants-in-aid—suggest other contrasts with the past and moves toward greater centralization.

Yet were the states and localities eclipsed or enervated by these developments? The answer, basically, is No. What the national government was doing during this period was responding gradually and with considerable uncertainty and conflict "to the new national dimensions of business enterprises and labor organizations, and to the consumer problems of an increasingly urbanized society."[37] Most of the newly assumed functions were part of this response and most of them, by their genuinely interstate and national scope, were beyond the effective control of the states' police power. At the same time, this left a wide range of functions primarily, if not exclusively, in state or local hands: primary and secondary education, public higher education, public welfare, public hospitals, police, fire protection, and local sanitation, to mention only the more obvious of state-local-provided and wholly or almost wholly-financed services. In all the federal-grant-aided areas, including the two largest—highways and vocational education—the states were the senior partners fiscally and administratively.

Toward the end of the era, the number of state and local personnel had grown to more than four times the federal figure.[38] In a similar vein, while federal per capita direct expenditures increased steadily over this period (beginning at $2.00 per capita in 1860 and rising to $7.23 in 1902, thence to $35.84 in 1927), overall state-local per capita expenditures soared from $13.83 in 1902 to $65.61 by 1927. In short, while the states' regulatory, intrastate commerce power, and in a few instances taxing authority were constrained by some of the federal regulatory efforts, these powers were not in any sense negated or undermined. In some cases, expansion of the state police power was sanctioned. Above all, perhaps, practically all of the growing number of public services provided directly to the public were decided upon, performed, and financed by state and chiefly local governments. In overall functional terms, the increase in national regulatory efforts vis-à-vis the private corporate sector was balanced by an increasing state and local direct servicing role (and without federal incentives or controls).

Conclusion

The dynamics of this era as reflected in the judicial, public-finance, servicing, and developmental areas all lead to the generalization that Madison's compound republic with its basically compartmentalized theory of functional assignment was still pretty much intact 140 years after it was established. It operated differently under the emerging industrial republic than it had under the old rural regime, but it definitely was a dual-federal system. The national government clearly was in a stronger position—constitutionally, judicially, fiscally, as well as in regulatory matters—than it was in 1860. The states and localities also had grown in power and authority during the same period. The emergence of servicing government, after all and quite naturally, began with these jurisdictions. Whether comparative revenue, expenditure, or personnel figures are used, the states and their localities were the senior partners under the federal system throughout the period.

What is more, hardly any of these expanding state and local

undertakings involved any regular interaction with the national government, though they did accelerate the interaction between them. Fifteen federal categorical grants amounting to a total of $100 million in 1930 did not add up to any major piercing of the traditional federal-state separation-of-services barrier. Moreover, the informal, ad hoc, and largely sporadic contacts between parallel regulatory and administrative agencies at the federal and state levels, while suggesting cooperation, were neither required (save in one instance) nor indispensable to the performance of either level's implementing and regulatory roles. Local governments, of course, had implementing and regulatory roles. Most local governments, of course, had no regular formal or significant informal contacts with the federal.

Dual federalism dominant—such was the operational theory of federalism that characterized most of the intergovernmental relations of this second era of America's emergence as a nation. Such was the ideal that the citizens of Muncie adhered to in the 1920s, believed they would return to in the 1940s (after the Depression was over), and pretend schizoidally to operate under even today.

THE RISE AND MATURATION OF
COOPERATIVE FEDERALISM (1930-1960)

The third phase of our evolving federal system encompassed the rise and maturation of cooperative federalism. Traditional dual federalism, for all intents and purposes, began its decline during the Depression. Cooperative federalism, seeds of which were sown in the previous era, evolved fairly rapidly and reached a high point of maturation and acceptance in the fifties. Yet, with the launching of the contemporary period in the sixties, a series of developments emerged that combined to undermine conventional cooperative federalism, and in its place substitute the overloaded system, described at the outset.

The concept of cooperative federalism emerged only a little later (e.g., the forties and fifties) than the idea of intergovernmental relations itself. And with good reason. Both primarily represented attempts to describe what had emerged with the New Deal, though diligent efforts to trace the roots of the concept to the Articles of Confederation were made.[39] As the two previous sections demonstrate, sustained interlevel interaction in administration, servicing, or finances—whether cooperative or conflicting—ranged from nil to minimal throughout the 140 years following the adoption of the Constitution, just as Madison intended.

What then are the postulates of cooperative federalism? In essence, as it emerges from the writings of its prime expositors, Grodzins and Elazar, it encompasses seven premises, which were meant to be descriptive, but which ultimately become prescriptive:

—— "The American federal system is principally characterized by a federal-state-local sharing of responsibilities for virtually all functions."
—— "Our history and politics in large part account for this sharing.
—— "Dividing functions between the federal government, on the one hand, and the states and localities, on the other," is not really possible "without drastically reducing the importance of the latter."
—— "No 'strengthening' of state governments will materially reduce the present functions of the federal government, nor will it have any marked effect on the rate of acquisition of new federal functions."
——Real and reliable decentralization is that which exists "as the result of independent centers of power and . . . operates through the chaos of American political processes and political institutions."
—— "Federal, state and local officials are not adversaries. They are colleagues. The sharing of functions and powers is impossible without a whole."
—— "The American system is best conceived as one government serving one people."[40]

In analyzing this theory, certain of its more distinctive features need to be emphasized. Primarily, it is a functional interpretation, focusing heavily on the funding, administration, and rendering of public services. The dominant pattern of service provision, so the theory holds, is a shared one including practically all governmental functions. The decentralized basis of our political parties and processes assures adequate representation and protection of state and local interests at the national level as well as a continuing "noncentralization," to use Elazar's apt term, within the peripheral governments. In terms of structure and power, the institutionalized pattern of collaboration had emerged within a "dualistic structural pattern" and "the relative balance between the federal government and the states [had] not significantly shifted" since the Constitution was adopted.[41]

Attitudinally, officials at all levels behave as allies, not as enemies, in that they need and rely on one another, as well as operate under one system and serve one people. The melding of the powers and functions of the American governments thus resembles the characteristics of a "marble cake," as McLean called it, rather than the "layer cake" of dual federalism.[42] So much for the theory, but what of its practice?

The real rise of cooperative federalism occurred during the Depression and the decade and a half following World War II. In terms of public finance, public programs, public administration and politics, a broadly collaborative pattern, or at least a pattern of sharing—whether done in a really cooperative fashion or not—emerged as the dynamic new feature of the intergovernmental relations of that period. The dollars, programs, and personnel involved as well as the sheer scope of expanded and regularized intergovernmental contacts were so much greater than the limited counterpart efforts of the earlier era that the cooperative federal label was a wholly appropriate one to apply. At the same time, and as will be shown, not all of the theory's premises were reflected in practice. Moreover, this basic shift in the development of American federalism would not have persisted for three decades (nor would the present pattern of intergovernmental relations have emerged as it has) without judicial sanction.

The Court Crushes Old Dual Federalism

Intergovernmental relations, as the analyses of the predecessor periods indicated, was and is conditioned by judicial decisions as much as by any other single factor. This is not to say that the judges are necessarily the paramount actors in the unfolding of the federal drama. But they were (and are) actors. For the first seven years of this period, the Supreme Court pursued a course that generally was the opposite of the political branches of the national government, resisting the rapidly emerging cooperative federal shift in direct regulation and intergovernmental relationships and enunciating variations on the older dual-federal principles.

Unlike President Hoover, who rejected a broad construction of the federal commerce power even as he urged certain relief measures (hence the 1930 dating of the beginning of this period), Franklin Roosevelt quickly scrapped his earlier states'-rights views and adopted a flexible approach to the constitutionality of the sweeping economic recovery and reform proposals he advanced in the wake of his first inauguration. In their entirety, the emergency programs enacted during 1933 added up to an extraordinary assumption of federal authority over the nation's economy and a major expansion of its commerce and taxing powers.[43] Two lines of precedents, in effect, were before the judges when dealing with the cases this legislation generated. The more limited one stretched back through the child-labor cases to E. C. Knight, while the more latitudinarian followed a different course, leading to those decisions that combined to create a broad federal regulatory power.

It was not until 1935 that a New Deal statute came before the Court. Beginning in January of that year and continuing for the next sixteen months, ten major cases or groups of cases were decided. In eight of them, the Court's majority voted against the New Deal. Only the emergency monetary measures and the Tennessee Valley Authority Act survived, largely on conditional terms.[44]

In the eight, the majority of the Justices rejected the New Deal's massive expansion of federal authority, some of it at the expense of the states. More specifically, they rejected

1. any delegation of broad rule making or regulatory authority to executive or especially to quasi-private agencies in the absence of clear congressional guidelines;
2. any real federal control over production whether by means of the commerce, taxing, or general welfare clauses, thus harkening back to the dual-federalism approach to the federal police power; and
3. any viable concept of constitutional growth in light of economic growth or emergency.[45]

The Court was not alone in its assault on the Roosevelt program, however. Political conservatives in both parties, business groups, and financiers, as well as former president Hoover, joined in a defense of limited constitutional government, the sovereignty of the states, and the free-market economy.[46] With Roosevelt's campaign against the "economic royalists" and his tremendous electoral triumph in 1936, overtones—but only overtones—of class politics began to emerge and the stage was set for a confrontation with the Court.

Various proposals to curb the Court were advanced in Congress. In early 1937, the president presented Congress with a bill that would authorize him to appoint another judge for each one who had served ten years or more and had not retired within six months after his seventieth birthday. A maximum of fifty such appointments were to be permitted and the Supreme Court's size was to be raised to fifteen.[47]

The plan was clearly constitutional and it split his own party, especially in the Senate. Yet the likelihood of its ultimate passage prompted some dramatically different decisions from the Court itself. In rapid succession, the Farm Mortgage Act of 1935, the amended Railway Labor Act of 1934, and the National Labor Relations Act and the Social Security Act of 1935 were upheld between March and June. The Court reorganization fight continued for a while, but its essential purpose already had been realized.

Thus, a new era of judicial construction was launched. The commerce power was given broad interpretation in the cases upholding the Labor Relations Act. The older distinction between direct and indirect effects was scrapped and the "stream of commerce" concept was adopted.[48] The scope of the federal taxing power also was broadened expansively. In sanctioning the Social Security Act, the unemployment excise tax on employers was upheld as a legitimate use of the tax power and the grants to the states were viewed as examples of federal-state collaboration, not of federal coercion.[49] The act's old-age and benefit provisions were deemed to be proper, since "Congress may spend money in aid of the general welfare."[50] When combined, these decisions obviously amounted to last rites for judicial dual federalism.

In overall judicial and constitutional terms, the post-1937 Court sanctioned a "permanent enlargement in the extent of Federal power."[51] Areas of authoritative action that previously had been left to the states' sphere of sovereignty or to the private sector now fell within the powers of Congress. The sale of securities, public-utility operations, agricultural production and marketing, labor-management relations (including wages and hours), flood control, and regional development were only some of the more obvious new federal policy areas that the New Deal carved out and that the Court ultimately found constitutional.[52]

The economy in all of its key phases had become a national responsibility and no later Court or set of new political leaders ever seriously questioned this. State authority in many of these areas was not nullified, but the regulatory activities of the national government generally far outweighed those of the states, either singly or collectively. Dual federalism as it had been applied judicially was a dead doctrine throughout the rest of this period. No longer could the Justices fall back on the two streams of precedents when dealing with commerce or taxing power cases, since only the broad, "liberal national tradition" was deemed authoritative.[53]

At the same time, the states' police power actually expanded during these thirty years, and well into the contemporary period. Moreover, as later analysis will show, the states became major implementors of several nationally initiated grant programs.

This judicial passivity in the economic and regulatory areas did not lead to passivity in all. Fears in the late thirties that the Court's role in the system would decline and that its traditional policy-making assignment would wither were proven groundless. Wide-ranging questions, after all, confronted it before, but especially following, World War II dealing with segregation, church and state issues, subversive activities, and segregation. As early as 1937, the Court began to enunciate a "preferred-freedoms" principle involving federal constitutional protection of those rights "implicit in the concept of ordered liberty" and those principles "so rooted in the traditions and conscience of our people as to be ranked as fundamental."[54] This libertarian doctrine provided the basis for a new judicial activism.[55]

In application, this led to a case-by-case gradual incorporation of various of the First Amendment guarantees within the "due process" and "equal protection" clauses of the Fourteenth Amendment, thus generating a new body of substantive due process in the civil-liberties area directed mainly against the states.[56] A few justices, notably Hugo Black, contended that the entire Bill of Rights should be covered by the amendment and that this was the intent of its framers.[57] The full Court, however, was not persuaded.

Reflective of the postwar period was the regularity with which civil-rights cases began to come before the Court. Thus, state-required segregation in interstate transportation was found unconstitutional in 1946 and state judicially enforced restrictive covenants were invalidated two years later.[58] Though earlier higher-education cases had begun to chip away at the "separate but equal" doctrine as it applied to education,[59] it took the landmark *Brown* v. *Board of Education* (1954) to relate the principle to primary and secondary schools and in the context of mid-twentieth century conditions, not those of the late nineteenth. It was, of course, found to be in violation of the "equal protection" clause of the Fourteenth Amendment, less on legal and historical grounds and more on the basis of the impact of segregation on black children.[60] The famous phrase "with all deliberate speed" was an attempt to recognize that implementation of the decision would not be instantaneous, but that flexibility and inevitable delays would be part of the effort to achieve what amounted to a social revolution in the South.[61] "Interposition" and "massive resistance" were but two aspects of a broad pattern of Southern formal and informal resistance to the decision. By the end of this era, the pace of school desegregation was still moving at a glacial pace.

In broad outline, what do these three decades of Court history suggest? They clearly indicate that federal-state questions arising in diverse areas were the dominant concerns of the Court. They demonstrate that judicial activism in one area may be accompanied by passivity in others, with a majority of the pre-1937 justices generally exhibiting a strong predilection to assert their narrow view of the federal commerce, taxation, and police powers, while rarely asserting themselves on civil rights or civil liberties issues. The New Deal Court, on the other hand, assumed a generally deferential posture vis-à-vis Congress's interpretation of its powers (thus leaving the question of constraint almost wholly to the political process), while civil liberties and a new version of substantive due process provided the basis for renewed judicial assertiveness.

In terms of the states, these various shifts in judicial outlook were not always threatening. The old Court's dual-federalism doctrine obviously was beneficial to them (at least in a judicial sense) and the new Court's abandonment of economic substantive due process expanded the scope of their police power. Moreover, the conservatism of the postwar years helped produce a series of decisions that were more protective of the police power than was the case during the years 1937-41.

Yet national authority in the economic area clearly was expanded massively during this period, and the Court ultimately found this crucial change to be within the framework of the Constitution. The desegregation cases in the fifties marked a renewal of this national assertiveness, though from the Court itself, rather than from the president or the Congress. Equally clear was the fact that some of this judicial enlargement of the federal "sphere" was at the expense of the states and the private sector. In short, despite relative state gains during the period, the national government in absolute and constitutional terms came out as the more authoritative partner in the system. Moreover, the high Court remained something of an umpire of the federal system, even though it abdicated its role in the economic regulatory area, leaving it to the determination of the political branches of the national government. Yet it also espoused—sometimes vigorously, sometimes softly—a new type of activism, if not interventionism, in the areas of civil liberties and civil rights.

Governmental Finances: Great Growth and Some Diversification

Major public finance shifts occurred during this third phase of the history of American federalism—shifts that paralleled developments in the other areas of intergovernmental activity. One authority put it in these dramatic terms: "The decade of the 1930's brought more drastic change to the intergovernmental financial structure in the United States than has the preceding 140 years."[62]

The prime fiscal fact of this era, perhaps, was the extraordinary growth of governmental outlays, especially during the thirties. Whether measured as a percent of gross national product (GNP) or in per capita terms or in constant dollars, the rate of growth between 1929 and 1959 exceeded that of either of the two preceding eras as well as that of the one we live in. In GNP terms, the percentage for the latter year was nearly three times (280 percent) greater than that of the earlier one and on a per capita basis, the $844 figure in 1959 (in constant dollars) was more than five times the 1929 amount. The growth rate since 1960 until now, though sizable, did not match these rates—suggesting yet another highly distinctive feature of these earlier three decades.

The expenditure patterns by level of government also highlight equally dramatic developments, with the federal government assuming, for the first time in American intergovernmental history, the dominant role, and its total outlays rising from 2.5 percent of GNP (or $42 per capita) in 1929 to 18.7 percent in 1959 (or $586 per capita). At the same time, the total state and local share of the GNP still surpassed the federal domestic proportion (8.2 percent versus 7.7 percent) at the end of the period, as it had by narrowing margins throughout.

The steady growth in state expenditures was especially noteworthy, with nearly a fourfold hike in per capita terms and almost a doubling of its proportion of the GNP. Total local expenditures, on the other hand, experienced a decline as a proportion of the GNP (from 5.3 percent in 1929 to 4.4 percent in 1959) as well as a slight decline in per capita terms between 1929 and 1949. The slight rise (to 4.4 percent of GNP) in the fifties still left them with a per capita 1959 figure that was only 64 percent higher than its 1929 counterpart. Yet when state and local outlays are combined, their total 1959 share of the GNP came to 8.2 percent compared to 6.9 percent in 1949.

The shift in the respective federal, state, and local shares of total and domestic expenditures during this period provides another means of dramatizing the significantly changed character of public finances. The jump in the federal share of domestic outlays from 17 percent in 1929 to 47 percent in 1939 to only a percentage point higher in 1959 really tells the story (see table 3–5). The relatively minor shifts in the state and local proportions in the latter two years also should be noted, suggesting rather stable trends during the period's last two decades and the continuing, though reduced, greater local expenditure role vis-à-vis the states.

In terms of specific revenue sources, the federal government relied somewhat less on income taxes during the thirties (thanks to

Table 3-5   Share of Total and Domestic Governmental Expenditures by Level, from Own Funds, 1929, 1939, 1959

Calendar year	Federal		State		Local	
	% Total	% Domestic	% Total	% Domestic	% Total	% Domestic
1929	25	17	21	23	54	60
1939	51	47	21	23	28	30
1959	70	48	14	24	16	28

Source: Adapted from Advisory Commission on Intergovernmental Relations, *Significant Features of Fiscal Federalism*, 1978-79 ed. (Washington, D.C.: U.S. Government Printing Office, May 1979), p. 7.

the depressed economy) than it did in the previous decade. Yet the income-tax share soared steadily during the forties and fifties, to assume an ever greater proportionate dominance than it had in the twenties (77 percent in 1948 and 79 percent in 1958).

State and local taxes also experienced major shifts. Overall, the state share of total state-local tax collections rose from 26 percent in 1927 to 41 percent in 1938, and then to a near parity status of 49 percent in 1958 (see table 3-6). This marked shift in the state role in one sense represents a continuation of a trend that began in the latter part of the earlier era. Yet the magnitude of the changed collections picture suggests a real departure from the earlier incremental growth pattern.

The adoption of new state taxes helps to explain this. Between 1930 and 1960 17 states enacted a personal income tax (16 of them in the thirties) and a like number adopted a corporate income levy (15 of them during the Depression years).[63] Moreover, and in complete contrast to earlier behavior, 35 passed general sales tax measures, with 20 acting in the thirties. In two specialized tax areas, 39 instituted distilled liquor excises (thanks to the repeal of Prohibition) and 15 enacted gift taxes.

Put differently, 114 separate new enactments in eight separate taxing areas took place in the thirties, along with 29 and 11 additional actions in the forties and fifties, respectively. The total of 154 separate tax actions for these three decades stands in contrast with the 183 for the entire pre-1930 period, of which 48 were death taxes and 49 were automobile registration fees. The mix and

Table 3-6   State and Local Tax Collections by Type of Tax

(Selected years)
(In millions of dollars)

Calendar year	Income	Consumption	Property	Other	Total
State 1927	162	445	370	631	1,608
1938	383	1,674	244	831	3,132
1948	1,084	4,042	276	1,340	6,743
1958	2,562	8,750	533	3,074	14,919
Local 1927	0	25	4,360	94	4,479
1938	0	120	4,196	157	4,473
1948	51	400	5,850	298	6,589
1958	215	1,079	13,514	653	15,461

Source: U.S. Bureau of the Census, *Historical Statistics,* pp. 722-24 and 727-29.

rate of taxes in any one revenue package varied considerably from one state to another, but unlike the earlier pattern, greater commonalities were emerging, since more states were making use of the same diverse sources of revenue.

At the local level, the property tax continued in its predominant position as the localities' chief revenue raiser, even as it experienced some gradual slippage (declining from the 97 percent mark in 1927 to 95 percent in 1938, 89 percent in 1948, 87 percent in 1958). This modest erosion of its near monolithic stance was due, of course, to the piecemeal and highly selective adoption (mostly by cities) of sales, earnings, and/or income taxes. Sometimes specific state authorization was needed in this and sometimes it was not, depending on whether "home rule" statutes conferred broad fiscal powers.[64] In absolute dollar terms, however, the property tax had regained all the ground by the fifties that it had lost in the thirties, demonstrating a strength that surprised some.

Despite all these charges, the overall tax system at the end of the period was only slightly more "intergovernmentalized" than it was at the beginning. Ninety-six percent of the income taxes went to the federal treasury in 1959, 94 percent of the property taxes were collected by local governments (a slight increase over the 92 percent figure for 1927); and while consumption taxes were levied by all levels, the general sales tax was almost exclusively in state hands and the selected excises oftener than not were different ones for the different levels. All this did not mean that there was not some increase in tax overlaps. There clearly was—thanks to the increasing diversification of state tax systems and, to a lesser degree, those of their localities.

Intergovernmental Fiscal Transfers: Major Increases with Some Systemic Impacts

Far more significant than the changes in tax systems was the great growth in grants-in-aid during these three decades. More than any other single factor—save for the Court's shift—this development with all its administrative, servicing, and fiscal implications was the one that gave this era its dominant intergovernmental character. Cooperative federalism, after all, depends heavily on grants as its chief means of reflecting functional collaboration in practice.

State aid to local governments witnessed a remarkable rise during this period. During the thirties, of course, its growth was modest, but its major postwar expansion made it the dominant intergovernmental system of fiscal transfers ($8.1 billion versus $4.7 billion for federal aid in 1958) by the end of this era (see table 3-7).

Explicit and implicit in table 3-7's figures are certain significant trends. First, the growing amounts both in absolute and relative terms were impressive. Even in constant dollar terms, it experienced a nearly fourfold increase,[65] a marked contrast to the slowly evolving state-aid pattern of the previous period.

Second, while the assisted functional areas aided were pretty much the same as the earlier ones, significant proportionate shifts occurred among them over time.[66] Welfare and general support payments (shared revenue and general revenue sharing programs) fluctuated irregularly; highways declined steadily in proportionate terms; and education began high and after some decline during the Depression rose again to an even more predominant position by 1958.

Third, school districts and counties continued to be the chief local governmental recipients of these aid programs, though cities that administered a school system or that were treated as counties

Table 3-7   State Aid to Localities by Function, Selected Years (In Millions of Dollars and in Percentages)

Function	1932		1940		1948		1958	
	Dollars	%	Dollars	%	Dollars	%	Dollars	%
Education	398	49.7	700	43.3	1,554	47.3	4,598	56.8
Highways	229	28.6	332	20.1	507	15.4	1,167	14.4
Public Welfare	28	3.5	420	25.4	648	19.7	1,247	15.4
Health & Hospitals	NA	NA	NA	NA	NA	NA	150	1.9
General Support	140	17.5	181	10.9	428	13.0	687	3.5
All Other	6	.6	21	1.3	146	4.5	390	4.8
Total	801	100	1,654	100	3,283	100	8,099	100

Source: U.S. Bureau of the Census, 1972 Census of Governments, Topical Studies, vol. 6, no. 3, "State Payments to Local Governments."

and performed county functions—like New York City, Philadelphia, Baltimore, St. Louis, Denver, and San Francisco—also benefited significantly.[67]

Fourth, the overwhelming bulk of state aid throughout the period was of the conditional variety, ranging from over 83 percent of the total 1932 amount to over 96 percent of the 1958 figure. This meant that the funds had to be spent for a specific purpose; that certain conditions had to be complied with (though these were far less intrusive, compared to their contemporary counterparts); that most of the conditional grant dollars were allocated pursuant to a legislatively determined formula; and that the cost-sharing approach was frequently the one used for determining how much a recipient jurisdiction actually received.

Finally, local governmental finances were helped and indirectly the pressures on the property tax were somewhat lightened by this rising tide of state aid. As a percentage of total local general revenue, it amounted to only 14.1 percent in 1932 and rose to 23.8 percent in 1940, thence to 28.9 percent in 1948, and finally to 29.2 percent by 1958. Moreover, as a percentage of the states' own direct general expenditures, the figures for this period reveal another steadily upward trend.[68]

All of these developments, however, are based on aggregate data and they conceal varying state-aid efforts in light of varying resources, varying preferences regarding program areas to be aided, varying degrees to which federal aid was incorporated in the state-aid figures,[69] and the varying extent to which some states relied more on the direct servicing approach (like Hawaii) rather than on intergovernmental fiscal transfers (like New York and California) as a means of responding to the growing servicing demands of their respective citizenries. These three decades, in essence, were the formative years in the evolution of these systems, since the states' intergovernmental transfer role ranged from miniscule to meager in the earlier era.

Overall, then, state revenue raising and aid expanded massively during the latter part of this period. While these developments reflected considerable variation among the states (in light of their differing resources, servicing preferences, and reliance on direct performance as against use of the grant device), each of the fifty far more resembled a single fiscal and functional system at the end of the period than at the beginning, because all of them became more intergovernmentalized to a greater or lesser degree. Real and widespread state-local fiscal/functional cooperation, then, was a distinctive and dynamic feature of this thirty-year period.

The federal-aid story for these years was almost as exciting as the state saga. For the thirties alone, it was the main attraction. Whether gauged in dollar amounts, the variety of services aided, or the perfecting of the mechanism, the growth in federal grants during these years marked a major turning point in the history of American intergovernmental relations. This growth, along with that of state aid, were major factors accelerating the operational decline of traditional dual federalism. The conditional grant-in-aid, after all, became a major weapon in the arsenal of a national government initially bent on relief, reform, and economic recovery and then on defense and postwar rehabilitation and development. During what some have called "The First New Deal" (1933–mid-1935), new grant programs were enacted for distribution of surplus farm products to the needy, free school lunches, emergency highway expenditures, emergency relief work, general relief, administration of employment security, and support of general local governmental costs.[70]

From mid-1935 to 1939, during "The Second New Deal," additional aid programs for child welfare, maternal and children's health, crippled children's services, old-age assistance, aid to dependent children, aid to the blind, general health services, fire control, wildlife conservation, public housing, emergency road and bridge construction, and venereal disease and tuberculosis control were passed.[71]

In dollar amounts, these Depression-born programs generated outlays in 1939 that were more than fifteen times the 1933 total, a figure that was not reached again until the early fifties. With the advent of World War II and the economic recovery it stimulated, six emergency relief programs were terminated and immediately following the conflict, five war-related aid programs were discontinued.[72] This partially explains the low aid figure of less than $900 million for 1946. Still, twenty-nine permanent grant programs had emerged from the New Deal years.

During the Truman years (1946–52), grant programs for agricultural marketing services (1946), airport construction (1946), scientific agricultural research (1946), hospital construction (1946), mental health (1946), disaster relief (1947), cancer control (1947), heart disease (1948), urban renewal and slum clearance (1949), civil defense (1950), aid to the permanently and totally disabled (1950), fish restoration (1950), school construction in federal impacted areas (1950), and school operation and maintenance in such areas (1950) were adopted.[73] The aid outlays consequently rose gradually to over $2.2 billion in 1950, then to $2.4 billion for the seventy-one separately authorized grant programs in 1952.

Despite the ostensibly conservative Eisenhower phase of this period (1953–60), more grants-in-aid were enacted, including a special school milk program (1954), watershed protection (1954), urban planning (1954), state and local preparedness planning (1954), waste treatment facilities (1956), water pollution control (1956), library services (1956), interstate highway system (1956), defense educational activities (1958), education for the mentally retarded (1958), forest and public-lands roads (1958), national guard centers construction (1958), and medical assistance for the aged (1960).[74] These new programs and changes in the ongoing ones produced 61 new separate authorizations for a total of 132 grants as of 1960, accounting for $6.8 billion in aid outlays, or two and a half times the figure when Eisenhower was inaugurated.

Table 3-8 Federal Intergovernmental Expenditures, by Function for Selected Years 1933–59 (In Thousands of Dollars)

Major Functional Area	1933	1936	1939	1946	1950	1956	1959
Veterans' Services and Benefits	758	568	720	20,238	15,277	8,091	8,316
Health, Welfare, and Labor	63,133	2,248,197	2,622,480	567,873	1,562,252	2,109,270	2,777,160
Education and General Research	10,349	13,055	24,678	25,308	38,614	208,672	296,747
Agriculture and Agricultural Research	12,966	21,656	92,370	92,427	106,276	389,277	322,470
Other Natural Resources	1,523	1,473	2,474	8,274	16,957	26,606	34,481
Commerce, Transportation, Housing, Communication	104,237	27,565	161,277	180,505	475,006	873,715	2,877,781
Total	192,966	2,312,514	2,903,999	894,625	2,214,382	3,615,631	6,316,955

Source: ACIR, *Periodic Congressional Reassessment of Federal Grants-in-Aid to State and Local Governments* (Washington, D.C.: U.S. Government Printing Office, June 1961), A–8.

In terms of program emphasis, health and welfare programs dominated the New Deal grants—a marked contrast to the highway and education predominance in the old pre-1933 package. Agriculture, agricultural research, and other natural resource programs experienced a slow but steady incremental growth over the entire period, while education and general research grants and, especially, transportation and housing made significant gains during its final years. What really stands out, however, is that as of 1960 four programs accounted for nearly three-quarters of the aid disbursements: highways (43.7 percent), old-age assistance (16.5 percent), aid to dependent children (9.1 percent), and employment security (4.7 percent). And, in geographic terms, only a little over half of the 1960 total went directly or indirectly to the nation's urban areas.

The "numbers game" in federal grants-in-aid is a perennial one, thanks to the problem of differentiating clearly between technical assistance and aid to individuals, private organizations, and businesses, on the one hand, and cash grants to state and local governments, on the other. Moreover, there is the quandary of whether to count separate authorizations, appropriations, and/or substantial amendments to existing grants. In terms of permanent aid programs, however, there were 15 separately authorized by 1930; 15 were added between 1933 and 1940; another 41 between 1941 and 1952; and 61 more during the period's last eight years. As of 1960, these produced a total of 132 separate grant authorizations that were subsumed under fifty-eight basic program headings.[75]

Despite the absolute growth in grant dollars and number of programs, the annual outlays during the period 1942 to 1958 hovered around the 1 percent of GNP mark throughout and only got to the 1.4 percent level during 1959-60. In addition, as a percent of state and local revenues, they remained steadily at the 10 percent level between 1952 and 1957 and only rose to 14 percent by 1959. As a proportion of all nondefense federal expenditures, they rose gradually from 11.2 percent in 1952 to 14.1 percent in 1956, finally to 17.1 percent by 1959.[76]

Regarding the recipients of federal aid, the states were the prime partners in all but a handful of the ongoing regular grant programs. Put differently, the "bypassing" of the states was an irregular and modest matter during most of this period, though it did occur frequently in the thirties thanks to the public works and local relief efforts. But these did not last, and the Housing Act of 1937 and 1949, the 1946 airport legislation, and the urban planning and renewal program of 1954 were the pivotal local programs of the postwar period. All told, some fifteen programs of local aid had been enacted prior to 1960 that involved no state role whatsoever. Yet the dollar amounts of all of these efforts were miniscule, rising from $298 million in 1950 (10 percent of the federal-aid total) to $473 million nine years later (7 percent of the total of federal grant funds).

In their design, all of the grant programs fell under the categorical or conditional grant heading. The only exceptions were shared revenues from western lands that were distributed back to the states involved on a "no strings" basis, and these never accounted for more than 1 to 2 percent of total aid outlays in any one year. Within the categorical designation, however, four separate grant types emerged. All of the 132 programs enacted fell under one of these headings.

There were (and are) three varieties of formula-based grants, wherein funds were made available automatically to eligible recipients who met the requirements and conditions established by statute or regulation:

— open-ended disbursements, under which the federal government matched approved expenditures without limit to the absolute amount (i.e., the 1911 assistance to state marine schools and the aid-to-dependent-children program started by the Social Security Act of 1935);
— formula grants, whose dollar disbursements were dictated wholly by a congressionally specified or required allocational formula (i.e., the highway programs of 1916 and 1956); and
— formula-project grants, under which a state area's funds were determined by an allocational formula, but the specific recipients and their precise disbursements were left to the process of state or federal administrators deciding among numerous individual competing applications (i.e., the 1946 airport legislation).

Pure project grants, of course, had no allocational formula and no state area distribution constraints. With them, potential eligible recipients had to submit specific individual applications in the form and at the times indicated by the federal grantor agency (i.e., the 1937 public housing and the 1946 scientific agricultural research programs). While formula grants always dominated the aid package in dollar terms, the number of project grants grew during the postwar period to the point where they exceeded the formula type by about a two-to-one margin at the end of the Eisenhower years.[77]

The conditions attached to federal grants reached a high level of maturation during this period. As one authority put it regarding the New Deal programs: "Many were additions to the already established programs of the 1910's and 1920's. Since many of the services were new, and since the funding was generous, there were additional incentives for the attachment of greater conditions. Plans were required by almost every act and permanent programs had detailed administrative regulations."[78] Of the fifty-eight basic programs in 1960, twenty-one required a state or other broad-gauged plan. Near the end of this period, the authors of the report of the Commission on Intergovernmental Relations (Kestnbaum Commission) to President Eisenhower could write:

The maturing of the grant as a means of stimulating and shaping particular programs, as distinct from a subsidy device, is reflected not only in increasing legislative attention to conditions, standards, sanctions, and methods of supervision, but also in the evolution of National administration machinery and procedures. The conditions attached to grants have not remained mere verbal expressions of National intent; National agencies have generally had funds and staff to make them effective.[79]

Closely linked to this maturing of the grant device was the attachment of certain protective conditions to certain programs, with a view toward enhancing the professionalism and political neutrality of recipient agencies and personnel. Thus, merit-system coverage was required in 1939 for state (and county) employees administering the Social Security Act programs and restrictions on political activities were placed on recipient employees paid wholly or in part with federal grant funds under the 1940 amendments to the Hatch Act. In an organizational sense, the "single state agency" requirement was used ostensibly to establish an administrative focus for the implementation of grant programs, but also to isolate and insulate the grant administrators and their personnel from the pressures—political and otherwise—from the rest of the state systems. Merit-system requirements (which by 1960 covered practically all of the health, welfare, and employment security programs), the political-activity prohibitions, and "single state agency" provisions combined to fashion a nonarticulated theory of grants administration that stressed the vertical, functional, bureaucratic linkages and the protective strengthening of administrative counterparts at the recipient level. Under it, the administrative role of elected chief executives and the administrative shaping powers of legislative bodies were deemphasized, if not ignored.

To sum up, the growth in conditional grants, both state and federal, was a major feature setting this period apart from its predecessor and serving as a prelude for its successor. It was this development that helped launch the study and definition of intergovernmental relations, even to the point of a temporary presidential commission on the subject being set up and statute creating the permanent Advisory Commission on Intergovernmental Relations (ACIR) being enacted in 1959. It was grants-in-aid, more than any other form of interlevel collaboration, that generated the cooperative federal theory and their operation prompted the "marble cake" metaphor.

That a "marble cake" had been baked during these three decades there can be little doubt. Whether it was done in a collaborative spirit by all the parties involved is yet another matter. And whether it was as "marbleized" as many of the writers contended it was is still another. The following analysis of the functional assignment issue will shed more light on the real character of this cake.

Functional Assignments in an Era of Growing Collaboration

That the orbit of national authority formally expanded considerably during these three decades, there can be no doubt. The foregoing judicial, fiscal, and grant analyses provide ample bases for this assertion. The Great Depression, the most devastating war we have ever fought, and their aftermath were sufficient—along with an ultimately supportive Supreme Court—to expand greatly the earlier, established, though skeletal roles of the national government as regulator, reformer, and promoter of the economy.

Legally, as we have seen, no real barriers were placed in the path of assuming these roles after 1937, to the extent that the political processes supported policies that furthered them. The power to spend for the general welfare and to regulate commerce produced a new concept of the national government's role in the entire economy—one that covered practically all of its most important phases: production, labor, unemployment, money and banking, social security, housing, public works, flood control, and conservation of natural resources.[80]

A national police power of far greater scope than its Progressive era predecessor thus emerged and, as Lowi has emphasized, the regulatory role that the national government assumed in the New Deal far outweighed the significance of the ballooning federal budgets.[81] The adoption of a range of new regulatory policies and the establishment over the entire period of fourteen new regulatory agencies (in addition to the fourteen established prior to 1930) were indicative of this new federal interventionist thrust.

Federal domination of banking, monetary, and fiscal policies was stretched to points unimaginable in the earlier period, thanks to the Depression, the establishment of the Board of Governors for the Federal Reserve System, and the gradual acceptance of Keynesian countercyclical concepts. Agriculture became a largely federally "managed" sector of the economy and a federal presence was established in private labor-management relations with the Wagner Act (1935) as well as its Republican-sponsored major modifier, the Taft-Hartley Act of 1947. Regulation of communications (telegraph, telephone, and radio) were lodged with the newly established Federal Communications Commission in 1934 and a little later the regulation of the operation of nonmilitary aircraft was assigned to the Civil Aeronautics Authority. The U.S. Maritime Commission was created to supercede the old Shipping Board, while the powers of the Federal Trade Commission were expanded to curb false or misleading advertising. The Securities and Exchange Commission (1934) was given regulatory authority over stock exchanges and public-utility holding companies. The Federal Power Commission (1930) was assigned the job of overseeing large electric-power companies in 1935 and of supervising the construction of interstate natural-gas pipelines and the rates charged big-city utility buyers. The Tennessee Valley Authority

(1933), of course, constituted a rare venture in government ownership in the means of energy production, and in the postwar period (1946) both the operating and regulatory facets of nuclear energy were lodged with the Atomic Energy Commission.

Despite this seemingly inexorable trend toward national regulation (and centralization), certain caveats need to be cited. First, most of these undertakings were of such a clear interstate nature that the states separately could not be expected to assume them. Second, the vigor with which the national regulatory policies were pursued varied considerably from agency to agency, from time to time, and from administration to administration.[82] Third, while the net effect of these legislative (and supporting judicial) actions was largely to keep the states out of interstate commerce, admiralty, bankruptcy, and currency matters and to prevent them from imposing burdens on federal instrumentalities, this did not mean, as was noted earlier, that the states' police power in intrastate commerce or even some aspects of interstate commerce was weakened.[83] The power to incorporate businesses, to tax and legislate in a way that established in very real terms the image of a "favorable" or "unfavorable" climate for expanding or relocating firms, to regulate insurance companies, to audit state-chartered banks, and to regulate the wide range of intrastate transportation activities (bus, rail, trucks, and ports) as well as such utilities as gas, light, telephone, and water were all left to the states. Fourth, no "constitutional no man's land" existed after 1937 wherein neither the national government nor the states could act in economic matters; either one or the other was, in effect, given the authority to legislate, thanks to the New Deal Supreme Court's interpretations of the federal commerce and taxing powers and of the states' police powers.[84] Fifth, the earlier practice of joint boards, representing regulatory agencies at both levels, was greatly expanded by law, to cover such areas as motor carriers, communications, electricity, and natural gas.

Above all, perhaps, the scope and degree of separation of the direct servicing responsibilities of the various levels must be weighed when considering the degree of centralization that emerged in this era. Here, the perspective of 1930 as well as that of now are needed to arrive at a balanced assessment. On the one hand, those state and local services that received federal aid and were subject to their accompanying conditions clearly were more numerous and more caught up with shared decisionmaking and shared implementation than ever was the case prior to the New Deal. On the other, major state and local servicing responsibilities were minimally affected or wholly untouched by the expansion of federal grants during this period.

The range of new social welfare, public health, natural resource and conservation, airport and highway construction, public housing and urban renewal, and selective, specialized educational programs of aid to the states, and in a few cases their localities, however, did give rise to the cooperative federal concept of a collaborative commingling of funds, personnel, and program purposes to promote common goals.

State highway, health and welfare, and natural resource and conservation agencies were most affected by this expansion of federal grants-in-aid. Yet even these units were by no means wholly dominated by the federal programs and their regulations.

- —With highways, maintenance and rural roads were wholly under state purview and subject to heavy state direct and grant expenditures.
- —In welfare, general assistance programs geared to filling the gaps left by the federal programs were under state control and funding, and they were frequently administered by local units. Moreover, state and local welfare outlays constituted 60 percent of the 1958 total (chiefly for matching and general assistance) and even within the aided programs, payment levels and certain aspects of eligibility were left to the states to determine.
- —Among state health programs, only one-fifth of the funds came from federal grants by the late fifties and state expenditures dominated the outlays for mental hospitals.
- —With natural resource conservation, only about 2 percent of all state expenditures were earmarked for these programs (excluding those for agriculture) and federal grants constituted only 7 percent of these funds.

All this suggests that some, not all, of the activities of these state agencies were conditioned by their heavy participation in federal grant programs. This was even more true of state agricultural and educational agencies.[85] Many of the U.S. Department of Agriculture programs, after all, were (and are) carried out directly with state and county committees of farmers and farm experts with no formal linkages to state or county agricultural agencies, though informal ties were not uncommon. Thus, while federal grants varied from 10 to 50 percent of the cost of running agricultural experimentation stations and extension work, they averaged only about one-fifth of the state's own outlays for agricultural activities in 1958, aside from soil and conservation undertakings.[86]

In the case of education—the largest state and local revenue consumer—comparatively modest amounts of federal aid were the prevailing pattern throughout this period. For state universities, aside from the original land grants, there was assistance for agricultural college programs and experimentation stations, for contract research, and special grants under the National Defense Education Act (1957), as well as indirect aid via tuition funds for veterans. With public primary and secondary education, there was the U.S. Office of Education's program of collecting statistics, specialized research and demonstration grants, vocational educational assistance, support for teaching agriculture and home economics in high schools, USDA's school lunch program, and aid to those school districts affected by the presence of a federal military or other installation within them. In short, state and local education efforts were only minimally affected by federal aid programs, which amounted to only about 4 percent of total state and local educational outlays in 1958.

Beyond these significantly and minimally aided state programs and agencies stood those that secured no federal grant funds: the attorney general's office, the state police, corrections departments, court systems, economic development units, licensing boards, and regulatory commissions, not to mention the offices of treasurer and secretary of state.

At the local level, informal contacts with federal officials increased, but ongoing intergovernmental administrative relationships grew only modestly. The pre-1930 pattern of receiving technical assistance from the Corps of Engineers, Public Health Service, Census Bureau, and the Department of Agriculture continued and expanded. Moreover, the emergency relief programs of the thirties (the Civil Works Administration, 1933; the Public Works Administration, 1933; and the Works Progress Administration, 1935) did pump sizable amounts of public-works funds to cities and counties in an effort to provide jobs for the unemployed.[87] These programs as well as the direct financial assistance for local relief expenditures, however, disappeared with the end of the Depression.

During the second half of this era, local contacts on an ongoing basis with federal officials and agencies were relatively limited. The number of assistance programs for which they were directly eligible, after all, were few. Only fifteen of these were wholly of the direct type, with no state role of any kind, and in only five of the twenty-five were local governments the sole recipients of assistance (low-rent public housing, urban renewal, the two impacted-area education grants, and community renewal).[88] The bulk of the $347 million, then, that was distributed directly to localities in 1957 was accounted for by these programs, along with some airport, water resources, and civil-defense aid funds. They represented a minuscule proportion (8 percent) of the 1957 total of federal grant funds and a pitiful proportion (1 percent) of overall local revenues.

In operational terms, of course, all of these (save for the impacted-area grants) were project grants which, in combination with the limited amounts of money, meant that comparatively few localities were continuing participants in these programs. Put differently, few local governments were continuing direct partners with the federal government in shared program undertakings and none of the major traditional functions of cities (servicing the physical environment and providing police and fire protection) were much affected by any of these aid programs. The same generalization, of course, could be applied to school districts, since even those benefiting from impacted-area aid received it in "no strings" disbursements. In the case of counties, direct grant relationships were restricted to a few of their urban units, and hardly any of their customary functions (in criminal justice, roads, elections, and natural resources)[89] were affected by these federal-local grants. On the other hand, counties were significantly affected by certain federal-state programs wherein the states mandated a county role, as in welfare and public health. Moreover, USDA's extension system with its county organizational basis indirectly affected these local jurisdictions. Regarding special districts and authorities, four of their categories (water and sewer, housing, renewal, and soil conservancy) expanded in number during this period, partially as a result of federal aid in these program areas. This, of course, provides some early examples of "bypassing" local general governments, albeit at their own instigation in many instances.

Overall, then, certain state functions and a few local services were "intergovernmentalized" by federal grants during this period and various forms of shared decisionmaking characterized the operations of these aided programs. But of equal importance was the fact that a significant portion of state services and the vast bulk of local governmental activities were not touched by this expansion of federal grants. The states were the prime recipients of what federal grant funds there were, and by 1960 nearly three-quarters of these monies assisted programs that had a lengthy history of federal-state collaboration behind them, ranging from forty-four years in the case of highways, to twenty-seven years with employment security, to twenty-five years with old-age assistance and aid to dependent children.

The localities, on the other hand, were far more affected by the growth in state aid and in state mandating than by federal programs. School districts and counties generally were the most heavily affected, given the state focus on education, highways, health, and hospitals. Regarding state mandates, one recent study shows that five states imposed a total of 531 separate mandates (by direct order or as a condition of state aid) during the period of 1941 to 1960, compared to fourteen federal mandates during the same period.[90]

The cooperative federal interpretation that emerged in the late forties and fifties, then, reflected the growth in federal-state as well as state-local sharing of functional responsibilities that had occurred since the early thirties. While its enunciators traced the historical roots of this development back to the Articles of Confederation, it seems clear that it was the 117 new federal-aid programs enacted during these three decades, not the fifteen of the previous period, that provided the dynamic environment in which the concept crystalized. The growing state-local interdependence provided yet another backdrop to this development, though the federal role initially was the chief focus of the cooperative federalism analysts. It was no accident, then, that the interpretation emerged when it did. If there is any doubt on this score, ponder the prospect of advancing it in the twenties. Impossible, given the dominant dual-federalist pattern of the intergovernmental relations of that decade.

Yet it did capture the relatively structured, simple, and stabilized, though obviously somewhat complex, pattern of the final decade of this predecessor period. The "ingredients," after all, were almost wholly the federal government and states; the chocolate and vanilla. The frequency of the major interweavings were few (four, in fact)—the cake of the fifties resembled the one that had been baked in the late thirties. None of these attributes characterize the contemporary cake, of course, for simplicity, relative stability, and structure are not among its ingredients. Unending complexity, some continuity but constant shifts, and a seemingly unstructured nonsystem are its main traits, and no culinary metaphor really expresses it.

Transcending and sometimes subsuming major aspects of the new federal regulatory and intergovernmental fiscal transfer efforts was the vast expansion during this era of its role as promoter of the economy and broker-subsidizer of major interest groups. In some respects, this was merely an extension of its previous 140-year record of subsidization, chiefly through tariffs, land grants, and maritime support. But in this period, the forms of subsidy multiplied, the cost in real dollar terms clearly escalated (though the real amounts were, and are, impossible to estimate), the benefiting groups expanded massively, and a very old political stratagem was given a very new application. The result was a drastic reformulation of the promotional role of the federal government—not merely in its intergovernmental relations but in its private-sector relations as well.

While the New Deal has been interpreted in terms of class coalitions and of redistributive politics and programs,[91] it also may be viewed as an effort to satisfy the aspirations and needs of weaker socioeconomic groups (labor, agriculture, the poor, the unemployed, and even the middle classes) by a range of responses, while not threatening the fundamental role of, nor the system that conferred that role on, the older ascendant groups (business, finance, the well-to-do).

This "concert of interests" approach dominated the "First New Deal" with its "something for everyone" strategy. As Hofstadter described it: "Farmers got the AAA. Business got the NRA codes. Labor got wage and hour provisions and the collective bargaining promise of Section 7(a). The unemployed got a variety of federal relief measures. The middle classes got the Home Owners' Loan Corporation, securities regulations, and other reforms."[92]

The "Second New Deal" did reflect more of a redistributive and less of a "pork barrel" thrust. The Wagner Act and Fair Labor Standards legislation was a boon to labor and led to massive and successful (10 million members by 1939) union efforts to organize. The AAA of 1938 carried forward the promise of the 1933 legislation (struck down by the Court) to agriculture. Trust busting was launched to appeal to the middle classes and an inheritance tax, an estate levy, gift taxes to prevent evasion of the inheritance tax, and more steeply graduated taxes on large incomes were enacted as redistributive measures. The Social Security Act aided the elderly and a range of other beneficiaries. All reflected the more social democratic tendencies of the second phase of the New Deal.[93]

World War II put an end to much of this and the "concert of interests" approach again became fashionable, thanks to crisis conditions, near full employment, massive government procurement and defense contracts, and rising corporate profits. In the decade and a half following VJ Day, it was the "concert of interests" approach far more than class politics that, in practical terms, conditioned the interventionist national role and especially its expanding subsidization activities.

Political rhetoric and political attitudes regarding the newly acquired class bias of the parties notwithstanding,[94] the statutory and institutional legacy of the New Deal, its extensions under Harry S. Truman's "Fair Deal" and during Dwight Eisenhower's conserving years—not to mention the Cold War defense budgets —stressed "distribution" and "pork barrel" politics far more than "redistribution" and class politics. The Full Employment Act of 1946, the Housing Act of 1949, its amendments of 1954, a cluster of other small categorical grants, some modifications in social security, and the desegregation decisions of the Court all nodded in the direction of redistribution. Yet the dominant practice was the reverse.

The fundamental reason for this, of course, was that the liberal nationalist ethic of the dominant political coalition throughout most of these years was a pragmatic one. With FDR, this meant: "It is common sense to take a method and try it: If it fails, admit it frankly and try another. But above all, try something."[95] With the next generation of national politicians, it became the pragmatism of the political process. In effect, whatever came out of the byplay among the basic socioeconomic interests by way of an agreement was legitimate and in the national interest.

This occurred because (1) no concept of a really authoritative national government emerged during the Roosevelt years; (2) the expansion of national governmental powers during this period was accompanied by attempts to deny it; and (3) the "concert of interests" strategy was more in harmony with the traditional "pork barrel" political ethic than variations on a redistributive theme and more in accord with the heterogeneous composition of the major parties than with any presumed socioeconomic homogeneity. And so it was that the agencies intended to regulate frequently collaborated with the regulated and direct assumption of a responsibility usually was rejected in favor of relying on subnational governments via the grant device or on quasi-private or wholly private organizations via contracts and subsidies.[96]

Reflective of this federal assumption and then abdication of authority was the relatively slow growth in its own bureaucracy during these years. Despite the ostensible accumulation of vast new federal "managing" authority and responsibilities, it rose from 600,000 in 1929 to only 1,100,000 a decade later, thence to 2,399,000 by 1959 (and this included postal, social security, and internal revenue service workers). As a proportion of the nation's labor force, federal employment peaked in World War II and declined by 1950 to the level it has maintained ever since.

Another prime result of this "concert of interests" strategy was the massive growth in the number of subsidy programs. On a formal level, these may be described as promotional efforts by the national government to encourage various sectors of the economy in order to further its development and to assist national defense.[97] At a more mundane and practical level, they reflected the interaction between an expanding number of interest groups and the national government and the brokerage response of a political process that was primarily conditioned by interest-group or pork-barrel politics.

In 1960, the Joint Economic Committee of the Congress compiled a listing of "subsidy and subsidylike programs of the U.S. Government."[98] It included various federal programs, past and then current, "which by one criteria or another, might be considered to partake of or involve an element of subsidy regardless of original intent of any particular programs."[99] Ten types of subsidies were identified: grants (five) to business firms and corporations to carry out specific objectives; farm subsidy programs (eight); tax benefits to specific economic groups; various forms of indirect assistance to specific economic groups; U.S. economic programs having incidental effects similar to those of subsidies; free or below-cost national services (other than loans or insurance programs); nineteen lending and at least thirteen loan guarantee programs; direct insurance programs undertaken by eleven different national agencies in eleven different areas; fifty-one federal grant programs to states and local governments; and seventeen federal payments to individual programs.

All told, about 140 of these programs were operational in 1960, and more than nine-tenths of these were enacted between 1930 and 1960. Not covered were federal regulatory efforts, some of which also had a subsidylike effect,[100] constituting an eleventh form of promotionalism.

Thus, to a far greater degree than merely regulation or grant efforts as such, the expansion of the federal government's subsidy-promotional role in this era stands out as the dominant form of national interventionism. Regulation itself was in part caught up with it, especially in the post–World War II years, and major federal aid programs were merely one of its many (eleven) basic manifestations. Of greater significance, of course, were the grants to firms, farm subsidy programs, specialized tax breaks for and indirect aids to specific economic groups, preferential lending and loan guarantee programs, and insurance programs.

The functional assignment picture changed greatly during

these three decades. The national regulatory role expanded, though not to the extent of really undercutting the states' police powers in a range of critical social and economic areas. Federal reliance on grants-in-aid as a means of achieving a range of specific programmatic (as well as fiscally supportive and especially stimu- lative) purposes became much heavier during these years and the cooperative-federalism metaphor served as a roughly accurate description of this novel development. Yet this did not reach the point of affecting even a majority of most state functions or even any of most cities', counties', or school districts' basic ser- vices directly. In the federal government's promotional efforts, however, a much more complicated, largely private-sector-oriented version of "cooperative federalism" emerged, which involved practically all of the basic organized sectors of the economy, plus some of the not-so-well-organized sectors of society. Diverse direct and indirect subsidy programs were developed, including certain regulatory and grant-in-aid undertakings. But, when viewed in their totality, they reflected an adaptation of promotionalism to the necessities of interest-group politics, especially of the economic variety, as well as the radical conversion of traditional promotionalism to the proliferating promotionalism of an activist national government. And it was this adaptation and this con- version that constituted the most significant shift in the functional responsibilities of the national government between 1930 and 1960.

NOTES TO CHAPTER 3

1. Edwin S. Corwin, "A Constitution of Powers and Modern Federal- ism," *Essays in Constitutional Law*, Robert G. McCloskey, ed. (New York: Alfred A. Knopf, 1962), pp. 188–89.

2. See Richard H. Leach, *American Federalism* (New York: W. W. Norton & Co., 1976), pp. 10–13.

3. Ibid., pp. 10–11.

4. See Alfred H. Kelly and Winfred A. Harbison, *The American Consti- tution, Its Origin and Development* (New York: W. W. Norton & Co., 1976), pp. 199–200.

5. See Harry N. Scheiber, "American Federalism and the Diffusion of Power: Historical and Contemporary Perspectives," *The University of Toledo Law Review* 9, no. 4 (Summer 1978): pp. 629–30; also *Gibbons v. Ogden*, 22 U.S. (9 Wheat.), (1824); *Willson v. Blackbird Creek Marsh Co.*, 27 U.S. (2 Pet.), 245 (1829); *Barron v. Baltimore*, 32 U.S. (7 Pet.), 243

(1833); *Ogden* v. *Saunders*, 25 U.S. (12 Wheat.), 213 (1827); *Providence Bank* v. *Billings*, 29 U.S. (4 Pet.), 514 (1830), respectively.

6. *Cohens* v. *Virginia*, 19 U.S. (6 Wheat.), 264 (1821).

7. Kelly and Harbison, op. cit., pp. 281-82; and Scheiber, op. cit., p. 630.

8. *Briscoe* v. *Bank of the Commonwealth of Kentucky* (11 Pet.), 257 (1837).

9. *Charles River Bridge* v. *Warren Bridge*, 36 U.S. (11 Pet.), 620 (1837).

10. Corwin, op. cit., pp. 200-201.

11. Quoted in Scheiber, op. cit., p. 630.

12. Kelly and Harbison, op. cit., p. 331.

13. *Abelman* v. *Booth* (21 Howard), 506 (1859).

14. See Morton Grodzins, *The American System*, Danial J. Elazar, editor (Chicago: Rand McNally & Co., 1969), p. 24.

15. Secretary Hamilton included an excise tax on liquor (1790) in his revenue program which produced a major confrontation in some states, including the Whiskey Rebellion (1794) and use of militia to suppress it.

16. *Congressional Globe*, 33rd Congress, 1st Sess., 3 May 1854, p. 1062.

17. Scheiber, op. cit., p. 632, and William Anderson, *Intergovernmental Relations in Review* (Minneapolis: University of Minnesota Press, 1960), p. 142.

18. See Samuel H. Beer, "Modernization of American Federalism," in *Publius: The Journal of Federalism* 3, no. 2 (Fall 1973) (issue entitled: "Toward '76, The Federal Polity"), pp. 68, 69.

19. See Kelly and Harbison, op. cit., p. 420.

20. 7 Wallace 700 (1869).

21. See Kelly and Harbison, op. cit., pp. 511-12; and Benjamin F. Wright, *The Growth of American Constitutional Law* (Boston: Houghton Mifflin Company, 1942).

22. See Scheiber, op. cit., p. 638; also *U.S.* v. *Cruikshank*, 92 U.S. 542 (1876); *Ex parte Virginia*, 100 U.S. 339 (1880); *Cummins* v. *County Board of Education*, 175 U.S. 528 (1899); and especially *Plessy* v. *Ferguson*, 163 U.S. 573 (1896); and *U.S.* v. *Reese*, 92 U.S. 214 (1876).

23. See Scheiber, op. cit., pp. 643-44 and 653-54.

24. See ibid., p. 639.

25. The states, after all, realistically could not grapple with great corporate power, even when the legal right was theirs. And, as has been demonstrated, the states' police power was expanded greatly into wholly novel areas during this period and many of their extensions were upheld.

26. William H. Riker, *Federalism: Origin, Operation, Significance* (Boston: Little, Brown, 1964), p. 51.

27. See Kelly and Harbison, op. cit., pp. 533-34.

28. *Pollack* v. *Farmers' Loan and Trust Co.*, 158 U.S. 601 (1895).

29. Advisory Commission on Intergovernmental Relations, *Significant Features of Fiscal Federalism 1976-77*, vol. 2 (Washington, D.C.: U.S. Government Printing Office, 1977), pp. 99-101.

30. Cf. James A. Maxwell and J. Richard Aaron, *Financing State and*

Local Governments (Washington, D.C.: The Brookings Institution, 1977), p. 85.

31. Cf. Arthur W. MacMahan, *Administering Federalism in a Democracy* (New York: Oxford University Press, 1972), p. 72.

32. See Earl Baker, Bernadette A. Stevens, Stephen L. Schechter, and Harlan A. Wright, *Federal Grants, The National Interest and State Response— A Review of Theory and Research* (Philadelphia: Center for the Study of Federalism, Temple University, 1974), pp. 25–28.

33. Ibid., p. 27.

34. Cf. ibid., pp. 28–29.

35. *Massachusetts* v. *Mellon*, 262 U.S. 447 (1923); and cf. Scheiber, op. cit., pp. 642, 643.

36. *Frothingham* v. *Mellon*, 262 U.S. 447 (1923).

37. See Harry N. Scheiber, *The Condition of American Federalism: An Historian's View.* A study submitted by the Committee on Government Operations, Subcommittee on Intergovernmental Relations, U.S. Senate, 89th Congress, 2nd Sess., 15 October 1966, p. 6.

38. Federal civilian employees numbered 579,559 in 1927 compared to 2,532,000 state-local personnel.

39. See Grodzins, op. cit., pp. 17–57.

40. Morton Grodzins, "The American Federal System," appearing in *A Nation of States*, Robert A. Goldwin, editor (Chicago: Rand McNally & Co., 1964), pp. 21–22.

41. Daniel J. Elazar, *The American Partnership: Intergovernmental Cooperation in the Nineteenth Century* (Chicago: University of Chicago Press, 1962), p. 297.

42. See Joseph E. McLean, "Politics Is What You Make It," *Public Affairs Pamphlet No. 181* (Washington, D.C.: Public Affairs Press, April 1952), p. 5.

43. Kelly and Harbison, op. cit., p. 688.

44. Ibid., pp. 693–94: and Swisher, *American Constitutional Development* (Boston: Houghton Mifflin, 1943), pp. 922–38.

45. Cf. Kelly and Harbison, op. cit., pp. 708–9.

46. Cf. ibid., pp. 710–11.

47. Ibid., p. 714.

48. See *NLRB* v. *Jones and Laughlin Steel Co.*, 301 U.S. 1 (1937) and *NLRB* v. *Friedman-Harry Marks Clothing Co.*, 301 U.S. 58 (1937).

49. *Steward Machine Co.* v. *Davis*, 301 U.S. 548 (1937).

50. *Helvering* v. *Davis*, 301 U.S. 619 (1937).

51. See Kelly and Harbison, op. cit., p. 747, *Consolidated Edison Co.* v. *NLRB*, 305 U.S. 197 (1938); and *NLRB* v. *Fainblatt*, 306 U.S. 601 (1939).

52. See Scheiber, "American Federalism and The Diffusion of Power," op. cit., pp. 644–55.

53. Kelly and Harbison, op. cit., p. 749.

54. *Palko* v. *Conn.*, 302 U.S. 319 (1937); see also Kelly and Harbison, op. cit., p. 753.

55. Scheiber, op. cit., p. 653.

56. Ibid.

57. See *Adamson* v. *Calif.*, 322 U.S. 46 (1948).

58. See *Morgan* v. *Virginia*, 328 U.S. 373 (1946) and *Shelley* v. *Kramer*, 334 U.S. 1 (1948).

59. See *Sipuel* v. *Board of Regents*, 332 U.S. 631 (1948); *Sweatt* v. *Painter*, 339 U.S. 629 (1950); and *McLaurin* v. *Oklahoma Bd. of Regents*, 339 U.S. 637 (1950).

60. *Brown* v. *Board of Education of Topeka*, 347 U.S. 483 (1954) and *Brown* v. *Board of Education of Topeka*, 349 U.S. 294 (1955).

61. See Scheiber, op. cit., pp. 654-55, and Kelly and Harbison, op. cit., pp. 863-64.

62. Maxwell and Aaron, op. cit., p. 18.

63. See ACIR, *Significant Features of Fiscal Federalism, 1976-1977*, vol. 2 (Washington, D.C.: U.S. Government Printing Office, 1977), pp. 99-101.

64. See Maxwell and Aaron, op. cit., p. 167.

65. The 1932 figure would have been $2.3 billion, while the 1958 amount would have been $8.1 billion.

66. See Maxwell and Aaron, op. cit., pp. 83-91.

67. As of 1957, counties received 27.6 percent of all state aid; school districts, 48.2 percent; cities, 20.2 percent; towns, 3.7 percent; and special districts, .3 percent.

68. Maxwell and Aaron, op. cit., p. 85.

69. The usual overall "guesstimate" for the fifties was 20 to 25 percent.

70. See Scheiber, "The Condition . . . ," op. cit., pp. 8-9.

71. Ibid., p. 9.

72. ACIR, "Periodic Congressional Reassesment of Federal Grants-in-Aid to State and Local Governments" (A-8) (Washington, D.C.: U.S. Government Printing Office, June 1961), table 4.

73. Ibid., table 1.

74. See Ibid.

75. Adapted from ACIR, *Fiscal Balance in the American Federal System*, vol. 1 (Washington, D.C.: U.S. Government Printing Office, 1967), A-31, pp. 140-42.

76. See ACIR, "Periodic Congressional Review . . . , " op. cit., table 3.

77. See ACIR, "Fiscal Balance . . . , " op. cit., p. 151.

78. Baker et al., op. cit., p. 34.

79. The Commission on Intergovernmental Relations, *A Report to the President for Transmittal to the Congress* (Washington, D.C.: U.S. Government Printing Office, June 1955), p. 120.

80. See Kelly and Harbison, op. cit., pp. 747-48.

81. Theodore J. Lowi, *The End of Liberalism*, 2nd ed. (New York: W. W. Norton & Co., 1979), p. 273.

82. See Louis M. Kohlmeier, Jr., *The Regulators* (New York: Harper & Row, Publishers, 1969), pp. 69-82 especially.

83. See Commission on Intergovernmental Relations, "A Report . . . , " op. cit., pp. 31, 32.

84. See ibid., p. 32.

85. See William Anderson, Clara Penniman, Edward W. Widner, *Government in the Fifty States* (New York: Holt, Rinehart & Winston, 1960), pp. 402-3.

86. Ibid., p. 404.

87. See Roberta Balstad Miller, "The Federal Role in Cities, The New Deal Years," *Commentary*, July 1979, pp. 11-13.

88. See ACIR, "Fiscal Balance . . . ," op. cit., p. 166.

89. Natural resources were aided minimally.

90. Catherine H. Lovell et al., *Federal and State Mandating on Local Governments: An Explanation of Issues and Impacts* (Riverside, Calif.: Graduate School of Administration, University of California, 1979), p. 71.

91. See Beer, op. cit., pp. 71-73, and Everett Carll Ladd, Jr., *American Political Parties* (New York: W. W. Norton & Co., 1970), pp. 180-83.

92. Richard Hofstadter, *The American Political Tradition* (New York: Vantage Books, 1954), p. 334.

93. See Ladd, op. cit., p. 188.

94. See the subsequent section of this chapter on the political dynamics of this period.

95. Samuel I. Rosenman, ed., *The Public Papers and Addresses of Franklin D. Roosevelt* (New York: Random House, 1938), vol. 2, p. 165.

96. See Lowi, op. cit., passim.

97. See Lloyd D. Muslof, *Government and the Economy* (Glenview, Ill.: Scott, Foresman, 1967), pp. 10-33.

98. See U.S. Congress, Joint Economic Committee, *Subsidy and Subsidylike Programs of the U.S. Government*, Joint Committee Print, 86th Congress, 2nd Sess.

99. Ibid., p. 18.

100. See James Q. Wilson, "The Politics of Regulation," appearing in *Social Responsibility and the Business Predicament*, James W. McKie, ed. (Washington, D.C.: The Brookings Institution, 1976), pp. 139-47.

4

Cooperative Federalism's Conceptual Offspring, 1960-1980

INTRODUCTION

The fourth, contemporary phase in the more-than-two-hundred-year evolution of American federalism witnessed the ultimate realization of many of the tenets of cooperative federalism—tenets that previously had never been put into practice. This, in turn, produced the collapse of the concept as an accurate descriptive theory of intergovernmental relations, but not as an ideal prescription of what these relations should be. In effect, the demise in the sixties of the residual and delimiting constraints imposed by dual federalism provided the basis for a near-complete triumph of cooperative federalism, both at the national and state levels. The forces that were unleashed by this sweeping victory in turn produced the "overloaded" system of the seventies, described at the outset, and the concomitant collapse of cooperative federalism.

This chapter and the following four deal with current intergovernmental relations. They provide the necessary background for the summary "findings" presented in chapter 1. Moreover, they set the scene for returning in the epilogue to Muncie and for examining the questions raised by the quandary its citizens and citizens everywhere find themselves in as a result of the dysfunctional, if not futilitarian, form of federalism that now prevails.

100

THE CONDITIONING CLUSTER OF "COOPERATIVE" CONCEPTS

Pragmatic Thinkers, Not Theoreticians

All of the dominant theories of federalism of these years were enunciated by or derived from the actions of leaders in the government's political branches (chiefly at the national level). They constitute a variation, but only a variation, on the cooperative federal theme. Despite their many differences in emphases, methods, and goals, the Creative Federalism of Lyndon B. Johnson, the "New Federalism" of Richard M. Nixon, the Congressional Federalism of the nation's legislature in the seventies, and the "New Partnership" of Jimmy Carter must be considered as subspecies of the generic cooperative federal concept.[1] All of them were functional theories that stressed governmental activism as well as intergovernmental collaboration, "sharing," and intricate interlevel linkages. Even the "picket-fence" and related operational concepts of the system that emerge from surveys of federal administrators indicate no real departure from these norms, but only other perspectives and approaches toward achieving them.

All of this is not to say that the spokesmen of the various "theories" were political theorists or even aware of all the principles implicit in their concepts of the system. "Creative Federalism," after all, never received a full presidential exposition. One of its best interpreters was not even a member of the Johnson administration, but a journalist, and another was an independent-minded senator, who was as much a critic as an ally of the administration.[2] Perhaps the best analysis of Johnsonian federalism lies buried in an unpublished doctoral dissertation at The American University.[3]

With the New Federalists, there were far more presidential explanations, beginning with a largely unheard radio address from Williamsburg, Virginia during the 1968 campaign, thence to presidential messages, and even to a televised presentation. There also were far more interpretative analyses from administration spokesmen[4] and from the media—both friendly and unfriendly. With

President Carter, dramatic labels were avoided for the most part, though the long-awaited and long-in-preparing "National Urban Policy," unveiled in March of 1978, did produce the "New Partnership" label.[5]

Most of the exponents of Creative, New, and New Partnership Federalism, then, were and are people of practical, not theoretic, bent—concerned with political, program, and/or administrative matters. Most did not attempt to formulate a comprehensive view of the system and none sought to use their interpretations as full explanations of how it "works" or how it used to "work." In the case of Congress, its principles had to be inferred from their actions. With the federal administrators, it was a cluster of concepts that emerged from opinion surveys that combined to suggest a certain view of the system.

All of them are operational theories and all of them must be classed as variations of cooperative federalism. Their chief differences arise primarily from their contrasting methods and values, differing views of the federal role, and varying views of the partnership ideal.

Creative Federalism

The first major variation to emerge was, of course, Johnson's Creative Federalism. Governor Nelson Rockefeller coined the phrase for the Godkin Lectures at Harvard in 1962, but it was Johnson's use and practical application of the phrase that made it a major molder of this era's intergovernmental relations.

With Johnson's expansive redefinition of the partnership principle to include cities, counties, school districts, and nonprofit organizations, as well as the states, the older, primarily federal-state focus of the cooperative federal concept as it was applied in the late forties and fifties was scrapped.

With the bypassing of the states (some seventy grant programs permitted direct disbursement to localities by 1968), and with the growing direct federal linkages with these substate units that this new partnership principle produced, a much more complex pattern of intergovernmental administrative and program relationships emerged than had been the case only a few years earlier.

With the greater emphasis on urban jurisdictions, especially cities, and on urban programs, the fifty-fifty split of federal aid to urban and nonurban areas of the fifties began to shift in favor of where seven-tenths of the people resided.

With the move into new program areas, some of which previously had been wholly state or local responsibilities and some of which had been handled, if at all, by the private sector, new intergovernmental and interest-group relationships and new approaches to the grant device emerged.

At the heart of the Johnson approach was a near monolithic reliance on the conditional grant device to achieve his Great Society goals, hence his Creative Federalism formulation. Nearly 209 new grant programs were enacted during his five-year presidency. Only one Great Society program enactment—Medicare—departed from his fundamental reliance on grants-in-aid as the means of implementing his domestic governmental programs.

Despite the massive expansion in categoricals, however, three "target grants" also were enacted (the Appalachian Regional Commission, the poverty program, and Model Cities) which departed from the categorical format in that they adopted a multifunctional approach to coping with the special problems of a specific region, a specific population group, and specific local jurisdictions, respectively. In addition, the first two block grants[6] were enacted in the Johnson years (the Partnership for Health Act of 1966, which merged seventeen previously separate narrow public health categoricals, and the Safe Streets Act of 1968, which began as a block grant).

Not to be overlooked in the new experimentalism of Creative Federalism was a massive expansion in the use of project grants (about four-fifths of the 1968 total), which stressed specific program purposes, contained eligibility provisions that encouraged a range of potential applicants to participate, and delegated considerable discretion to middle-level federal grants' administrators, including the power to decide what units had passed muster in the competition for project awards.

Unlike the New Deal period, no real debate occurred within the administration (or Congress) as to whether the federal government itself should administer any of the proposed new programs. More than anything else, this silence stands as weighty evidence of the consensual character that the conditional grant mechanism had

assumed as it entered the sixties. The only real debate was over
recipients and here, as we have seen, an open-ended approach was
adopted as often as not. Not to be ignored in this massive outpouring of new federal intergovernmental initiatives, surpassing in number all of the grant programs enacted prior to 1964, was the
doubling of the dollars going to subnational grant recipients during
these five years.

The president couched his efforts in terms of federal actions
needing "the cooperation of the State and the city, and of business
and of labor, and of private institutions and of private individuals."[7] In most of his messages, he indicated that intergovernmental cooperation had its roots in nineteenth century as well as
in New Deal practice. In some, however, he sensed the novelty of
certain of his proposals and talked of "new federal partnerships."[8]

Despite Johnson's tendency to harken back to the intergovernmental norms of the previous period (which he had done so
much to shape as Senate majority leader), the theory and practice
of Creative Federalism was markedly in contrast with the practice
of its Cooperative Federalism predecessor. It differed in its range
of new grant programs, in its diversity of participating state and
especially local units and nonprofit agencies, in its expanding federal outlays, and in its urban and city emphasis (though states still
received over four-fifths of all the grant funds during the Johnson
years).

Yet it outwardly conformed to some of the key tenets of the
theory of Cooperative Federalism. It did, after all, reflect a belief
that the system was chiefly characterized by a federal-state-local
sharing of responsibilities for practically all governmental functions (which the earlier practice of cooperative federalism did not).
It assumed implicitly that no division of functions between levels
was either possible or desirable. It trumpeted the ideal that officials
at all the levels were allies, not adversaries, under the system. And
it accepted the concept that the system was "first conceived as
one government serving one people," hence the president's call for
the Great Society.

The New Federalism

With Nixon's New Federalism, a reaction set in to many of the
thrusts of Creative Federalism. It was ostensibly anticentralization,

anticategorical, and anti–administrative confusion. In positive terms, it supported: greater decentralization within the federal departments to their field units; a devolution of more power and greater discretion to recipient units; a streamlining of the service delivery system generally; a definite preferring of general governments and their elected officials; and some sorting out of some servicing responsibilities by governmental levels. Moreover, there was some relationship between the theory and practice of the New Federalism, though less than was the case with Creative Federalism.

With decentralization, the field structure was reorganized in 1969, with ten standardized regions and common headquarters cities established. By the end of Nixon's administration, nine domestic departments or agencies were covered by this structure. In addition, their key field representatives served as members of the federal regional councils (FRCs) which were assigned both an interdepartmental coordinative and an intergovernmental liaison role. Attempts to delegate "sign off" discretion in managing grants from Washington to the field produced the claim, in 1972, that at least 190 grant programs had been decentralized administratively.[9]

Devolution took the form of general revenue sharing (GRS) and six special revenue-sharing proposals. The former became law in 1972, becoming the New Federalism's greatest legislative victory. With it, the discretion of states and general units of local government was strengthened, since it could be, was, and is used for a range of purposes—tax reduction, supplementing existing services, and/or launching new projects. While none of the special revenue proposals were enacted in their original form, these Nixon initiatives did lay the groundwork for block-grant compromises, which contained more conditions (the essential difference between a block grant and special revenue sharing) than the administration sought. Yet the Comprehensive Employment Act of 1973 and the Community Development Act of 1974 provided recipients with far more programmatic discretion than their categorical predecessors.

Streamlining of the grant delivery system largely was subsumed by the Federal Assistance Review (FAR), which explored various ways to standardize and simplify administrative procedures and requirements. Its chief accomplishment was the Office of Management and Budget Circular A-102, which sought to establish uniform phases of the grant application and management process. In addition, FAR launched the Integrated Grant Administration project and twenty-seven pilot undertakings resulted from this experiment in jointly funding state, areawide, and local grant application projects. This, in turn, helped provide some of the momentum required to achieve enactment of the Joint Funding Act of 1974, a measure that had been proposed initially in 1967.

The New Federalism's preference for generalists and general governments was reflected in the eligibility provisions of general revenue sharing and the new block grants (which flowed from the special revenue sharing proposals). In all of these new programs, special districts were excluded and elected officials of general governments favored.

The attempt to sort out the system somewhat was reflected in three endeavors. First, the special revenue sharing proposals, while continuing federal funding, gave recipient state and local governments the bulk of the real decisionmaking in the six functional areas covered—law enforcement, rural development, urban development, primary and secondary education, manpower, and transportation. Second, the unsuccessful but innovative Family Assistance Program (FAP) would have replaced a range of older welfare categoricals with a national system covering all low-income families with children. Third, the federal takeover of the financing of the adult public assistance categories (old-age assistance, aid to the blind, and aid to the permanently and totally disabled—authorized by the 1972 Social Security Amendments) marked the first real sifting out of functions that occurred during this entire period.

In these diverse ways, the Nixon administration's New Federalism sought to reverse some of the trends in Creative Federalism, while not returning to the laissez-faire and narrow dual federalism of Herbert Hoover or to the mere conservative acceptance with a few adaptations and a few new departures of the inherited intergovernmental system, as was the case with Eisenhower. The inherited legacy, after all, was that left by the Johnsonians, and much of it was deemed unwise, unmanageable, or undermining of state and local governments by the Nixonians. Hence, their reform proposals—some fairly drastic (the special revenue sharing proposals and FAP) and others milder (unemployment insurance and manpower training). This assertive, revisionist stance on the part of the Nixon administration generated a range of initiatives for congressional consideration. While only a few survived, they managed to dominate much of Congress's attention, to raise the suspicion of Creative Federalists among the congressional Democrats, and to generate a climate wherein halfway objective assessments of the Johnson programs proved nearly impossible.

All this is not to say that there were no continuities between Creative and New Federalism, for there were several. The former, after all, was not all programmatic wind; it did have a managerial rudder and this was shaped during LBJ's last two years in office. During that period, the "managing" problem was given major emphasis. Witness:

—— the launching of the A-85 process in 1967 to give state and local elected chief executives a chance to react to proposed grant regulations;

—— the issuing in 1967 of the Bureau of the Budget Circular A-80, which encouraged states to form substate districting systems by promising to conform federal substate regional programs to them, to the maximum extent possible;

—— the staff work in the Bureau of the Budget during 1968 on reorganizing the federal regional boundaries and field structures; and

—— the administration support for and the passage of the Intergovernmental Cooperation Act of 1968, which sought in various ways to lessen friction in the administration of federal grants-in-aid.

In these and other ways, the Johnsonians began trends that the Nixonians continued, suggesting that Creative and New Federalism had some things in common. Yet the real story of the Nixon effort must be placed alongside that of the Democratic Congress, with which the New Federalism had to contend.

Congressional Federalism: Creative Federalism Resurgent

The primary architect of the contemporary pattern of intergovernmental relations is, of course, Congress. As was noted earlier, Congress's operational concept of federalism must be inferred from its actions. Yet these reveal a theory that, more than any other, dominates the workings of today's system.

What are the hallmarks of this theory? Its essential features

may be described as incremental, confrontational, strongly categorical (as well as anti–block grant and anti–general revenue sharing), heavily conditional, and politically cooptive. An explanation
of each of these attributes clearly is in order.

The incrementalism inherent in the concept merely reflects the
perennial congressional tendency to cope with problems, programs,
and pressures in an ad hoc, largely piecemeal fashion. This trait is
heavily reflected in dozens of discrete grant enactments and reenactments over the past decade, with little attention paid to the
side effects of or the interrelationship among the programs. It also
has helped to conceal the drastically altered thrust of Congress's
approach to intergovernmental relations, even though the many
separate actions when combined clearly indicate the remarkable
degree to which Congress now plays the role of state legislature,
city council, and school board.

The confrontational character of the Congress's concept of
federalism suggests something fairly novel, however, since it underscores a newfound assertiveness of the national legislative body
vis-à-vis presidents, departmental secretaries, federal administrators,
and interest groups—both private and public. This trait is distinctly
a phenomenon of the seventies and of the dramatically different
political conditions of the past decade.

The antipresidential overtones of many of the congressional
actions were probably the most familiar. The Nixon initiatives,
especially the special revenue sharing proposals and their seeming
threat to the legacy of Creative Federalism, was the first conditioner of this congressional attitude. It was sustained by later
presidential vetos and impoundments of appropriated grant funds
which triggered court cases. President Ford's effort to achieve enactment of three "block grants"[10] continued it, with the proposed
merger of fifty-seven categoricals in health care, elementary and
secondary education, and child nutrition areas.[11]

Nothing, perhaps, illustrates this congressional assertiveness as
well as the countercyclical programs. The chief federal response to
the recession of the mid-seventies, after all, was largely a congressional one, and it took the form of three enactments: the Local
Public Works program (authorized by Title I of the Public Works
Employment Act of 1976 and expanded by the Intergovernmental
Anti-Recession Act of 1977); the Anti-Recession Fiscal Assistance

Program (established as an add-on to GRS by Title II of the 1976 omnibus legislation and extended as part of the 1977 measure); and a major extension of the public service programs (Titles II and VI) of the Comprehensive Employment Act of 1973 in June of 1977. The first two programs were almost wholly a product of congressional initiatives, while the last was a joint presidential (Carter)–congressional effort, and like many of the Creative Federalism programs, they heavily favored local governments. Finally, while President Carter did not confront Congress with any really revisionist programs in the intergovernmental area, the earlier distrust of the White House remained, for reasons that will be discussed later.

The antibureaucratic thrust of many of Congress's intergovernmental actions reflected the rapid erosion in the seventies of the trust that formerly characterized federal middle-management–congressional-committee (and subcommittee) relationships. With Nixon, and to a much lesser degree Ford, it was partly a matter of the congressional Democrats' belief that these posts had become politicized (e.g., Republican). With all three presidents, there was the feeling that in all too many instances competent professionals did not occupy key administration posts. This attitude, along with the heavy turnover among the political executives in the various departments, generated a sentiment among many congressional committees and their expanded staff that their own expertise was at least equal to, if not superior to, that of the executive branch. A tendency to treat the administrators as mere functionaries, if not administrative agents of the Congress, emerged. Witness the tendency to include regulations in the authorizing legislation (as with the Elementary and Secondary Education Amendments of 1978) and to specify in detail federal agency as well as recipient government organizational relationships (as with the Vocational Rehabilitation Amendments of 1973). In these and other ways, the Congress confronted what it took to be hostile forces and developed its own oppositional approach to intergovernmental relations.

At the heart of this congressional approach was an expanded and eager reliance on the categorical device. While attention in the seventies tended to focus on general revenue sharing and the enactment of three new block grants, an equally significant development was the passage of more than sixty new categoricals during President Nixon's years in office and approximately thirty more under President Ford.[12] Some of these reflected major new federal initiatives (as in the case of the environment beginning in 1970), but most of them were by-products of the process by which the Great Society programs were reauthorized (as the dozens of programs that now are part of federal aid to primary and secondary education demonstrate).

Part of this intensified preference for categoricals is mirrored in Congress's hostility to the two newer forms of intergovernmental fiscal transfer: general revenue sharing and the block grant. Enactment of the former, of course, was the result of the coming together of an unusual cluster of political pressures and in an unusual political year: 1972.[13] Its renewal in 1976, while not thwarted, was marked by the addition of several new strings, including auditing, citizen-participation, and tough civil rights requirements.

In the case of the block grants, the first—the Partnership for Health program—degenerated during the seventies into a minor part of the federal government's overall efforts in public health. Beginning in 1970 and despite the protests of then HEW secretary Elliot Richardson, new categoricals began to be enacted, to the point where a score of such grant programs now surround what in 1966 was trumpeted as the federal government's prime aid program in this functional area. The Safe Streets program acquired new conditions and earmarks within and functionally related new grants outside of it during the seventies. While Title XX, CETA, and CDBG were of more recent vintage, the familiar tension between achieving national purposes (i.e., "strings") and maximizing recipient discretion (i.e., cutting "strings") emerged in all three, with the resulting tilt favoring more conditions. In all but a handful of instances, either administrative fear of congressional reaction or direct congressional action produced this binding of the block grants.

Closely linked with this concentration on categoricals was Congress's newer proclivity to enact ostensibly national-purpose conditions and to extend them to all or nearly all grants-in-aid. In a wholly incremental fashion, Congress, over the past decade and a half, has established across-the-board requirements in the areas of equal rights, equal access, the environment, handicapped, historic preservation, relocation payments, contractor wage rates, and personnel, to cite only the more obvious, and in the process produced a new era and a new form of federal regulation.[14] These conditions are much more intricate, more intrusive, and more pervasive than the programmatic strings that were attached to the grant programs of the fifties. In many instances, the direct impact of the requirements was not gauged; in practically all of them, the secondary and tertiary effects were not explored; and at no point has the cumulative impact of these national-purpose conditions on individual recipient jurisdictions been fully gauged by Congress.

The political process from which all of the substantive intergovernmental traits of the congressional theory emanates was, of course, that of the seventies. With the quadrupling—at least—of the interest groups located in Washington, the initial breakthrough into several new program areas during the sixties, and the decline in Congress's traditional techniques for coping with outside pressures, a new method—a cooptive political one—emerged during the reauthorization process wherein all groups that are directly or even indirectly affected by the initial program are "pacified" one way or another. The typical vehicle was an omnibus bill that reflected the concerns of a wide range of interests—primarily functional, subfunctional, and even sub-subfunctional, but also generalist public interest, sociomoralistic, and demographic. Categoricals, especially project grants, were the perfect device for satisfying the divergent claims of such diverse interests. And an across-the-board requirement or specific grant condition frequently was a valuable stratagem to employ when confronting interests who were more concerned with moral issues than with money, program mechanics, or practical effects.

Reflective of the vigorous representational efforts of all local governments was the congressional tendency to place all governments on a par, and to channel funds directly to substate units as frequently as to channel them through the states. This greatly expanded concept of partnership produced a "pinwheel pattern" of grant administration, with each of the governmental and quasi-governmental recipient groups constituting a separate spoke in the wheel and with Washington (and by implication, Congress) serving as its hub.

This special brand of cooptive politics was, in a sense, only an extension of traditional "logrolling," but in a vastly expanded area and with infinitely more players. That it was congressional in character and in focus is undeniable. That it changed, if not clogged, the legislative process is also undeniable. And that it shaped heavily the presently overloaded intergovernmental network is again undeniable.

Incrementalism, confrontation, more and more categoricals, as well as conditions, and a new variant of interest group-cooptive politics—these are substantive and procedural hallmarks of the congressional approach to and theory of contemporary federalism. In combination, they have tended to place Congress at the center of the system and to make it the major molder of the present pattern of intergovernmental relations.

The failure on the part of many to recognize the differences between Nixon's New Federalism and Congress's expansion of Creative Federalism explains many of the confused interpretations of the 1969–76 phase of this period. When the two are joined, certain very understandable paradoxes emerge:

1. A conscious presidential effort to curb categorical grants was mounted, yet their number only multiplied.
2. A serious presidential drive was launched to "devolve" greater decisionmaking authority to subnational governments, yet intrusive conditions of various types increased.
3. New forms of federal aid emerged, but in time most of them came to resemble the older, categorical form.
4. An effort was made to streamline the grant delivery system, but greater managerial confusion resulted—thanks to more programs, more recipients, and more conditions (both programmatic and across the board, as well as procedural and institutional).
5. Generalists and general governments were favored by presidential efforts, yet these, along with those of Congress, made no effort to distinguish among subnational governments that were genuinely general, as in the case of general revenue sharing, and both branches failed to confront the array of special program people and districting units at the substate regional level, which federal grant programs with a regional component had encouraged.
6. Finally, some sorting out of governmental functions was contemplated, with the special revenue sharing and the federal take-

over of the "adult categories," but the overall tendency was a massively expanded commingling of governmental functions.

"The New Partnership"

To chronicle the components of Jimmy Carter's approach to inter-governmental relations is hazardous at best, given the relatively brief time involved, the eclectic character of his initiatives, and the secondary emphasis given to federal-state-local relations by his administration. Most of the basic themes subsumed under the Carter concept were enunciated in his campaign address to the United States Conference of Mayors in the summer of 1976 at Milwaukee.[15] In it, echoes could be heard of both Creative and the New Federalism, as well as of the man himself.

An expanded federal-state-local-private sector partnership, a heavily urban/city focus, a wide range of expanded and new inter-governmental programs, bypassing of state governments, greater targeting, and a leadership role for the national government in the system—such were the Johnsonian tenets that were reiterated in the Carter address.

Fiscal caution, greater devolution, curbing categorical growth by grant consolidations, overhauling the federal executive branch, and injecting some rationality into the organization and behavior of its bureaucracy—these were the New Federalism themes that crept into what otherwise would have appeared to be a latter-day Creative Federalist paper. The speech, then, like most of the follow-up efforts, reflected an artful effort to synthesize key concepts from both of the predecessor presidents' approaches to federalism, as well as from his own arsenal of technocratic and populist beliefs, while avoiding the inconsistencies (at least in the address) that such a merger necessarily entails.

During the transition period following his election, the new president-elect focused his goals for improving intergovernmental relations and stressed (1) the need for a more precise targeting of federal aid to the most hard-pressed communities, (2) greater use of public funds as levers in stimulating private investment, and (3) his intent to mount a full-fledged attack on red tape and the paper-work morass hindering efficient government at all levels.[16] While he promised the governors not to "preside over an administration which ignores the lessons of my own personal experience," the pressures on the new president were such that some of these lessons had to be ignored.

There was the legacy of an extraordinarily complex, costly, and heavily interest-group-conditioned federal-aid and regulatory system. There was the coalition of diverse interests that put him into office—some that wanted more "targeting," more federal aid, and more access; others that wanted a streamlining and simplification of the nonsystem; and still others that sought more of a private-sector role in resolving the nation's domestic social and economic challenges. Above all, perhaps, there was the pressure from the president himself to achieve a more efficient and more simple system—structurally, administratively, and programmatically.[17]

Four basic themes emerge from the Milwaukee and transitional press conference addresses: managerialism, greater access and improved intergovernmental procedures, fiscal prudence, and better older, as well as some newer, federal program initiatives (especially to urban jurisdictions and genuinely needy people). These four themes, in fact, dominated the Carter approach to intergovernmental relations during his first three years.[18]

Managerialism

Extraordinary efforts were mounted on the organizational and reorganizational fronts. In a strict sense, however, these had little to do with federal-state-local relations as such, since they were largely based on the old public administration notions of executive leadership and of the president's obligation to structure the federal bureaucracy "into a manageable hierarchy, establish firm control over expenditures, and render the civil service accountable to him."[19]

As applied by President Carter, this old-style public-administration philosophy produced five reorganizational undertakings:

——a renewal of the president's reorganization authority;
——a restructuring (à la Brownlow) of the Executive Office of the President (EOP);[20]
——the establishment of two new departments (Energy and Education);

——the launching of a twenty-one-month President's Reorganization Project (PRP), which produced some thirty-one studies in seven broad functional areas and four major recommendations, but not legislative proposals, for shifting most of the economic and community development, natural resources, food nutrition, and trade programs to a like number of cabinet departments;[21] and

——another experiment (the last being Eisenhower's) with "cabinet government," with full-dress weekly meetings, significant personnel decisions left to the department secretaries, and no members of the scaled-down White House staff dominating or acting "in a superior position to members of the Cabinet."[22]

Carter's managerialism also led to a revamping of the executive budget process with the introduction of zero-based budgeting (ZBB), beginning with the preparation of the budget for FY 1979. Touted as a technique for prioritizing all expenditures—for existing programs and activities as well as for new proposals—ZBB was geared to providing each successive level of administrative authority (starting at the lowest) with the information needed to make more astute judgments about future spending plans.[23] Though a new technique, ZBB's goals were and are wholly compatible with the economy and efficiency objectives of traditional executive budgeting. Whether the "savings" have been as great as the original claims promised is a matter of some debate.

The third angle of Carter's managerial triangle was formed by his Federal Personnel Management Project, which ultimately came up with his civil service reform proposals. These "reforms" were largely accepted by Congress, and in the process the old public administration concept of personnel as a vital tool of executive management was given something of a boost. A key argument in gaining congressional enactment was the claim that the old civil service system had erected "a pretty firm wall against effective management."[24]

In launching these many administrative reforms, attention was focused on the internal operations of the federal executive branch, and especially on the president's position as its chief administrator. Traditional public administration concepts were applied, along with a few new adaptations (ZBB and civil service reform). Ostensible success was achieved as they related to the structure of the executive office of the presidency, its functions, and its presumed capacity to "manage" the system, but save for the Education Department, they fell afoul of strong interest-group political pressure in matters not falling within the EOP (as with the President's Reorganization Project's final proposals and, in effect, the experiment with cabinet government). In none of these efforts (save for PRP's) was state and local relations a key factor, and certainly no theory of federalism resulted from any of them.

Proceduralism

A second major theme of the Carter administration was its stress on accessibility and on improved intergovernmental procedures. Here, there was a clearer federal-state-local focus and set of assumptions. One of the president's first acts was the appointment of Jack Watson, a long-term Carter associate, to the dual role of secretary of the cabinet and assistant to the president for intergovernmental relations. This honored his campaign promise to improve communication with the states and localities and to make the presidency more accessible. It also reflected the continuation of a practice that had begun with Eisenhower—though admittedly Carter's predecessors followed somewhat different formats in structuring this liaison function.

A directive to the departments shortly thereafter sought to assure that similar points of contact would be available to state and local officials throughout the executive branch and that such posts would be staffed with "high-ranking" officials. Accompanying this action was a presidential memorandum that specified that state and local inputs should be sought on any major policy, budgetary, and reorganization proposals.[25]

In related efforts, the Undersecretaries Group, which had been established in the early seventies to coordinate federal activities through the FRCs in the ten regions, was reactivated (it had become moribund during the Ford years) under Watson's direction. While the FRCs were subject to three different studies (even as some of the departments—Interior, Labor, Justice, HEW—were recentralizing the management of many of their programs), they finally received presidential authorization to continue in his executive order of July 20, 1979. In it, their older interagency coordination and intergovernmental liaison responsibilities were reiterated along with new assignments in the economic development and anti-inflation areas.[26]

Carter administration efforts to simplify and enhance the coordination of the many procedural and some substantive requirements attached to federal assistance programs were varied, but persistent. The first major step was taken on September 9, 1977 with a presidential memorandum geared to launching "a concentrated attack on red tape and confusion in the Federal grant-in-aid system."[27] It called for

—reduction in the amount of duplicative information required in applications for grant renewals;
—reliance upon standard application and financial reporting forms;
—combination or elimination of unnecessary reports and sharing of information among the agencies;
—increased use of advanced funding, letters of credit, and electronic fund transfers;
—coordination of audit procedures (by making departmental audit schedules available to grantees, conducting single audits wherever possible, and using state and local audits more often); and
—expanded use of the joint funding procedure (which permits potential recipients to package grant applications).

Most of these "reforms" reflected a renewed commitment to various provisions of the Intergovernmental Cooperation Act of 1968, existing OMB A-circulars, and the Joint Funding Simplification Act of 1974. The memorandum also called for a "lead agency" to compile and examine existing agency practices relating to three "across-the-board" grant requirements that are intended to help achieve national goals in the environmental impact, equal opportunity employment, and citizen participation areas. An earlier (June) presidential directive had called for a "zero-based" revision of all federal planning requirements (more than 3500 in some 160 aid programs) and a later (March 1979) executive order called upon existing agencies to adopt procedures that will produce regulations that are simple and clear, will achieve legislative goals efficiently and effectively, and will not impose unnecessary burdens on the economy, individuals, public or private organizations, or state and local governments.[28]

At the request of the president, the Advisory Commission on Intergovernmental Relations (ACIR) was asked to monitor the implementation of the goals set forth in his September 9, 1977 memorandum. ACIR's specially convened panel of state and local administrators found overall departmental and agency compliance with the memorandum's reform goals "mixed but disappointing."[29]

The basic dilemma confronting any administration that now relies primarily on improved and uniform procedures and processes to strengthen intergovernmental management is that such efforts cannot be separated from the drastically expanded size, scope, and substantive concerns of today's intergovernmental programs and of their recipients. Thanks to the legacies of Creative, New, and especially contemporary Congressional Federalism, no mere effort on the process and access fronts alone—no matter how persistent and massive—can bring uniformity, simplicity, and manageability to intergovernmental administration.[30] Combined with consolidation, abolition, and devolution, proceduralism would have been a viable management strategy for the late seventies; alone it was ineffective.

Fiscal Conservatism

Fiscal constraint and control comprised another basic, albeit sometimes wavering, theme of the Carter approach toward intergovernmental relations. Perhaps its firmest features were the budgeting procedures: ZBB, multiyear budgeting, and better use of existing programs. After ZBB's first year in operation, an OMB assessment claimed that it had facilitated explicit identification of agency priorities, helped curb the size of agency budget requests, and increased management participation throughout the process.[31] Shortcomings were conceded, however.

The more substantive, but less consistent, feature of Carter's fiscal-constraint theme was his campaign pledge of a balanced budget by fiscal year 1981, which was reiterated after his inauguration. Yet austerity was not part of his revisions of the Ford budget. He called for a nearly $20 billion hike in spending

and an increase in budget authority of $27 billion, even as defense
was cut by $3 billion and talk of a balanced budget continued.[32]
Some cuts were reflected in his FY 1979 proposals, in response to
growing concern about inflation, but it produced a chorus of out-
raged protests from union leaders, civil rights groups, and specific
program people. The end result was a proposed tax cut of $24.5
billion, $8 billion in proposed new outlays, and almost $30 billion in new budget authority (or $33 billion in spending and
nearly $50 billion in budget authority more than the figures
projected for FY 1979 by the Ford administration).

With his proposals for FY 1980, a more concerted effort was
made to reduce spending. Inflation now was recognized as a far
more pressing problem than unemployment; in an October 1978
televised address, the president called for wage and price guidelines, but not controls, and in November he warned the mayors
in an address to the National League of Cities that little new
federal aid could be expected in his forthcoming budget message.

At the heart of his FY 1980 budget proposals was the pledge
to hold the federal deficit to $29 billion, down from $33.2 billion
in FY 1979 and $48.8 in FY 1978. Inflation was to be brought
under control and governmental restraint was needed. In political
terms, this Carter thrust was intended to immunize Washington
from Proposition 13 fever and to slow the mounting momentum
behind a drive for a constitutional amendment requiring balanced
federal budgets.

In real dollar terms, the Carter proposals added up to less than
one percent in growth and even an actual decline, if the modest
hike in defense spending is set aside.[33] Under them, federal aid
was slated to rise by less than one billion dollars over the $82.1
billion 1979 figure. Yet no grant consolidations surfaced, and
many among the intergovernmental lobby—both functionalist
and generalist—were delighted that more drastic budget actions
had not occurred.

Programmatic Flexibility

The final concept that conditioned the Carter "New Partnership" was a concern with improving and sometimes expanding
the operations of old programs and with launching some new ones,

but all in a highly flexible fashion. In a real sense, the other three themes all reflected Carter's technocratic bent, but this one reflected his party affiliation. In his first year, a range of program and policy initiatives were launched (too many, some said), including a national energy plan, welfare reform, an economic stimulus package, food stamp reform, an increase in the minimum wage, hospital cost containment, energy fuel assistance, a proposed consumer protection agency, increased housing for low- and moderate-income families, expansion of the Community Development block grant and enactment of the Urban Development Action Grant (UDAG) to provide additional funds to the most distressed cities, and legislation to curb Medicare and Medicaid fraud.

These by no means exhausted the list of early administrative initiatives, nor did they include congressionally instituted measures "supported and signed" by the president. But they highlight the diversity of initial program concerns of the president and they reflect the traditional tendencies of a Democratic president to curb unemployment, to aid in one fashion or another the divergent interests that helped elect him, and to rely heavily on conditional grants as the basic means of doing this. The chief Carter legislative defeats in 1977—energy, welfare reform, a consumer protection agency, and hospital cost containment—were all new initiatives that (save for consumer protection, perhaps) had no clear link to the Johnson past, that were hastily (and in two instances poorly) drafted, and that appeared threatening to various of the congressional Democrats.

Other than energy, probably the most prominent of Carter's new program undertakings during his first two years, and certainly the most significant from an intergovernmental perspective, was his promised national urban policy. Responsibility for devising it was lodged in the Urban and Regional Policy Group (URPG), set up in March of 1977 and chaired by then HUD secretary Patricia Harris, but the group soon encountered major obstacles.[34] The former included meager initial White House direction or participation, internal rivalries within HUD, lack of HUD authority over the other participants (Treasury, Commerce, Labor, HEW, and Transportation), and a seemingly unending consultative process that involved literally hundreds of hours and people.

There were basic substantive difficulties as well. The causes of the urban crisis, after all, are diverse (human, physical, jurisdiction, and fiscal) and each has different roots and frequently conflicting solutions.

The final report, "New Partnership To Conserve America's Communities," called for:

— improvements in local planning and management capacity and in the administration of existing federal programs;
— fiscal assistance for the most distressed communities;
— greater state involvement in aiding their urban communities;
— increased participation of neighborhood and volunteer groups;
— improvement of urban physical and cultural environments;
— incentives for private-sector investment and development;
— job opportunities for the long-term unemployed;
— increased opportunities for the disadvantaged; and
— improved and expanded health and social services.

Missing in these proposals and in the background report was any real recognition that federal urban aid already was at an all-time high (thanks to the three countercyclical programs) and was moderately well targeted.[35] Neither was there any real assessment of the vast array of existing urban programs, nor any proposed consolidation or elimination of any older programs. Moreover, no proposal relating to the federal government's multiple and conflicting substate regional programs was advanced. Instead, certain of the existing grant programs were expanded; several new programs were proposed, chiefly of a conditional character; and a new cluster of members (the neighborhoods) were added to the already expansive membership of the old partnership.

The policy's defenders[36] emphasized that its policy roots were quite different from those of early urban assistance efforts. They stressed its procity emphasis and its striving to shift certain older federal programs out of their former anticity role (transportation, infrastructure subsidies, etc.). They contended that a new urban-conserving ethic was a basic conditioner of the policy and that more of a targeting and less of a formula allocation strategy was reflected in it. They maintained that the policy for the first time rationally recognized the critical position of the states in their urban areas as well as the pivotal private-sector role.

By the end of 1978, some thirteen urban-related measures had become law (five of which were not part of the original urban policy package).[37] In the arena of administrative actions, four executive orders were issued as a follow-up to the urban policy. Under the provisions of two, federal agencies were to target purchases of goods and services to areas of high unemployment and to assign priority to locating their offices and facilities in central-city areas. Under a third, urban and community impact analyses were required of agencies to identify the potential impacts of their major programs on cities, counties, and other communities. With the fourth, an Interagency Coordinative Council (IACC), chaired by Jack Watson, was established; its chief assignment was to identify and resolve interagency conflicts that undermine the urban policy's goals.

While it would be going too far to compare the interest-group-conditioned product to FDR's "concert-of-interests" strategy, this prime example of Carter's "New Partnership" certainly resembled it. The only really distinctive features of the policy were its "targeting" and private-sector leveraging features, and it is not at all clear that the programs enacted and the administrative actions taken pursuant to these two tough goals will be permitted to succeed.

An Inconclusive Conclusion

The confused and conflicting effects of Carter's managerialism, proceduralism, fiscal conservatism, and program flexibility underscore the absence of any consistent theory of federalism or approach to intergovernmental relations in his administration. The ambiguities arose partly because within the president the technocrat was in steady conflict with the need to be a Democrat. The technocrat had not moved much beyond the traditional public-management precepts and had not confronted the intergovernmental administrative realities that previous Democrats, both presidential and congressional, largely had shaped. His fiscal conservatism also was at war with his Democratic self, though really only recently and with little recognition of its possible use as an alternative means of achieving greater manageability in the system.

Despite these conflicting personal pressures, as well as the equally conflicting external ones, what ultimately emerged from his principles and practices was not wholly unclear in intergovernmental terms. Some tentative tenets *can* be inferred from the record, including:

——Categorical grants are the preferred intergovernmental transfer mechanism.
——Reorganizational and procedural reforms, if properly implemented, are the appropriate approaches to improving the grant delivery system and the regulatory process.
——The existing general revenue-sharing and block-grant programs should be continued, but major new mergers and consolidations are either unnecessary or politically unwise.
——The national government must have direct access to those local jurisdictions who provide a vital membership in the "New Partnership."
——The national government has no responsibility for building authoritative decisionmaking units at the substate regional level, though it should help to improve the processes under which federally encouraged units at this level operate.
——Fiscal circumstances dictate a gradually reduced federal fiscal role in intergovernmental programs, but this need not include any reduction in the number or variety of assistance programs nor require any curbs on federal government's regulatory thrusts in the grant-in-aid area.

These are some of the "principles" that can be inferred from the Carter record. Whether they in fact add up to a "New Partnership" or a new approach to federalism is debatable. In broad terms, they resemble the tenets of Johnson's Creative Federalism, with an extra emphasis on managerial and procedural reform. Some of Nixon's fiscal conservatism is there, but none of his stress on restructuring the grant system itself is present. In many respects, this resembles the current congressional approach to federalism, though again, with more of a technocratic tone than Congress would ever allow itself.

From "Picket-Fence Federalism" to "Bamboo-Fence Federalism"

Federal aid administrators also are primary participants in present intergovernmental relations (IGR) in the United States, thanks to the accelerating significance of federal assistance programs. How influential a role these administrators occupy and how significant their views of the system are depend not only on one's assessment of their power, influence, and position within the system, but also on the formal and informal constraints placed upon them by other key IGR actors—the executive office of the president, the Congress and its oversight and appropriations committees, departmental political executives, nationally based public and functional interest groups, and state and local political and program leaders.

One fairly conventional interpretation is that federal-aid officials form an angle in a series of "functional triangles" that also include affected interest groups, and relevant congressional committees and subcommittees.[38] Sometimes, but not always, this horizontal view is given a downward "vertical functional autocracies" dimension.[39] The linkage between the two is not wholly consistent, since the latter is chiefly a bureaucratic interpretation involving "clear and unbroken lines of communication between and among functional specialists and their counterparts in the field."[40] Hence, some treat this view as a wholly separate explanation of federal-aid officials' influence and behavior.

More recently, and partly stemming from these two earlier views, a pair of "whipping boy" interpretations have emerged. Both embody the belief that aid administrators are the paramount actors in the current intergovernmental drama.

From the executive branch, as the earlier analysis demonstrated, has come the view that severe measures must be taken—in terms of personnel actions, administration reorganizations, budgetary and other fiscal actions, and program reformulation—if these officials are to be rendered accountable. From the Congress has come a range of antibureaucratic opinions that tend to lead to common conclusions: the federal bureaucracy is out of control and the will of Congress, as reflected in grant statutes, is not being honored. Detailed statutory prescriptions of proper administrative behavior, better congressional budget procedures, "sunset" legislation, and/or legislative review (or veto) of administrative regulations have been utilized or proposed as means of establishing a pattern of proper accountability.

In one sense, both of these recent interpretations stem from the constitutionally based dual theory of administrative accountability, wherein the president and the Congress share the responsibility for organizing, directing, and controlling the civil administration. In another, they reflect the institutional and partisan conflicts of the 1969–76 period. But from a systemic vantage point, they tend to reflect presidential and congressional frustrations, if not bewilderment, throughout the past dozen years, with the massive change in federal-assistance efforts.

But what of the views of the bureaucrats themselves? In 1975, the Advisory Commission on Intergovernmental Relations conducted a survey of federal grant administrators as part of its multivolume probe of the intergovernmental grant system. This poll, along with the pioneering 1964 effort of the Senate Subcommittee on Intergovernmental Relations, are the only two of their kind and provide the basis for this attitudinal analysis.[41]

Respondents to the subcommittee's mid-sixties survey tended to reflect four behavioral themes in their replies.[42]

——*Functionalism,* or the administrator's preoccupation with protecting and promoting the purposes of individual grant programs, was the most important single conditioner of comments.
——*Professionalism,* or a deep faith in the merit-system principle and to the ethical and technical standards of the specialized group to which they belonged, conditioned answers to numerous questions relating to intergovernmental personnel and state organization.
——*Standpattism,* or the vigorous defense of traditional practices and program principles, dominated many of the replies to items covering federal aid, financial management, and metropolitan area problems.
——*Indifference,* or the seemingly "cavalier" dismissal of serious questions or broader intergovernmental, managerial, and fiscal significance, was another theme embodied in the administrator's survey replies. This attitude was viewed as partly an extension of the other three, but was singled out for special treatment in the subcommittee report because of its special significance for those seeking to reform the grant system.

In most respects, then, the federal-aid administrators of the mid-sixties matched the bold behavior assigned to them in Terry Sanford's "picket-fence federalism" metaphor.[43]

But how did the general attitudes of federal-aid administrators in the seventies compare to those of their counterparts of more than a decade ago? While the areas of inquiry in the later survey differed in many respects from some covered by its 1964 predecessor, certain identical questions were included in both. Moreover, broad attitudinal themes can be gleaned from both surveys and used for comparative purposes, even though specific items in the two polls differed.[44]

While the four earlier behavioral norms were present in the pattern of responses to the 1975 poll, they were much less striking and strident. And certain new themes can be detected in their collective responses to several survey items.[45] Of the earlier four, functionalism, or program protectionism, emerged most fully intact. The moderate to strong negative responses on consolidating programs, standard application and preapplication forms, the staffing size and organization of counterpart recipient units, congressional cuts in authorizations and appropriations, and departmental reorganizations highlight the continuing and not surprising strength of this collective attitude. Not to be overlooked here was the respondents' overwhelming satisfaction expressed about most of the features of their individual grant program's design and fairly strong tendency to rate highly the performance of special-purpose, public and quasi-public recipients over and above that of general-purpose governments. Yet this functional theme still emerged less strongly from the 1975 survey than it did in the 1964 poll.

Some of this can be explained in terms of the chastening effect of various efforts to curb narrow program commitment during the previous ten years. Equally significant was the emergence of other themes in the later survey—themes that do not necessarily reinforce the functionalist tendency.

Standpattism figured predominantly as a major bureaucratic norm conditioning a heavily status quo orientation on a range of items in the earlier poll. But it was more than matched by a countervailing tendency toward greater flexibility in the later one. Admittedly, the basic contentment with most aspects of the design of their grants (noted earlier), the negative to merely passive reactions to efforts geared to speeding up the grant application process, and the strength of the "not applicable" and "negative" views on decentralization efforts—all suggest that the older norm had not disappeared.

At the same time, the moderate to favorable views on the management circulars, the A-95 process, and others clearly suggest adaptability and, in some cases, a shift of attitude from that of their predecessors. Greater flexibility, then, especially on managerial and procedural issues, emerged from various response patterns in the ACIR survey, and this served to undercut somewhat the standpat stance reflected in replies to other items.

Professionalism, or the strong attachment to vocational and program standards or goals, was very much present in the 1975 attitudinal probe. But it presented a far less paternalistic image, vis-à-vis state and local program personnel, than it did in 1964. This was due primarily to the many positive changes that the later generation of federal-aid administrators found in recipient governments' personnel practices. Salaries, training, personnel turnover, and merit systems were all given much more favorable ratings than they received earlier. More negative judgments about the "overall capacity" of recipient units suggested some continuing concerns chiefly of a professional nature. But even here, the dominant views were not caustically critical.

Finally, the earlier collective sentiment of indifference toward serious questions of broad intergovernmental concern can hardly be discerned in the responses to the 1975 poll. Instead, it was replaced almost wholly by a spirit of skepticism—if not a sense of "hard-headed realism." The strong "no appreciable effect" response to the management circulars, to incentives for improved recipient program administration or servicing, and to many of the regionalization and decentralization efforts underscores this, while the self-criticism reflected in the response pattern on agency monitoring of recipient performance and on the issuance of regulations suggested a realistic awareness of internal management difficulties, rarely found in the previous attitudinal probe. The perceptive, nondefensive replies to the two questions relating to general revenue sharing suggest another dimension of this realism.

Overall, then, the 1975 aid administrators adhered to some of the behavioral norms of their predecessors. But their lesser commitment to standpat positions, their greater flexibility in confronting broad managerial and interlocal issues, their much more moderate professional concerns regarding state and local counterpart personnel, their rejection of their predecessors' cavalier indifference toward certain basic intergovernmental management challenges, along with a certain skepticism regarding some efforts to reform grants management, clearly indicate changed attitudes. And, for the most part, these basic opinion shifts reflected the reduced influence and unclear sense of purpose of the federal-aid managers of the seventies.

What kind of an operational theory of federalism emerges from all this? Only a minority of the 1975 respondents implicitly favored the old "picket fence" theory with all of its rigid, vertical functionalism that was endorsed by three-quarters of the respondents to the 1964 survey. But what of the majority?

A fence still would appear to be the proper metaphor, but not the sturdy, solid wood variety. One of bamboo would be more apt—given its somewhat softer materials, its elaborate horizontal wiring system, and its greater capacity to bend to prevailing winds. Whether "bamboo-fence" federalism accurately captures the vertical functionalism, continuing professionalism, greater flexibility, and realism of these contemporary administrators depends in part on one's taste in metaphors. Yet it clearly suggests a marked contrast with the more rigid "picket-fence" variety, and a similar contrast was reflected in the general attitudes embodied in the two surveys of federal-aid administrators.

CONCLUSION

Creative Federalism, New Federalism, Congressional Federalism, New Partnership, picket-fence and bamboo-fence federalism—such were the diverse range of intergovernmental interpretations and ideas that helped shape the contemporary era. All were derivatives of cooperative federalism; none of them paid any homage to dual federalism; and all of them were more than theories, since all had an impact on the system. Some would say that the confused and conflicting character of today's intergovernmental relations in large measure is a direct by-product of the intellectual confusion that these diverse, though ostensibly "collaborative" concepts reflect.

NOTES TO CHAPTER 4

1. See Richard H. Leach, *American Federalism* (New York: W. W. Norton & Co., 1976), pp. 14–17.

2. See Max Ways, "Creative Federalism and the Great Society," *Fortune,* January 1966, and Sen. Edmund S. Muskie, "The Challenge of Creative Federalism," *Congressional Record,* Friday, 25 March 1966.

3. Richard Warner, "The Concept of Creative Federalism," Washington, D.C., American University, unpublished doctoral dissertation, 1970.

4. See *Publius* 2, no. 1 (Spring 1972): 98–146.

5. The term *balanced national partnership,* of course, had been used in some of his campaign speeches.

6. A block grant is an intergovernmental fiscal transfer that covers a wide functional terrain and that seeks to achieve broad national purposes, while maximizing the discretion of recipient jurisdictions.

7. Lyndon B. Johnson, Speech to the N.Y. Liberal Party, 15 October 1964, *Public Reports,* pp. 1350–51.

8. See Harry N. Scheiber, *The Condition of American Federalism: An Historian's View.* A study submitted by the Committee on Government Operations, Subcommittee on Intergovernmental Relations, U.S. Senate, 89th Congress, 2nd Sess., 15 October 1966, pp. 14–16.

9. Given the difficulty of gauging whether such delegations actually take place, this estimate must be viewed with some caution. See Advisory Commission on Intergovernmental Relations, *Improving Federal Grants Management* (A-53) (Washington, D.C.: U.S. Government Printing Office, February 1977), pp. 187–91.

10. Despite their designation, these lacked many of the strings associated with block grants, thus making them a latter-day version of "special revenue sharing" in the eyes of most members of Congress.

11. See *Special Analysis, Budget of the United States Government, Fiscal Year 1977* (Washington, D.C.: U.S. Government Printing Office), pp. 256–57.

12. See Advisory Commission on Intergovernmental Relations, *Categorical Grants: Their Role and Design* (A-52) (Washington, D.C.: U.S. Government Printing Office, 1978), pp. 31–43 and ACIR, *A Catalogue of Federal Grant-in-Aid Programs to State and Local Governments: Grants Funded FY 1978* (A-72) (Washington, D.C.: U.S. Government Printing Office, February 1979), p. 1.

13. See Samuel H. Beer, "The Adoption of General Revenue Sharing," *Public Policy* 24, no. 2 (Spring 1976): 127–95.

14. See ACIR, "Categorical Grants . . . ," op. cit., pp. 233–72.

15. See Jimmy Carter, "Address on Urban Policy to the United States Conference of Mayors," 29 June 1976.

16. See Rochelle L. Stanfield, "Is the Man from Georgia Ready to Help the States and Cities?", *National Journal*, 22 January 1977, 137–41.

17. See Jack Knott and Aaron Wildavsky, "Jimmy Carter's Theory of Governing," *The Wilson Quarterly*, Winter 1977, 49–67.

18. This analysis does not cover the year 1980.

19. See David R. Beam, "Public Administration Is Alive and Well and Living in the White House," *Public Administration Review*, January/February 1978, 72–77.

20. See Reorganization Plan No. 1 of 1977.

21. See Rochelle L. Stanfield, "The Best Laid Reorganization Plans Sometimes Go Astray," *National Journal*, 1 January 1979, 84–91.

22. Less than two years later, the White House began tightening up on its control over the departments, their personnel policies, public relations, and program planning and by the summer of 1979, the wholesale reshaping of the cabinet itself (and the White House Office) occurred.

23. See Donald F. Haider, "Zero Base: Federal Style," *Public Administration Review* 37 (July/August 1977): 400–607.

24. See Joel Havermann, "Can Carter Chop Through the Civil Service System?" *National Journal* 23 (April 1977): 616.

25. "The President's Memorandum for the Heads of Executive Departments and Agencies: Involvement of State and Local Officials in The Administration's Policies and Programs," 25 February 1977, *Weekly Compilation of Presidential Documents*, p. 283.

26. See *Fact Sheet, Federal Regional Councils*, Washington, D.C., The White House, 20 July 1979.

27. "Memorandum for the Heads of Executive Departments and Agencies: Administration of Federal Aid Systems," 9 September 1977, *Weekly Compilation of Presidential Documents*, 12 September 1977, pp. 1318–19.

28. See *Federal Aid Simplification*, White House Status Report, September 1978.

29. See ACIR, *Streamlining Federal Assistance Administration, The Final Report to the President* (Washington, D.C.: U.S. Government Printing Office, 1978).

30. See *Fact Sheet, Grant-in-Aid Planning Requirements*, Executive Office of the President, Office of Management and Budget, Washington, D.C., 25 March 1979; Office of Management and Budget, *Paperwork and Red Tape: New Perspectives—New Directions, A Report to the President and the Congress* (Washington, D.C.: U.S. Government Printing Office, September 1979); and Office of Management and Budget, *Improving Government Regulations, A Progress Report* (Washington, D.C.: U.S. Government Printing Office, September 1979).

31. See "Assessment of the First Year of Zero-Base Budgeting," *The White House, Office of the Press-Secretary*, 2 May 1978.

32. See Karl O'Lessker, "Carter: The First Two Years," *The American Spectator* 2, no. 12 (December 1978): 5–8.

33. See Timothy B. Clark, "Lobbying Over the 1980 Budget—Can Congress Say No?" *National Journal,* 24 March 1979, 464–69.

34. David R. Beam and David B. Walker, "Can Carter Cut The Marble Cake?: 1977 in Intergovernmental Perspective," paper prepared for presentation at the 1978 Annual Conference of the American Society for Public Administration, 9–12 April 1978, Phoenix, Arizona.

35. See ACIR, *Intergovernmental Perspective,* Winter 1978, pp. 8–9.

36. See Lawrence O. Houstoun, Jr., "The Carter Urban Policy A Year Later," memo dated 8 February 1979, U.S. Department of Commerce.

37. See ACIR, "The National Policy: One Year Later," *Information Bulletin* No. 79–4, May 1979.

38. See Harold Seidman, *Politics, Position & Power: The Dynamics of Federal Organization* (New York: Oxford University Press, 1970), p. 136.

39. See ACIR, *Tenth Annual Report* (Washington, D.C.: U.S. Government Printing Office, 1968), p. 8.

40. U.S. Senate Committee on Government Operations, Subcommittee on Intergovernmental Relations, *The Federal System as Seen by Federal Aid Officials,* 15 December 1965, pp. 98–101.

41. The latter involved a survey of 125 program administrators, responsible for disbursing a little over $12 billion in grants in 1964, 109 of whose responses were used in the subcommittee's report. The ACIR surveyed 440 administrators, 276 of whose responses were deemed "usable" for analytical purposes.

42. U.S. Senate Committee on Government Operations, Subcommittee on Intergovernmental Relations, *The Federal System as Seen by Federal Aid Officials* op. cit., pp. 93–102.

43. Terry Sanford, *Storm Over the States* (New York: McGraw-Hill Book Co., 1967), p. 80.

44. David B. Walker, "Federal Aid Administrators and the Federal System," in Advisory Commission on Intergovernmental Relations, *Intergovernmental Perspective* 3, no. 4 (Fall 1977): 10–17.

45. See ACIR, *The Intergovernmental Grant System as Seen by Local, State, and Federal Officials* (Report A–54) (Washington, D.C.: U.S. Government Printing Office, 1977), chapter 5.

The Dynamics
and Dimensions
of Today's
System

5

The
Federal
Judiciary

Each of three earlier eras in the evolution of American federalism revealed a significant, if not dominant, role for the federal judiciary, and the current one obviously is no exception. Any notions that the federal principle and intergovernmental relations are discrete and somehow disconnected, that the judges deal with the former but exert little impact on the latter, are swept aside by the Supreme Court's record of the past two decades. Moreover, the nearly complete demise of dual federalism and the concomitant tendency to thrust nearly every type of public policy question—large or small, paramount or puny—into the intergovernmental arena was heavily conditioned (if not in some areas actually shaped) by decisions of the Supreme Court.

While the activism of the Warren Court obviously predated 1960, it was the addition of four new members (Byron R. White, Arthur J. Goldberg, Abe Fortas, and Thurgood Marshall) by presidents Kennedy and Johnson that strengthened the Court's libertarian and equalitarian tendencies. To a far greater degree than in the fifties, the Supreme Court of the sixties not only sanctioned controversial congressional enactments, but assumed "a novel role as a leader in the process of social change quite at odds with its traditional position as a defender of legalistic tradition and social continuity."[1]

For the most part, these decisions "expanded federal power fundamentally by placing much stricter limits on the states."[2] Yet some of the Warren and Burger court cases, notably in the reapportionment and educational finance areas, had the effect of strengthening the states, and as recently as 1971 one of the Court's most pronounced libertarians, Justice Hugo L. Black, could speak fondly of "Our Federalism" and of the necessity of understanding that "the entire country is made up of a Union of separate state governments."[3] He went on to caution in dual-federalist terms that "the National Government will fare best if the States and their institutions are left free to perform their separate functions in their separate ways."[4]

On occasion, then, the Court has revealed some sensitivity to the concept of state autonomy, and inferentially to the old dual-federal view that presumed such a sensitivity. At the same time, it also has relied on such phrases as "cooperative federalism" and "state cooperation in a joint federal-state program" to underpin some of its decisions in the grant-in-aid area.[5] Finally, the Court on many occasions, and especially during the sixties, has appeared to be totally oblivious to the systemic effects of its decisions. The following will attempt to determine how these varying judicial views on federalism fared with the "new" Warren Court (1960-69) and with its successor under the leadership of Chief Justice Burger (1969-——).

THE WARREN COURT IN THE SIXTIES

Four basic commitments, as Cox has pointed out, dominated the Warren Court, and especially its decisions during the sixties: to achieving greater racial justice, to securing civil liberties, to reforming criminal procedures, and to strengthening political processes.[6] Far oftener than not, it was the states and their localities that were affected most directly by the Court's actions in these four areas.

What emerges from the Warren Court's record of the sixties is a federal judiciary determined to end racial discrimination and segregation, to carry the protection of civil liberties to the outermost bounds of the individualistic ethic, to reform totally criminal-justice procedures, to afford new and controversial protections to the accused and to the convicted, and to establish an egalitarian standard for representation in all of the nation's deliberative bodies, save for the United States Senate. With this, the federal system was transformed. National judicial power was asserted in ways and by means never before contemplated or practiced. Frequently, the Court was ordering respondents, especially subnational governmental respondents, to do something, rather than simply negating what was held to be unconstitutional. Throughout, the Fourteenth Amendment became a vehicle for revising the Constitution and for transforming the federal system.[7] Not only the First Amendment but most of the procedural guarantees of the Bill of Rights were "absorbed" within it, and even new constitutional rights were found that could be brought within its orbit. The Warren Court, then, generally "seemed to come down squarely on the side of progress for individual rights, even if these decisions were harmful to the principles of federalism."[8]

The basic dilemma that this reformist record raises is how far a tribunal whose authority ultimately rests on a historic national consensus regarding the nation's purposes, philosophy, and frame of government can move into essentially controversial political areas. Judicial lawmaking is as old as the system itself, but continuous judicial lawmaking on several, not a few, controversial fronts suggests a faith in the results and in the stability of the system that many would question. If the Court, not the political processes, serves as the instrument of social change, rather than the stabilizing agent, what then do the concepts of a responsible citizenry operating through the representational processes and of the resulting roles for the political branches of the national government, not to mention those of subnational units, signify?

To sum up, the Warren Court, more than any of its predecessors, furthered the cause of individual rights and racial justice, but in the process it left a legacy of institutional problems that its critics have highlighted and its defenders have preferred to ignore or argue away. One major facet of the resulting institutional dilemma was the cluster of problems the court itself was faced with as a result of its particular style of activism. Its abandonment of the traditional "step-by-step process that long characterized the common-law and constitutional forms of adjudication" and its alternative preference for carrying nearly "every proposition . . . to its logical extreme" and "to write codes of conduct rather than resolve particular controversies" was one manifestation of this.[9]

Another was its failure to acknowledge the weaknesses in its own structure: its difficulties in gathering the data required for broad rule making, its difficulty in administering the broad rules it promulgates, and its difficulty in commanding the support of the political branches of the national government when its rules affect those who have not resorted to the judiciary for their protection—to cite only some of the more obvious.[10] Above all, perhaps, was the Warren Court's tendency to ignore the counsel from Hamilton to Brandeis that a judge may advise and persuade, but should not coerce or comment.[11]

In the broader, societal and systemic areas, however, the Warren Court's decisions and procedures produced even greater problems. In its zeal to assert its own version of individual liberty and social equality, and to bind the political branches of all levels of government as well as the lesser federal and state-local judiciaries to them, it failed to recognize the highly problematic nature of many of its positions and the equally problematic results that flowed therefrom. To illustrate:

——How can individual liberty and social equality be merged either in judicial decisions or philosophic debate, when the long history of both suggests that the concepts are antithetical, not complementary and certainly not identical?

——How can majority rights be reconciled with those of the minority (to go back to a Madisonian proposition) in the political processes of a federal system, when a simple majoritarian ethic is applied to the former and an absolutist protective stance is adopted regarding the latter?

——How can the political branches of any level of government behave more responsibly, if basic policy questions confronting them are judicially preempted?

——How successful can new judge-made laws be in changing citizen and official behavior, when multiple efforts on diverse fronts are mounted at the same time?

——How can a federal system survive, if the ultimate umpire of the system assumes that practically all of the subnational governments are controlled by racists, reactionaries, and/or rural folk and where the principle of interlevel comity becomes the principle of preemption?

These are but a few of the paradoxical and profound questions raised by the Warren Court's legacy. In the past, correctives usually had taken the form of a side glance by the Court at election results, and it could be argued that its decisions in the sixties were in rough harmony with the results of the 1960 and especially the 1964 presidential contests. But what of 1968 and the election of a president who campaigned against the Court's libertarian and egalitarian tendencies?

THE BURGER COURT

In June of 1968 Chief Justice Warren announced his resignation, to take effect once his successor had been confirmed by the Senate. President Johnson's appointment of Justice Fortas to the chief justiceship, however, was defeated by a Senate filibuster, and in December Warren indicated he would retire the following June. Judge Warren Earl Burger of the Federal Court of Appeals for the Eighth Circuit was selected by President Nixon to succeed Warren. The forced resignation of Fortas in May[12] and the retirements of Justices Black and Harlan in September of 1971 ultimately brought about three other Nixon appointments: Judge Harry A. Blackmun, Judge Louis Powell, and Deputy Attorney General William H. Rehnquist. Along with Justice Potter Stewart, the last of the Eisenhower appointees, some felt these new appointees would constitute a new conservative majority. The appointment of Lewis Paul Stevens in 1975 by President Gerald R. Ford, following Justice Douglas's reluctant retirement, only buttressed this impression for some. But let the Burger Court's record speak for itself.

Continued, If Not Greater, Activism

Analysis of a cluster of key cases in the civil rights and civil liberties areas suggests an activism and sensitivity to the libertarian and racial justice norms nearly as great as, if not, in a few instances, greater than, its predecessor.[13]

These decisions reflect no major retreat from the Warren Court's egalitarianism, especially when issues of racial justice were involved. Pretty much the same generalization applies to a range of civil liberty questions.[14] Most of its cases in the civil liberties and rights areas, then, indicate no counterrevolution on the part of the Burger Court. If anything, they suggest strong lines of continuity to it and, in some instances, some logical (and liberal) extensions (as with the death penalty, antipatronage, abortion, and equal employment opportunity decisions). No special consideration was given to the states and their police powers here. Yet the Burger Court obviously was and is no carbon copy of its predecessor. Its own special positions and policy preferences, then, must be found largely in its decisions relating to other constitutional issues and in its approach to the Court's procedures.

Some Contrasts, a Different Assertiveness, and Some Sensitivity to the Federal Principle

One clearly identifiable area where the Burger Court instituted significant changes involved the procedural guarantees of the Bill of Rights. In a series of cases beginning in 1971, the Court began to narrow the Fourth Amendment's protections by limiting its exclusionary rule. As a result, it expanded the discretion of state and local law-enforcement officers.[15]

While *Miranda* was never overturned, its strict rules against forced disclosure of evidence by a criminal suspect were weakened, but not to the extent claimed by the most vociferous critics of the Burger Court.[16] The right to counsel in pretrial interrogations, another *Miranda* standard, was also limited.[17] Yet the Warren Court's extension of the jury trial right to all state criminal cases was further expanded during the transition to the Burger Court to cover petty misdemeanors punishable by six or more months imprisonment.[18] But later decisions voided the twelve-person and unanimous verdict requirements.[19] Both of these actions marked a rediscovered recognition by the Court's new majority that the diversity of state criminal-justice procedures and practices need not lead to injustices.

With the new procedures initiated by the Warren Court, its successor in 1971 began to curb the availability of federal injunctions against alleged state violations of civil rights.[20] In most of these cases, however, some form of state action had commenced, unlike the situation in the earlier *Dombrowski* case (1965), wherein the Warren Court sanctioned federal injunctive relief in a situation where no state prosecution was pending.[21]

In a somewhat similar vein, the Burger Court severely curtailed habeas relief for prisoners who claimed Fourth Amendment violations.[22] Federal habeas corpus review of seizure and search claims of convicted and incarcerated criminals had been pioneered by the Warren Court as a means of ensuring the "integrity of proceedings at and before trial where constitutional rights are at stake."[23] In *Schneckloth* v. *Bustamonte* (1973), the Burger Court held that this "collateral relief" practice tended to ignore societal values that are significant for individual justice, including "(i) the most effective use of limited judicial resources, (ii) the necessity of finality in criminal trials, (iii) the minimization of friction between federal and state systems of justice, and (iv) the maintenance of the constitutional balance upon which the doctrine of federalism is founded."[24]

In its decisions relating to pornography, the Burger Court stepped back from the "constitutional quagmire" its predecessor had created and been caught in. The concept of a national community standard for obscenity was rejected and trial courts were urged to gauge obscenity by local community values, which clearly vary from locale to locale.[25]

With school desegregation, the Court sounded no retreat, but trumpeted a blast for busing. Yet, when it confronted the question of approving a multidistrict affirmative action plan as a remedy for de jure segregation in a single district (Detroit), the strategy was rejected.[26]

In an entirely different area—state taxation as it affects commerce—the Court in 1976 upheld state levies on all imports, as long as they "were imposed equally on all goods foreign and domestic" and were not applied to goods still in transit.[27] Decisions to the contrary going back for more than a century were overruled here and the states clearly were strengthened as a result.

The Burger Court's handling of federal preemption marks another area of contrast with its predecessor. In a number of cases, it has permitted state law "to govern questions thought preempted by the national lawmaking power."[28] All of these decisions have had the practical effect of expanding the authority of the states' police power. Yet a note of caution must be injected here, since this trend has by no means been consistent or across the board.[29]

In its reapportionment cases, the Burger Court has been less literally equalitarian than its predecessor. Slightly larger disparities in the size of electoral districts have been upheld than would have been permitted in the sixties.[30] Moreover, the "one man, one vote" rule was not extended to invalidate various extraordinary majority requirements.[31]

Of critical import from the vantage point of those concerned with the federal principle, however, have been the small cluster of recent cases wherein the Supreme Court refused to extend federal authority. In the pivotal case of *San Antonio Independent School District* v. *Rodriguez* (1973), the Burger Court by a 5-4 vote refused to hold that the local property-tax method of financing public education necessarily operated to the disadvantage of some "suspect class." Whatever discrimination that might arise as a consequence of unequal property values in various school districts is relative, not absolute, hence, the equal protection clause does not require "absolute equality or precisely equal advantages."[32]

The Burger Court also has been cautious in automatically holding that sex is a suspect classification in state statutes.[33] Moreover, in a cluster of local zoning cases, the Court has reflected a significant "degree of deference to referendums and other forms of state and local government decisionmaking designed to distill and reflect the particular will of local majorities."[34] It has left to the states and localities the task of deciding the proper balance between majority wishes and minority rights in the zoning area, just as it did in the educational finance realm.

Of greater significance was the Court's dismissal in 1978 of the appeal generated by a ruling of the Pennsylvania Supreme Court that state laws forbidding the state treasurer from disbursing federal-aid funds unless they have been specifically appropriated by the legislature do not violate either the state or federal constitution.[35] During the seventies, the question of legislative appropriation of federal-aid monies had become a major issue between the executive and legislative branches of certain states (and some localities) as the proportion of state (and local) revenues coming from Washington grew. In addition to this separation of powers issue, federal-state questions also were raised, since some grants (in the instant case, the 1968 Omnibus Crime Control and Safe Streets block grant) focused on executive branch recipients and overtly or tacitly ignored the state legislature. The Court dismissed the appeal "for want of a substantial federal question." In effect, the traditional theory of a grant-in-aid was used here to reject the appellant's claims that the supremacy clause and the intent of an act of Congress had been subverted by the state statute.

Finally, in the most controversial of these denying decisions (*National League of Cities* v. *Usery* [1976]), the Supreme Court voided the 1974 amendments to the Fair Labor Standards Act that extended the wages and hour provisions of that act to nearly all state and local employees.[36] This was the first time in four decades the Court held a congressional regulation of commerce to be unconstitutional, and it created more than a slight flurry of attention in legal circles and the law schools.

Some of the Court's liberal critics have dubbed *National League of Cities* an aberration that will be corrected by the addition of another liberal Justice to the Court, while others view it as a welcome signal that the Court finally has begun recognizing the need for federalism-based constraints on what heretofore had been a largely unchecked congressional power to regulate state conduct and to impinge on state autonomy.[37]

An Assessment

As the foregoing suggests, the Burger Court has been neither completely unmindful of its role as inheritor and interpreter of its predecessor's racial justice and libertarian legacy, nor oblivious to some of the many institutional difficulties that this legacy generated. Hence, there has been no real retreat from the Warren Court's defense of the First Amendment and of the equal protection clause, especially in matters involving racial justice. The current Court, however, has been less prone to place all of the procedural guarantees of the Bill of Rights on the same plane as the First Amendment and to apply them with the same degree of vigor as its predecessor to constrain the police power of the states and their localities. Moreover, the Burger Court has been somewhat more sensitive to the concept of state autonomy than its predecessor ever was and arguably because some of the reformist decisions of the latter now permitted such a stance.

In any event, some sense of the older judicial concepts of intergovernmental "comity" and "forbearance" clearly are reflected in its efforts to bar federal court interference in state judicial proceedings in order to protect individual constitutional rights, to restrict interpretations of the scope of constitutional protection in areas where decisions that might find a state or local government in violation of a right protected by the Fourteenth Amendment would place the federal courts in direct conflict with on-going state or state-regulated operations (as in the *Rodriguez* decision), and to gauge the possible effects of its decisions on state and local governments in its approach to remedies for still other alleged constitutional violations (as it did in *Milliken v. Bradley*).[38]

Above all, perhaps, the National League of Cities (NLC), lower court EPA, and the Thornburg decisions suggest some awareness of contemporary intergovernmental trends and a growing understanding that unbridled congressional authority can lead to the gradual destruction of the states as quasi-sovereign political entities.[39] Moreover, the NLC and EPA cases begin to suggest some of the bases for determining when the commerce power infringes unconstitutionally on state prerogatives. Yet this feeling for federalism has not been consistent, constitutionally well grounded, or carried over into related subject areas.[40] Nowhere is this last trait revealed more clearly than in the Court's handling of federal grant-in-aid cases—the subject of the final phase of this chapter.

THE RECENT GROWTH IN GRANT-IN-AID CASE LAW

In modern times, three major areas of Supreme Court action have critically affected the states and their localities. The expansion in the commerce power following the 1937 "revolution" and a few signs of its contraction in the mid-seventies and the massive extension largely in the sixties and seventies of what is subsumed under the equal protection and due process clauses of the Fourteenth Amendment, as the foregoing indicates, constitute two of these. The third was the emergence, mostly in the seventies, of a rather massive, but largely ignored (by the legal community), body of case law relating to federal grants-in-aid and their administration.

The "Old Court" and Its Not Always "Conservative" Decisions

Prior to 1937, as chapter 3 indicated, the old Court had handed down three basic decisions regarding federal grants. In a pair of Massachusetts cases in the early twenties, two principles were established: 1. Congress's spending power, as utilized to finance grants-in-aid, does not "require the States to do or yield anything," since states may defeat any alleged "ulterior purpose" by "the simple expedient of not yielding" and of withholding "their consent";[41] and 2. an individual has no right to question the specific purposes for which his federal taxes are used, "since after funds have been brought into the Treasury and mingled with other funds, Congress has sweeping power to dispose of these funds."[42]

In the controversial *Butler* case (1936), an equally conservative Court voided the Agricultural Adjustment Act of 1933 in a somewhat convoluted opinion which held that its processing tax was not really a tax but a means of regulating agricultural production, and that, while Congress had broad power to appropriate for the general welfare and was not confined to the enumerated legislative fields committed to it, the crop benefits authorized by the act were in fact a system of agricultural regulations, not a matter of voluntary compliance or rejection, hence clearly a violation of the Tenth Amendment.[43]

The "New Deal Court" and Its Legacy

The first evidence of a change in Court opinion regarding the spending power came in late 1937 with the *Steward Machine Co. v. Davis* decision. In sanctioning the Social Security Act, its unemployment excise tax on employers was upheld as a legitimate use of the tax power and the grants to the states were viewed as examples of federal-state collaboration, not of federal coercion. Hence, they were deemed to be fully within Congress's power to appropriate for "the promotion of the General Welfare" and constituted no infringement on the states' "reserved powers."[44]

From 1937 until the mid-sixties, relatively few cases arose regarding federal aid. Those that did focused chiefly on whether certain conditions attached to specific grants (Hatch Act prohibitions and equal treatment of recipients under a grant's regulations) violated the Tenth Amendment.[45] This absence of justiciable grant controversies, however, only reflected the times. The growth in grants both in dollar terms and numbers, as chapter 3 indicated, was glacial during the period 1945–63. Moreover, the conditions attached to them were relatively unintrusive and far more clearly related to program purposes, compared to those of today.

A summary of the state of grant case law just prior to 1960 would have included the following principles:

1. Congress's power to spend for the general welfare programs is not restricted to the enumerated power detailed in Article I, Section 8 of the Constitution.
2. Conditions attached to grants are a legitimate exercise of Congress's power to fix the terms by which federal funds are expended, though lurking in the background here was Justice Cardozo's warning that "the location of the point at which pressure turns into compulsion and ceases to be the inducement, [is] a question of degree—at times, perhaps, of fact."[46]
3. The grant device is essentially a cooperative venture entered into freely by the subnational partners, with the latter's right to refuse to participate constituting the chief means of protecting the powers reserved to the states (and localities indirectly) under the Tenth Amendment.

Implicit in these principles were potential dangers to the long-term viability of federalism as a constitutional principle, but these can be seen most clearly with the benefit of hindsight.

The Building of a New Body of Law

The real body of grant-related case law, then, is a product largely of the past decade and a half.[47] As such, it mirrors the extraordinary changes that occurred in the federal role and in the federal system—politically, programmatically, administratively, fiscally, and above all attitudinally—during this relatively brief span of time. The nature, scope, and purposes of the federal grant system have been transformed in the process and in ways that have produced an intergovernmental system that dominates the provision of domestic governmental services. Against this backdrop of a seemingly uncontrollable tendency to intergovernmentalize everything, where has the Court stood, and for what?

In large measure, the Warren and Burger courts have adhered to the earlier concepts relating to Congress's power to spend for any program it deems necessary for promoting the general welfare, to Congress's concomitant right to attach conditions to such programs, and to the grant-in-aid as a collaborative and voluntary, not a coercive and unrefusable, mechanism for achieving Congress's promotional goals. Unlike the Court's assertive stance in nearly every other area of its constitutional concerns (save for the commerce power),[48] in this one its posture ostensibly has been one of complete restraint and of deference to Congress. Yet the practical effect has been to help further changes in the grants' realm, as drastic and as qualitatively different as the Court itself has initiated in such areas as civil rights, civil liberties, criminal procedures, and reapportionment.

To put it differently, the Court's somewhat atypical reliance on precedents and past principles here have not helped to stabilize intergovernmental relations or really to reconcile the old with the new. Instead, it has simply ratified, with a few exceptions, the novel course that was launched politically in the mid-sixties and that has continued unabatedly in the seventies, with little to no attention to the secondary, tertiary, or certainly the long-term systemic effects of their decisions.

How has the federal judiciary applied its traditional grant-related precepts in the rash of recent cases?[49] First, regarding Congress's power to spend to promote the general welfare, a few constraints have been imposed. Yet these have related to violations of the First, Fifth, and Fourteenth Amendments,[50] not to the Tenth. Moreover, deciding what programs promote the general welfare still is held to be a distinctly congressional function.

Second, the authority of Congress to attach all sorts of conditions to federal-aid programs also has been upheld in several cases, even though many of these conditions are of a type and have an effect that contrast markedly with their predecessors of the fifties or the forties. Thus, a requirement that would necessitate a state to amend its constitution to authorize its police power to regulate certain private institutions was upheld by a federal district court as no violation of the Tenth Amendment.[51] Similarly, a requirement that had the practical effect of leaving basic public health decisions in the hands of a county planning unit and beyond the authority of the county executive and board of commissioners was sanctioned as merely part of a "cooperative venture among the federal and state and local authorities."[52] In still another case, a grant requirement stipulating a specific (and many would say arbitrary) pattern of headquarters-field relationships within a state's bureaucracy, which contravened a duly enacted and highly commended state reorganization and which overlooked a provision of the Intergovernmental Cooperation Act of 1968, was found valid. Here the district court reiterated the traditional theory of grants and contended that it was not "coercive" or "mandatory" and that the state had the right to refuse to participate in the program.[53]

Third, the grant device clearly is still defined in nearly the same basic terms as it was in the early 1920s: that is, as a quasi-contractual relationship, freely entered into but with differing obligations for the grantor and the grantee. Moreover, the Court has maintained this interpretation even in instances where (1) all aid funds in a functional area, not merely in the specific program involved, would be cut off if a recipient failed to meet all the requirements in one of them (National Health Planning Act), and (2) the grant program involved probably had more federal regulations and requirements attached to it than any other (AFDC).[54]

Fourth, the Court has moved forward and fleshed out the obligations and rights that a grant places on the grantor, grantee, and, in the case of transfer payments grants, on the ultimate recipients. Thus, several procedural due process rights of grant applicants and recipients have been upheld, clarified, or established by the Court.[55] Moreover, agency regulations concerning eligibility in and rights established by certain grants have been scrutinized in light of their statutory bases, their mode of development and promulgation, and the extent to which they aid the intended beneficiaries.[56] In these decisions, the Court has exhibited some of its more habitual assertiveness, though almost always in the context of presumably interpreting a grant statute. Finally, the Court has sanctioned the application of several of the sixty-odd national social and environmental standards to grant recipients and, in the process, the rights of third parties have been strengthened.[57]

Conclusion

To sum up, thanks to the explosion in federal grants since the mid-sixties, along with the real ambiguities regarding grant requirements, responsibilities, and rights that have accompanied this development, the federal courts—especially the High Court—have assumed a major role in grants management. Procedural and even certain substantive due process rights have been injected into the process, sometimes to the grantor's benefit, sometimes to the grantee's, sometimes to the ultimate recipient's, and sometimes to that of an affected third party.

The paramount thrust of the Court's decisions, however, has been to reaffirm the supremacy of Congress's power to spend in furtherance of the general welfare, rarely to curb its authority to attach almost any conditions to grants—whether reasonably or unreasonably related to the program's basic purpose[58]—and to leave the protection of reserved powers almost wholly to the political process and to the states' and localities' presumed capacity to refuse or to withdraw from participating.

A tenuous theory of cooperative federalism may be deduced from some of these recent decisions. Yet it lacks content and seems only to suggest that the Court "feels" that grants are a collaborative, not coercive, way of enlisting recipient participation and that "considerable autonomy remains vested in grantees to deal with the shape, content, and administration of the aided programs despite mandated federal standards."[59]

In leaving the prerogative of determining what best promotes the general welfare in this area almost wholly to Congress and in refusing thus far to apply any test for the conditions attached to grants as to what is really reasonable and really related, the Court implicitly has endorsed Congress's all-encompassing and intrusive, but politically astute, approach to and prime control over contemporary intergovernmental relations. By assuming a passivity in this area, while aggressively asserting ever greater authority for itself in nearly all others, the federal judiciary may have avoided some confrontations with the political branches and with various powerful pressure groups. But it has won few friends in the process, and the specter of legal sophistry has been raised. After all, the political process of the seventies (as chapter 8 will demonstrate) is a far different one from that of the early sixties or the fifties, with state and local interests not as well represented now as they were then.

Of greater significance, of course, is the fate of the system that the Court has sworn to uphold. When one ponders the loose legislative and rampant interest-group politics that dominated the enactment of many of the recent grants (notably, the Vocational Rehabilitation Amendments of 1973 and the National Health Planning Act of 1976) whose arbitrary requirements have been upheld, the need for some form of judicial arbitration seems clear. It could well begin with cases involving conflicts between such conditions and provisions of other congressional statutes. It might lead eventually to assessing those conditions that are attached to grants which involve a significant infringement on the integrity of the political processes of states and local governments,[60] thus complementing the decision in *National League of Cities*.

To leave grants and their conditions wholly to a political process which, in this decade, successfully coopts practically all of the affected functional interest groups in each aided area during the course of renewals, and which ignores, far more times than not, the institutional needs of state and local governments, is to suggest that the old and outdated textbook theory of the national lawmaking is the one to which the Justices still adhere. (See chapter 8 for a more detailed analysis.) To focus so heavily on the responsibilities of granting agencies and of grantee governments, while ignoring the more fundamental responsibilities the Congress and the Court have under the Constitution to assure the continued vitality of the federal system, is to dally with symptoms and not to deal with remedies. To accord a higher place in the order of things to a narrowly based social-interest group operating under the cloak of an Act of Congress—over and against the elected officials of the state demonstrably bent on improving its overall social-services delivery system and with other congressional statutory provisions supporting its case—reflects little concern for programmatic outcome and no sensitivity to reforms in the states.[61]

In short, the system needs more than a confectionary judicial theory of cooperative federalism. It needs one that is rooted in the realities—political, fiscal, administrative, programmatic, and procedural—of today's intergovernmental relations. Above all, it needs a judicial approach and theory that reflects a genuine sense of reasonableness and of balance.

THE COURT IN RETROSPECT

The Supreme Court's record over the past two decades indicates a degree of judicial leadership in so many areas of public policy that it is safe to state that none of its predecessors matched its degree of assertiveness. In effect, three very different interpretations emerge as to the essential nature and direction of this record. The differences between and among the interpretations relate to the contrasting ideological stance of their formulators and their concomitant capacity to be highly selective in their reading of the cases.

With Nathan Glazer, a neoconservative critique of the Court emerges. For him (and others), there has been little difference between the Warren and Burger courts. Instead, the entire period is characterized by the emergence of a seemingly permanently activist, nonconservative federal judiciary.[62] This continuing activism was a result of the decline, especially in the seventies, in "angry reactions from the people and legislatures," the favorable image of the Court projected by the mass media, the expansion of government itself (especially its regulatory role), and the proliferation of legal advocacy groups of all kinds. The continuing nonconservative course is rooted more in the need for the later Court to work out "the logic of positions . . . taken" by its predecessor and in the difficulty of withdrawing from the implications of earlier decisions. Both situations clearly confronted the Burger Court in its consideration of certain classes of cases. The record, then, suggests that this neoconservative view is partially correct, especially as it pertains to decisions of the current Court relating to racial justice and certain facets of the First Amendment.

Yet the opposing liberal critics are not wholly in error. Their charge of a "retreat from the vigorous defense of liberty and equality" is not totally without foundation, though their claim that "the primary victims of this shift in judicial attitude have been our society's oppressed" is subject to considerable doubt and debate.[63] The Burger Court's stance on habeas corpus and injunctive relief procedures and its less rigid stand on the need to incorporate all of the procedural protections of the federal Bill of Rights within the confines of the Fourteenth Amendment are what is usually cited to buttress this contention. But what of its equalitarian decisions on busing, equal opportunity, compensatory educational programs, and the vote? What of its libertarian stands on abortion, speech, and the spoils system? These cannot be dismissed in any overall assessment of the complex behavior of this Court. Only by focusing on some decisions and by ignoring other equally significant ones can the liberal charge of a judicial "counterrevolution" begin to be sustained. Neither the neoconservative nor the liberal assessments tell the whole story, then.

A third perspective is provided by those who assess the Court in terms of its capacity to balance institutional needs and individual rights—to return to the basic dilemma raised by Cox in his analysis of the Warren Court a dozen years ago.[64] For some, like McFeeley, the Burger Court has concerned itself more "with the protection of the traditional institutional relationships such as federalism."[65] In support of this view, its decisions in the obscenity, fair labor standards, federal preemption, privacy as it relates to personal reputation, and school finance cases are highlighted.[66] In addition, the current Court's efforts to restrict the jurisdiction of federal courts by limiting class actions, federal injunctive relief, and "standing" are cited as procedural ways by which it, in contrast to its predecessor, has served to reduce the federal judicial role in the interpretation and protection of individual rights.[67] Yet, though the evidence cited demonstrates a greater sensitivity to the federal principle and to the notion of state autonomy than the Warren Court exhibited, it is at least arguable that civil rights and liberties have not fared that much worse and federalism that much better under the Burger regime.

If anything, its record would suggest rough attempts at balancing institutional needs as against individual rights, at reconciling societal concerns with minority protections, at toning down a bit the Court's new role of progressive and persistent lawmaking and elevating somewhat its traditional one of serving as a stabilizing agent for the entire system. This attempt to weigh conflicting basic values and principles inevitably infuriates both the liberal and conservative critics of this Court, for neither group has much patience with this balancing process, given their respective mind sets and fairly rigid sets of values.

But has this difficult balancing act really served to meet better the institutional needs of the system, especially those of the federal system? If the slightly expanded scope of the states' police power and criminal justice processes as a result of some of the decisions of the seventies are singled out, and if the sole set of contrasting values used for assessment is individual rights as against those of the government, the answer would be in the affirmative. Yet institutional needs now encompass far more than placing these two on the scales of justice and performing a corrective balancing act that favors somewhat more governmental authority.

The system now needs a clarification of the national government's role and the reach of its constitutional powers, of the constitutional meaning of state autonomy and the integrity of its processes, of the constitutional bases for judicial intervention and nonintervention in the political process. Little of this deals directly with questions of individual rights as against the police power of the states. Most of it involves questions of power, particularly of recent shifts of power within the governmental and political system, and of the new forms in which governmental power and political influence now are expressed. These institutional issues of the eighties reflect conflicts between groups and governments, governments and governments, and groups and groups. They are primarily political and intergovernmental matters, then, and they flow directly from the drastic changes—political, fiscal, programmatic, regulatory, and administrative—that transformed the federal system in the seventies.

These institutional difficulties resurrect older value conflicts —national rights versus state (and local) rights, the need for unity and uniformity versus the benefits of diversity, and the role of the court as arbiter versus the role of the court as a member of the national triumvirate. Those who find a deference to the federal principle and to the concept of state autonomy in the record of the Burger Court focus largely on the issues raised and cases decided by its predecessor and on how the current Court has reacted and behaved differently. But this places the assessment largely within the parameters of the governmental authority versus individual rights debate, not within the arena of intergovernmental conflict. In the latter, only a handful of cases relating to curbing the commerce clause can be cited to demonstrate any balancing of institutional concerns and interests.

No case can be found where a curb has been placed on the spending for the general welfare power or the coercive and quasi-regulatory conditions attached to certain federal grants. But this dynamic federal assistance area is where many of the most crucial issues confronting contemporary federalism arise, including the mandated "use" of states by the national government for some of its own regulatory purposes, a reliance on the spending power and the conditions that may be attached thereto to achieve regulatory purposes beyond the scope of the commerce power, and the use of grant conditions to force constitutional and institutional changes in recipient governments—to mention only the more obvious. These raise many of the same kinds of questions that the federal judiciary has cautiously begun to explore within the context of the commerce power.

Whether it is a matter of rigidly defining activities that are integral and indispensable to the integrity of the states (and their localities), of arriving at some point of curbing those federal actions that coerce or intrude in a blunderbuss fashion on vital state-local political processes, or simply of balancing federal as against state/local interests, the Court potentially could play a significant role in applying one or more of these approaches to the conditional spending power and in fleshing out their application to the commerce power. Whether this will occur, only time will tell, along with the Court's own evolving view of whether this form of activism is needed to correct what this author takes to be some serious imbalances and malfunctions in the system.

NOTES TO CHAPTER 5

1. Alfred H. Kelly and Winfred A. Harbison, *The American Constitution, Its Origins and Development* (New York: W. W. Norton & Co., 1976), p. 856.

2. Harry N. Scheiber, "American Federalism and the Diffusion of Pow-

er: Historical and Contemporary Perspectives," *The University of Toledo Law Review* 9, no. 4 (Summer 1978): p. 654.

3. *Younger* v. *Harris*, 401 U.S. 37 (1971).

4. Ibid.

5. See *King* v. *Smith*, 329 U.S. 316 (1968) and *Shapiro* v. *Thompson*, 394 U.S. 618 (1969).

6. See Archibald Cox, *The Warren Court: Constitutional Decision as an Instrument of Reform* (Cambridge, MA: Harvard University Press, 1968).

7. See Raoul Berger, *Government by Judiciary* (Cambridge, MA: Harvard University Press, 1977).

8. Neil McFeeley, "The Supreme Court and the Federal System," *Publius: The Journal of Federalism* 8, no. 4 (Fall 1978): p. 12.

9. See Philip B. Kurland, *Politics, the Constitution, and the Warren Court* (Chicago: University of Chicago Press, 1969), p. xx.

10. Ibid., p. xxi.

11. Ibid.

12. A minor scandal prompted this.

13. See *Swann* v. *Charlotte-Mecklenburg Board of Education*, 402 U.S. 1 (1971); *Keyes* v. *School District No. 1, Denver*, 413 U.S. 189 (1973); *Milliken* v. *Bradley*, 418 U.S. 717 (1976) (as will be noted later, this case also rejected a central city-suburban school district merger as a means of furthering desegregation); *Lau* v. *Nichols*, 414 U.S. 563 (1974) (the legislative history of the act indicated no such concern on the part of its formulators; see Donald L. Horowitz, *The Courts and Social Policy* [Washington, D.C.: The Brookings Institution, 1976], pp. 15-17); *Griggs* v. *Duke Power Company*, 401 U.S. 424 (1971); *Oregon* v. *Mitchell*, 400 U.S. 112 (1970); Kelly and Harbison, op. cit., p. 1010; and *U.S. Department of Agriculture* v. *Moreno*, 413 U.S. 528 (1973).

14. See *Cohen* v. *California*, 403 U.S. 15 (1971); *Elrod* v. *Burns*, 965 U.S. 2673 (1976); *Hynes* v. *Borough of Oradell*, 96 S. Ct. 1755 (1976); *Roe* v. *Wade*, 410 U.S. 113 (1973) and *Doe* v. *Bolton*, 410 U.S. 179 (1973); and *Furman* v. *Georgia* and *Gregg* v. *Georgia*, 478 U.S. 153 (1976) and *Coker* v. *Georgia*, 433 U.S. 584 (1977).

15. *United States* v. *Harris*, 403 U.S. 629 (1971); *Cady* v. *Dombrowski*, 410 U.S. 952 (1973); *United States* v. *Robinson*, 412 U.S. 936 (1973); and *United States* v. *Calandra*, 414 U.S. 338 (1974).

16. *Harris* v. *New York City*, 401 U.S. 222 (1971); *Oregon* v. *Haas*, 420 U.S. 714 (1975); and *Ybarra* v. *Illinois*, no. 78-5937 (1979).

17. *Kirby* v. *Illinois*, 406 U.S. 682 (1972).

18. *Baldwin* v. *New York*, 399 U.S. 66 (1970).

19. *Williams* v. *Florida*, 399 U.S. 78 (1970); *Johnson* v. *Louisiana*, 406 U.S. 356 (1972); and *Apodaca* v. *Oregon*, 406 U.S. 404 (1972).

20. *Younger* v. *Harris*, 401 U.S. 37 (1971).

21. *Dombrowski* v. *Pfister*, 380 U.S. 479 (1965).

22. See McFeeley, op. cit., pp. 23-34.

23. *Kaufman* v. *United States*, 394 U.S. 217 (1969).

24. *Schneckloth* v. *Bustamonte*, 412 U.S. 218 (1973).

25. See *Miller* v. *California*, 413 U.S. 151 (1973) and *Paris Adult Theater I* v. *Slayton*, 413 U.S. 49 (1973).

26. *Milliken* v. *Bradley*, 418 U.S. 717 (1974).

27. See C. Herman Pritchett, *The American Constitution* (New York: McGraw-Hill, 1977), p. 213, and *Michelin Tire Co.* v. *Wages*, 96 S. Ct. 535 (1976).

28. Louise Weinberg, "The New Judicial Federalism," *Stanford Law Review* 29 (July 1977): 1193. See *DeCanas* v. *Bica*, 424 U.S. 35 (1976); *Kewanee Oil Co.* v. *Bicron Corp.*, 416 U.S. 470 (1974); *Askew* v. *American Waterways Operations, Inc.*, 411 U.S. 325 (1973); and *Goldstein* v. *California*, 412 U.S. 546 (1972).

29. See, for example, *Ray* v. *Atlantic Richfield Co.*, 96 S. Ct. 988 (1978) and *City of Philadelphia* v. *New Jersey*, 98 S. Ct. 2531 (1978).

30. *Mahan* v. *Howell*, 410 U.S. 315 (1973).

31. See *Gordon* v. *Lance*, 403 U.S. 1, 7 (1971) and *Bogert* v. *Kinzer*, 403 U.S. 914 (1971).

32. *San Antonio Independent School District* v. *Rodriguez*, 411 U.S. 1 (1973).

33. See *Reed* v. *Reed*, 404 U.S. 71 (1971); *Stanton* v. *Stanton*, 421 U.S. 7 (1975); *Frontiero* v. *Richardson*, 411 U.S. 677 (1973); and *Kahn* v. *Shevin*, 461 U.S. 351 (1974).

34. "Developments in the Law: Section 1983," *Harvard Law Review* 90 (1977): 1180.

35. *Thornburg* v. *Casey*, No. 78 642 (1978).

36. *National League of Cities* v. *Usery*, 426 U.S. 833 (1976).

37. See Lawrence Tribe, "Unraveling National League of Cities: The New Federalism and Affirmative Rights to Essential Governmental Services," *Harvard Law Review* 90 (1977): pp. 1067-68, and McFeeley, op. cit., p. 22; it should be noted that the lesser federal judiciary in a series of cases in the mid-sixties voided those provisions of the Environmental Protection Agency's regulations for the Clean Air Act that mandated state implementation of federal standards and state regulation of private action on grounds that they were an unconstitutional encroachment on states' rights, hence beyond the reach of the commerce power. See Jeffrey Kessler, "Clean Air Act," *Columbia Law Review* 76:990 (1976): 1007-10.

38. See Lewis B. Kaden, "Politics, Money, and State Sovereignty," *Columbia Law Review* 79:847 (1979): 885.

39. See *Maryland* v. *Wirtz*, 392 U.S. 183 (1968).

40. Kaden, op. cit., p. 886.

41. *Massachusetts* v. *Mellon*, 262 U.S. 456 (1923).

42. *Frothingham* v. *Mellon*, 262 U.S. 467 (1923).

43. *United States* v. *Butler*, 297 U.S. 1 (1936).

44. *Steward Machine Co.* v. *Davis*, 301 U.S. 548 (1937).

45. See *Oklahoma* v. *Civil Service Commission*, 330 U.S. 1276 (1947) and *Ivanhoe Irrigation District* v. *McCraken*, 357 U.S. 275 (1958).

46. *Steward Machine Co.* v. *Davis*, supra.

47. Of the almost five hundred cases dealing with grants identified by the Department of Justice's Law Enforcement Assistance Administration in 1979, 80 percent had been handed down since 1975. See Thomas J. Madden, "The Law of Federal Grants," Washington, D.C., prepared for the Advisory Commission on Intergovernmental Relations's Conference on Grant Law, 12 December 1979, p. 2.

48. Though even with it, the Court, as was noted earlier, has placed few curbs as it impacted on states and localities.

49. The lesser federal judiciary has been far more involved with these cases than the Supreme Court; hence the reliance here on several of their decisions.

50. See *Shapiro* v. *Thompson*, 394 U.S. 618 (1969) and *Tilden* v. *Richardson*, 403 U.S. 672 (1971).

51. *North Carolina* v. *Califano*, 445 F. Supp. 532 (E.D.N.C. 1977).

52. *Montgomery County, MD* v. *Califano*, 469 F. Supp. 1230 (D. MD 1978).

53. *Florida Department of Health* v. *Califano*, 449 F. Supp. 274 (N.D. Fla. 1978) aff'd 585 F. 2d 150 (5th Cir. 1978).

54. See *North Carolina* v. *Califano*, supra, and *King* v. *Smith*, 392 U.S. 309 (1968), respectively.

55. See Richard B. Cappalli, *Rights and Remedies Under Federal Grants* (Washington, D.C.: Bureau of National Affairs, Inc., 1979), pp. 180-243, and Thomas J. Madden, "The Right to Receive Federal Grants and Assistance," *Federal Bar Journal* 37 (Fall 1978): 27-29.

56. See Madden, op. cit., pp. 29-35 and 50-52.

57. See ibid., pp. 49-50.

58. The liberal dissenters to the *Butler* decision, it is to be noted, were the first to enunciate clearly a "reasonably related" test for grant conditions; see "The Federal Conditional Spending Power: A Search for Limits," *Northwestern University Law Review* 70, no. 2 (May-June 1975): 298-303.

59. Cappalli, op. cit., p. 12.

60. See Kaden, op. cit., p. 896-97.

61. See *Florida Department of Health* v. *Califano*, supra.

62. Nathan Glazer, "Towards An Imperial Judiciary?" *The Public Interest*, no. 41 (Fall 1975): 112-21.

63. See Tribe, op. cit., p. 1065.

64. See Cox, op. cit.

65. McFeeley, op. cit., p. 6.

66. See ibid., pp. 19-22.

67. Ibid., pp. 23-34.

6

Fiscal Federalism

The current era has witnessed a continuance of most of the drastic shifts in intergovernmental finances that were launched in the thirties. At the same time, some developments unique to these two decades also emerged. When the continuing trends blended with the newer developments, the highly problematic condition of America's current public finances resulted.

CONTINUED PUBLIC SECTOR GROWTH

Total governmental outlays soared during this period, but not quite at the same rate as during the years 1930–60. As a proportion of the gross national product (GNP), the figure had reached the one-third mark by 1979 and had gone even higher in 1975 and 1976, compared to the 27 percent share in the early sixties. This overall 6 percent increase for the past two decades, however, obviously does not match the 17 percent expansion that occurred between 1930 and 1960.

On a per capita and constant dollar basis, the size of public outlays nearly doubled between 1959 and 1979; in the previous three decades they quintupled. The growth in the public sector since 1960, then, has been impressive, but not spectacular. Yet, in cumulative terms, it reached a level in the late seventies that some economists found alarming and some politicians, a source of campaign debate.

The Intergovernmental Split

The manner in which these outlays were divided among the governmental levels, in terms of expenditures from their own funds, reflects some previous trends as well as some different developments. For example, while the federal government had assumed the dominant overall fiscal position by the late thirties, it went on during the late sixties to gain a comparable role in domestic outlays as well, with the federal proportion reaching 15 percent of GNP by 1979, compared to a combined state-local share of 11 percent.

At the same time, the earlier expansion in state expenditures continued fairly steadily. The states' 3.8 percent of GNP in 1959 rose to 5.3 percent by 1969, and finally to 6.2 percent (or $145 billion) by 1979. In per capita constant dollar terms, the 1979 figure represented more than two and one-half times the 1959 one. Local outlays, on the other hand, experienced a more erratic pattern of growth. They rose from 4.4 percent of GNP in 1959 to 5.1 percent in 1969 and then to 5.3 percent six years later. Yet a decline to 4.8 percent occurred by 1979, which still amounted to a higher proportion of the GNP than its 1959 counterpart. In other words, the previous trend of a gradual decline in the local share of the GNP was halted in the current era. When the state and local shares are merged, they produce an overall 2.2 percent increase in their share of the GNP over their 1959 combined proportion of 8.2 percent.

Shifts in the Federal, State, and Local Shares

The changes in the federal, state, and local shares of total outlays and of domestic expenditures provide yet another way of highlighting certain broad intergovernmental fiscal trends of this current period. Unlike the previous three decades, the figures here reveal a fairly stable federal share of total outlays, but nearly a 10 percent hike in its share of domestic expenditures (see table 6-1). The state proportion of domestic outlays, on the other hand, remained fairly stable throughout, while the local share declined by nine percentage points between 1964 and 1979.

Table 6-1   Share of Total and Domestic Governmental Expenditures by Level, from Own Funds

Calendar year	Federal		State		Local	
	% Total	% Domestic	% Total	% Domestic	% Total	% Domestic
1964	67.0	48.3	15.5	24.3	17.5	27.4
1969	66.0	49.0	17.4	26.0	16.6	25.0
1974	65.3	55.0	18.6	24.0	16.1	21.0
1979	66.3	57.8	19.0	23.8	14.7	18.4

Source: Adapted from Advisory Commission on Intergovernmental Relations, *Significant Features of Fiscal Federalism, 1978–79 Edition* (M-115). (Washington, D.C.: U.S. Government Printing Office, 1979), p. 7.

If comparisons are made with the previous era, the stable state pattern appears to be one long continuation of what prevailed in 1929 and continued throughout the next three decades. The local also reflects a projection of the earlier trend line, but instead of a mere 9 percent decline, more than forty percentage points must be subtracted from the 1929 figure. Moreover, the federal share of domestic outlays not only surpassed the combined state-local proportion by the early seventies, it reached the point by 1979 where the spread between them amounted to more than fifteen percentage points.

Revenue Sources: Changes and Continuities

Turning to specific revenue sources, the federal government relied to an even greater extent on the income tax during the past twenty years than it did in the previous thirty. The proportionate reliance rose from over 80 percent in 1960 to 85 percent in 1975, and to 87.5 percent in 1978.

The federal government also relied increasingly on two other funding sources: deficit spending and social security taxes. To a far greater degree than in the earlier periods (wartime years excepted) large annual federal deficits were incurred. The seventies, thanks in part to the recession of 1975–76, witnessed an annual growth both in percentage and absolute dollar terms that would have been unacceptable in the fifties and early sixties. Moreover, annual interest payments on the debt soared from $6.4 billion in 1954 to $9.5 billion six years later, thence to $20.0 billion by 1970, and finally to an estimated $73.7 billion in 1980. And this was reflected in an ever-increasing proportion that interest payments constituted in federal budget outlays (up to an estimated 10.6 percent in 1980).[1] At the same time, the federal debt has declined steadily as a proportion of the GNP, prompting some to view this dramatic expansion in the debt with some complacency.

Contributions for social insurance were another major source of federal funding. At present, it is the second largest source of federal sector receipts ($152.4 billion in 1979), whereas in the early fifties it was the smallest of the big four (personal income taxes, corporate income levies, indirect business taxes, and contributions for social insurance).[2] The increases were caused by the expansion of the nation's work force, by wage rates, by the coverage of existing social insurance programs, and by congressional enactment of new ones and periodically of higher tax rates to finance the liberalization of benefits.

State Taxes: More Growth, but Continuing Diversity

State taxes also saw some shifts during this period, with the state share of the state-local total surpassing the local, for the first time in the early sixties. The margin between them subsequently widened steadily, to the point in 1978 where the difference stood at seventeen percentage points (or 58.5 percent versus 41.5 percent). The sustained strength of both general and selected sales taxes and the significant hike in the income tax's share of total state taxes (from 19 percent in 1969 to 35 percent by 1978) help explain the emergence of this dominant state role.

As the above suggests, the adoption of new state taxes during this period was a key factor producing this stronger state fiscal position. Between 1960 and 1979, 11 states adopted personal income taxes (to join the 17 that took similar action between 1930 and 1960, and the 15 in the 1911–30 period), and 9 enacted corporate income levies. In addition, 10 moved on the general sales front. These thirty major enactments helped produce a fiscal picture in 1979 wherein 41 states had a broad-based income tax, 45 a corporate income levy, and 45 a general sales tax.[3] Overall, 37 states possessed all three of these levies in 1979, compared to 19 in 1960.

New enactments, along with rate hikes, do not explain all of this growth in state tax collections, however. Economic factors, like growth in economic activity and inflation, played a role as well. In 1966, for example, it was estimated that new enactments and rate raises accounted for one-third of the hike in overall state collections that year, while real economic growth explained 48 percent of the increase and inflation 19 percent.[4] By way of contrast, political actions accounted for only 19.5 percent of the growth in 1978 over 1977, while inflation explained 59 percent of the increase and expanded economic activity 41 percent. Overall, between 1966 and 1978, new enactments and rate hikes accounted for 23 percent of the total growth in state collections, while economic factors were responsible for 77 percent, with the latter dividing between 26 percent for real growth and 51 percent for inflation.[5]

This steep rise in state collections, especially in the past decade, prompted fifteen states since 1976 to enact tax "cap" or expenditure lids.[6] The most notable, of course, was California's Proposition 13. Prior to its adoption by the voters in June 1978, four other states had adopted expenditure limits and subsequently eleven more caught some variant of Proposition 13 fever. Of the fifteen enactments, seven were constitutional, and all but two occurred in regions outside the Northeast and Great Lakes. In addition to these tax and expenditure lids, six states in the late seventies (Arizona, Colorado, and California in 1978 and Wisconsin, Iowa, and Minnesota in 1979) indexed their personal income taxes. By requiring that certain fixed-dollar features of their income tax code be adjusted annually in light of the rate of inflation, these states sought to curb the collections "windfall" that occurs simply by inflation's capacity to push a family's income into a higher tax bracket. These various actions, then, along with the growing pressure for fiscal constraint in various of the states not enacting such measures, can be expected to produce some lowering of the rate of state collections in the eighties.

Local Levies: Modest Diversification and Some Limits

Among the local levies, the property tax retained its traditional predominant position. Yet, the erosion in its earlier near-monopoly status that began in the forties and fifties continued, with its 87 percent share in 1960 slipping to 82 percent in 1975, thence to 80 percent in 1978. The somewhat greater diversification of the local revenue base provides one explanation for this. By 1976, twenty-two states had authorized some or all of their general units of local government to levy a sales tax and 4150 cities and 685 counties utilized this additional revenue source.[7] Moreover, eleven states authorized some or all of their cities to levy a local income tax. At least 3000 cities made use of it in 1976, but approximately 2960 of these were located in five states—Indiana, Kentucky, Michigan, Ohio, and Pennsylvania. At least sixty-three counties also made use of this tax, with all but two located in two states (Indiana and Maryland). All this suggests a limited broadening of the local tax base and largely in a handful of states.

Still another factor explaining the reduction in the role of the property tax in the seventies was the enactment by seventeen states (for a total of twenty) during the last decade of limits on the amount of levy.[8] This recent move, in part, reflected the ineffectiveness of tax rate limit actions in the forty states having them, due to generally rapidly rising property values. In addition, six states during the seventies took the more restrictive step of placing limits on annual assessment increases.

State-Local Tax Efforts

The rates and specific combination of these various state and local taxes, of course, differed considerably from state to state, just as they did in the previous period. As figure 6-1 indicates, the resulting tax effort among the fifty varied greatly. Twelve fell 15 percent or more below the overall fifty-state average, while eight were in the 9 percent or more above-average group. The overall typical tax bite of 7.6 percent of state personal income in 1953 rose to 12.8 percent by 1977, but these national averages concealed the

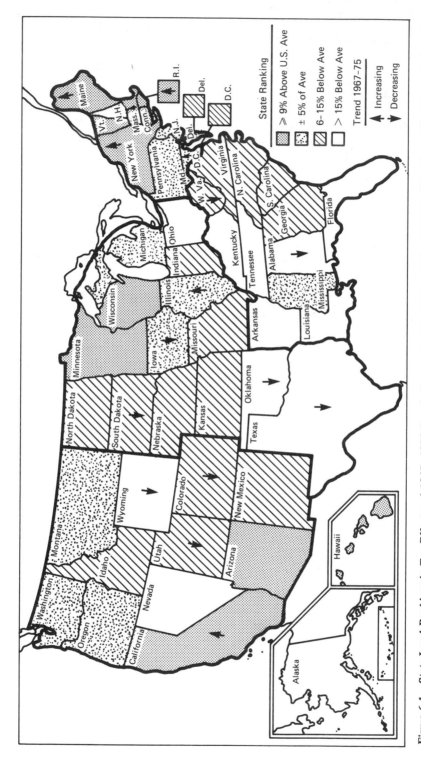

Figure 6-1 State-Local Rankings in Tax Effort and 1967–1975 Trends (Source: D. Kent Halstead, *Tax Wealth in Fifty States* [Washington, D.C.: U.S. Department of Health, Education, and Welfare, 1978] p. 21)

State Ranking

≥ 9% Above U.S. Ave

± 5% of Ave

6–15% Below Ave

> 15% Below Ave

Trend 1967–75

← Increasing

→ Decreasing

wide variations, as well as declines and sharp increases. In the earlier year, for example, Delaware's typical state-local tax burden in relation to personal income stood at 56 percent of the national average, while North Dakota's was 149 percent. In 1977, the spread extended from Alabama and Ohio with 78 percent and Missouri with 80, on one extreme, to Alaska on the other, with 183.[9]

In terms of their degree of dependence on one or another of the major direct taxes, five states (New York, Delaware, Maryland, Wisconsin, and Minnesota) placed heavy reliance on the income tax in 1977, while twelve made meager use of it.[10] All states in New England and the Great Lakes areas made greater relative use of the property tax than did the "average" and all but one state in the southwest and southeast regions underutilized this revenue source. Twelve of the sixteen southern states, on the other hand, placed a heavier emphasis on the general sales tax while nine in various other parts of the country made meager or no use of this levy. Interstate differences, with all their equity, economic development, grant-in-aid, and servicing implications clearly were not eliminated by the tendency during this period of more states to adopt more balanced revenue systems.

How Regressive?

At the same time, widespread state efforts were made to render two of the main and more regressive components of state-local tax systems more equitable. By 1977, all states had enacted property-tax-relief measures, most of them since 1970. Thirty-four were state-financed programs and twenty-nine of these were of the "circuit breaker" type. Like its counterpart in an electrical system, this type cuts in where there is an "overload," that is when the property tax reaches a percent of family income that a state deems to be onerous. Fifteen of these relief programs benefited elderly renters as well as homeowners; six aided elderly homeowners; one was designed to assist all homeowners and another all renters; six provided relief to all homeowners and renters.[11] The total cost of these programs jumped from $447 million in 1974 to $943 million three years later. Nearly all of these enactments, it should be noted, occurred during the seventies when property tax values and rates were rising rapidly. In addition to these efforts, twenty-three of the states by 1978 had exempted food and drugs from their sales taxes and three provided an income tax credit for such payments.[12]

Despite these reforms, however, most states did not possess progressive state-local tax systems by the late seventies. Using the tax burden from the major direct taxes for "typical" families whose income levels ranged from $10,000 to $50,000, only five such systems in 1976 could be classed as "progressive" (i.e., the burden increased significantly as family income increased); eighteen fell in the "proportionate" category (i.e., the tax burden grew but not as greatly as family income); and the remainder fell in the regressive grouping (where the tax burden for the more affluent was actually less than that for the average family).[13] Again, the variations among the fifty states seem to equal, if not outweigh, the commonalities.

This generalization applies with comparable force to the taxes imposed by local government. The pressure during the seventies of nonschool taxes on a per capita basis, for example, was heaviest in the central cities of the East, heavy in the West, with a lighter load in the Midwest and the lightest in the South.[14] During the early seventies, such taxes for central cities rose more rapidly than did those of their overlying counties and neighboring municipalities in all regions but the South.

The Toll on the Taxpayer

Perhaps the most vivid evidence of the overall impact of the many changes that have transpired in intergovernmental finances during the current era is found in their effect on the citizenry. As table 6-2 indicates, the direct tax burden on the average family nearly doubled between 1953 and 1977, with most of the increase occurring after 1960. While the tax load of higher-income families also became heavier, it did not match the average family's rate of increase (91 percent versus 50 percent for the upper-middle-income family and 91 percent versus 55 percent for the higher-income family).

The basic reasons for these differences, as table 6-2 suggests, were the significant hikes in social security and state-local taxes during the past two decades. The regressive features of most of these levies clearly have impacted most heavily on the lower-middle-income family and this has had political repercussions.

Some Summary Observations

What do these various trends and shifts in intergovernmental finances mean? They suggest, among other things, that:

—— The federal government began the period with a much stronger revenue system than that of the states and localities, but during the seventies the state-local systems (especially the state component thereof) achieved a greater degree of strength than they possessed in 1960.

—— The strength of federal finance in the sixties was based on its reliance on the broad-based income tax, the responsiveness of this levy to conditions of economic growth (and of inflation), the growing acceptance of deficit spending, the separate system for financing social insurance, and the ability to shift funds from defense to the domestic sector; yet by the late seventies the earlier illusion of a federal cornucopia was beginning to disappear—thanks to the troubled condition of the social security system, the growing demands of the Department of Defense, and mounting popular concerns about inflation, social security taxes, federal spending generally, and federal deficits specifically.

—— The growing state-local fiscal strength was a by-product of the emergence of more balanced and somewhat less regressive tax systems in thirty-seven states, the emergence of the states as the senior (over 50 percent of their combined general expenditures, from own revenue sources) partner in all but seven instances (as of 1977), and the rapid rise of the income tax as a major state revenue resource.

—— Despite this overall picture of growing fiscal power, many states in the Northeast and Midwest have experienced and continue to confront strong pressures due to their heavy tax, welfare, and urban burdens and to the slow growth in their economies.

—— In addition, while their revenue systems have become more responsive to economic growth and less in need of rate hikes in "good" or inflationary periods, thanks to the growing reliance

Table 6-2 A Comparison of Direct Tax Burdens Borne by Average- and Upper-Income Families, Calendar Years 1953, 1966, and 1977

Item	Average family[1]			Twice the average family[2]			Four times the average family[3]		
	1953	1966	1977	1953	1966	1977	1953	1966	1977
Total family income	100%	100%	100%	100%	100%	100%	100%	100%	100%
Decrease due to direct taxes	11.8	17.8	22.5	16.5	19.3	24.8	20.2	23.4	31.4
After tax income	88.2	82.2	77.5	83.5	80.7	75.2	79.8	76.6	68.6
Percentage decrease in after tax income:									
1953–1966	...	6.8		...	3.4		...	4.0	
1966–1977	...	...	5.7	...	...	6.8	...	...	10.4
1953–1977	...	...	12.1	...	...	9.9	...	...	14.0
Direct taxes as a percent of family income:									
Fed. pers. income tax	7.6	9.5	9.6	12.8	12.7	14.8	16.6	17.3	22.6
Soc. sec. tax (OASDHI)	1.1	3.2	5.9	0.5	1.6	3.0	0.3	0.8	1.5
Local res. prop. tax	2.2	3.1	3.9	1.8	2.6	3.2	1.7	2.4	2.6
State-local personal income tax	0.3	1.0	1.8	0.9	1.6	2.9	1.2	2.4	4.0
State-local general sales tax	0.6	1.0	1.3	0.5	0.8	0.9	0.4	0.5	0.7
Total	11.8	17.8	22.5	16.5	19.3	24.8	20.2	23.4	31.4

[1] Estimates for average family earning $5,000 in 1953, $8,750 in 1966, and $16,000 in 1977 assuming all income from wages and salaries and earned by one spouse.

[2] Estimates for twice the average family. Family earning $10,000 in 1953, $17,500 in 1966, and $32,000 in 1977 and assumes that earnings include $125 (interest on state and local debt, and excludable dividends) in 1977, $50 in 1966, and $25 in 1953; also assumes the inclusion of net long-term capital gains of $1,200 in 1977, $625 in 1966, and $350 in 1953.

[3] Estimates for four times the average family. Family earning $20,000 in 1953, $35,000 in 1966, and $64,000 in 1977 and assumes that earnings include $1,100 (interest on state and local debt, and excludable dividends) in 1977, $525 in 1966, and $265 in 1953; also assumes the inclusion of net long-term capital gains of $7,300 in 1977, $3,360 in 1966, and $1,730 in 1953.

Note: In computing federal personal income-tax liabilities, deductions were estimated to be 14 percent of family income for the $5,000 and $8,750 families, and 12 percent of income for the $10,000 family. Estimated itemized deductions were assumed for the remaining families. Interest on state and local debt, dividends, and one-half of capital gains (estimated, based on I.R.S. Statistics of Income) were excluded from family income for these computations.

Residential property tax estimates assume average housing values of approximately 1.8 times family income for the average family in both 1953 ($5,000) and 1966 ($8,750), and 2.2 times in 1977 ($16,000). The ratios for the remaining family income classes are: 1.5 for $10,000 income (1953) and $17,500 income (1966); 1.4 for $20,000 income (1977); 1.8 for $32,000 income (1953) and $35,000 (1966); and 1.5 for $64,000 income (1977); with average effective property tax rates of 1.75 percent in 1977, 1.70 percent in 1966, and 1.20 percent in 1953. Based on U.S. Bureau of the Census, Governments Division, various reports and *U.S. Census of Housing;* Commerce Clearing House, *State Tax Reporter;* Internal Revenue Service, *Statistics of Income, Individual Income Tax Returns;* and ACIR staff estimates.

In computing state income tax liabilities, the optional standard deduction was used for the $5,000, $8,750, and $10,000 income families, and estimated itemized deductions for the remaining families.

Estimated state-local general sales tax liabilities are based on the amounts allowed by the Internal Revenue Service as deductions in computing federal personal income taxes.

The percentages shown for state-local personal income and general sales taxes are weighted averages (population) for all states including those without a sales or income tax.

Source: ACIR, *Significant Features of Fiscal Federalism, 1978–79 Edition* (M-115) (Washington, D.C.: U.S. Government Printing Office, 1979), p. 31.

on income taxes, such systems also are more exposed to downward turns in the economy.

——Local revenue systems have become somewhat more diversified, much more reliant on intergovernmental fiscal transfers,
and much less of a proportion of overall domestic outlays in
terms of expenditures funded from local levies.

——Tax effort and tax burdens still vary widely among states and
among localities within the states, even though state per capita
income differentials have narrowed greatly.

——Most major cities in the Northeast and Midwest are in worse fiscal condition than most of their counterparts in other regions.

—— Finally, the earlier view that the public sector was starved for
funds has been scrapped; the ever-mounting burdens on the
American taxpayer, especially those in the lower-middle-
income sector, have generated initiatives for relief, particularly
in the property-tax area, and for fiscal restraint—in the form of
expenditure and tax lids at both the state and local levels and
of calls for a balanced federal budget and even for a constitutional amendment (sanctioned by thirty-one states as of mid-
1980) requiring it.

INTERGOVERNMENTAL FISCAL TRANSFERS: DRAMATIC
EXPANSIONS WITH PROFOUND SYSTEMIC EFFECTS

As the foregoing analysis suggests, the explosive growth in intergovernmental fiscal transfers marked shifts in federal expenditures,
radically reshaped both the revenue and expenditure actions of
state government, and provided the most rapidly growing revenue
source for most local governments during the past two decades.
Moreover, it was the administrative, programmatic, and political
implications of this extraordinary development, as much as its fiscal, that have conditioned and characterized this current era of
American intergovernmental relations.

State Aid

While attention all too frequently focuses on federal assistance
programs, the state-aid story cannot be ignored. It tells much

about the role and strength of the states in this period, and it highlights intergovernmental trends that both differ from and parallel federal-aid actions.

The rate of increase in state aid was nearly as impressive for this period as it was in the earlier one (a sevenfold increase versus a tenfold hike for 1930-60). In constant dollars, the growth rates were nearly the same (427 percent for 1940-60 versus 350 percent for 1960-78). Despite this impressive growth record, however, federal aid by 1971 surpassed it as the dominant system of intergovernmental fiscal transfers. Moreover, the reported figures overstate the amount of state aid coming from their own sources. In any recent year, 20 to 22 percent of the total would represent federal aid that was channeled to the states and then "passed through" to their localities, four-fifths or more of it typically going into the traditional state-assistance programs.[15] In 1972, for example, federal-aid pass-through funds comprised 20.8 percent (or $7.3 billion) of state aid and in 1976-77, it represented 20.3 percent (or $13.3 billion).[16] This pass-through phenomenon, however, suggests that the figures on federal aid to the states overstate (by one-third in 1977) the extent of state reliance on this funding source.

These developments in federal aid, however, do not undercut the continuing significance of state aid. Witness the following basic trends that have emerged over the past two decades.

First, the functional areas assisted remained pretty much the traditional ones (education, highway, public welfare, general support), but the proportionate shifts among them reveal some critically important developments. The steadily increasing proportions for educational aid stand out and by 1974 for the first time the states became the major provider of funds for primary and secondary education. The proportionate declines for highways and welfare were partly a by-product of the upward surge in educational outlays and growing state assumption of the full nonfederal welfare responsibility, while the hike in the "all other" category is partly suggestive of the growth in some states of aid to urban services.

Second, as in the earlier period, school districts and counties tended generally (though not in New England) to be the prime local governmental recipients of state aid, given their special functional focus and the servicing arrangements in most of the states.[17]

Third, the figures for general support payments clearly indicate that while this "no strings" assistance grew slightly in percentage terms during the seventies (compared to the sixties), the bulk of state aid continued to be of the conditional type (90 percent in 1978). Moreover, the overwhelming proportion of the funds were distributed according to a formula, not on a competitive project grant basis.

Fourth, equity considerations (i.e., efforts to compensate for variations in local fiscal capacity and/or effort) received somewhat greater attention in some state-aid formulas during the seventies than in the sixties or in the earlier era. A recent study of state aid to cities assessed the differing assistance systems in light of state-local relationships, traits of each system, and the social-economic differences among the substate governments.[18] It concluded that

—Nine states have consistently (from 1967 to 1977) targeted their aid allocations to needier and fiscally strained cities.
—Eleven others in 1967, 1972, and 1977 achieved some measure of targeting, but these varied in each of the years and the number of need variables for this group wherein a statistically significant relationship was found were always fewer than with the above nine states.
—The size of the state-aid package to cities, more than the other traits of each aid system, and municipal tax effort, more than varying social-economic characteristics, were related closely to equalization efforts.
—The extent of federal "pass-through" aid was not found to be a significant factor in explaining state aid allocations in this study, probably because most of it focuses on functions (welfare, education, and highways) that municipalities typically do not perform.

In short, what this study suggests is that the targeting of aid to distressed cities is chiefly a concern of nearly a fifth of the states and it is their performance that in large measure prompts the generalizations in other analyses of an expanding pattern of greater equalization.

Somewhat clearer evidence of state efforts to reduce disparities by their aid systems is found in the area of primary and secondary education. In addition to the general increase in state funding, half the states took action during the seventies to narrow the resource gap between the poorer and the more affluent school districts, thanks to court cases, the threat of them, and the interplay of political forces. This was reflected statistically in the increase between 1970 and 1977 in the number of central cities, largely in the East and Midwest, that received greater amounts of educational aid on a per capita basis.[19] Only fourteen central cities within the sixty-eight largest SMSAs enjoyed this status in 1970, while the number rose to 26 by 1977.

To summarize this brief analysis of state aid over the past twenty years:

——It grew significantly both in absolute and constant dollar terms, though it lost its first-rank position to the federal-aid system in the early seventies.

——Its functional focus shifted somewhat with education and the "all other" category gaining and highways and welfare declining.

—— Its prime recipient beneficiaries nationwide continued to be school districts and counties, though the cities' share increased somewhat in the seventies.

——Its preferred device for transferring funds continued to be the conditional grant (chiefly the cost-sharing type of categorical).

——Its capacity to focus on unequal local fiscal capacity and/or effort, in some cases, seems to have improved during the seventies.

——Finally, when compared with federal aid, it is far less diversified in its functional pattern, has experienced far fewer program shifts over time, and is far more dominated by a single function, by formula grants, and by the alternative ability of states to provide a function directly.

Federal Aid: Explosive Expansion with Major Implications for the System

As chapter 1 emphasized, it has been the extraordinary expansion in federal assistance and a series of developments directly related to it which, more than any other single factor or force, "explains" and symbolizes the near total transformation of the intergovernmental system since 1960. Federal assistance to state and local governments grew phenomenally in dollar amounts, number of programs, types of aided functions, activities aided, and eligible recipients. Equally significant, it experienced major changes in program emphasis, in the forms of fiscal transfer, in the kinds of conditions attached thereto, and in its allocational disbursements. When combined, these crucial changes in federal assistance, along with their many intended and unintended effects, highlight the remarkable expansion of the federal government's role in the federal system over the past two decades and help explain the "overload" of the current intergovernmental system.

Dimensions of Growth

While the Kennedy years witnessed only a gradual hike in grant outlays (from $7.1 billion in 1961 to $8.6 billion by 1963; see table 5-9), the five years of Lyndon Johnson saw a doubling of the dollars (from $10.1 billion in FY 1964 to $20.3 billion in FY 1969) and the passage of 209 new grant programs.[20] During the Nixon-Ford period, as was noted in chapter 4, a strong presidential emphasis was placed on curbing the growth in categoricals. Yet, despite some mergers and more vetoes, the number of federal-aid programs rose to 448 by 1976 and the outlays grew by more than two and one-half times (from $24 billion in FY 1970 to $68.4 billion in FY 1977), thanks largely to congressional initiatives. Finally, in the Carter years, the outlays reached the $88.9 billion mark by FY 1980 and the number of grants continued to increase, passing the five hundred mark by 1980. In constant dollar terms, however, the seemingly spectacular expansion in outlays during this twenty-year period was somewhat less impressive—growing by a factor of 3 rather than 12.5.

For state and local recipients, *the annual growth rate of federal aid* was greater than that of their own revenues for thirteen of the twenty years (see table 1-1). The tapering off during the late seventies is but one more sign that federal aid in the eighties will be less bountiful than it was in the sixties and early seventies.

Similarly, federal aid *as a percentage of state-local revenues* experienced a fairly steady increase between 1964 and 1978, save for FY 1969 (see table 1-1). Yet the proportionate decline that began in FY 1979 serves as still another signal that the salad days of federal aid may be over.

This expansion in federal aid also was reflected in *the variety of assisted activities*. Creative Federalism, as was noted earlier, moved beyond the federal efforts in traditionally aided program areas (largely certain state functions) into new state efforts, a range of novel and familiar local services, as well as activities previously provided by the private sector.[21] Many, though not all, of these new grant programs reflected an attempt to move state and local governments into new fields in light of what was deemed a national need. National purpose, of course, had always been a rationale for launching grants, but with Johnson's Creative Federalism it extended to so many new areas—in economic and regional development, transportation (especially urban mass transit), community development and housing (notably water and sewer facilities and model cities), dozens of education and manpower programs, health (particularly mental health, health services delivery, manpower, and medical assistance), and income security (with Medicaid, child nutrition, special milk and food stamps predominating) that the concept bore little relationship to the one that had been applied previously.

This proliferation in aided program thrusts did not end with President Johnson's departure, as chapter 4 indicated. Despite attempts by both Nixon and Ford to curb the categoricals, their number increased, their level of subfunctional and even sub-subfunctional specialization became deeper, and older aided efforts of secondary concern became major ones—as with environmental, social services, manpower, and income security programs. With the congressionally initiated and presidentially (under Carter) embraced countercyclical programs, states and localities (especially the latter) assumed a major role in implementing national economic policies in a time of serious recession.

In short, by 1980 hardly any governmental activity at the subnational levels was ineligible for some form of federal assistance, albeit in many instances meager, and practically all of the most national of services were caught up in the grant-in-aid system as well as the plainly intergovernmental (like energy, the environment, and transportation) along with an array of presumably local, if not private, concerns. Among the last, there were programs for urban gardening, noise control, snow removal, police disability payments, aqua-culture, displaced homemakers, rat control, education of gifted children, residential repair services for the elderly, the development of bikeways, pothole repair, runaway youth, art education, rural fire protection, and school security. National purpose as defined through the national political process clearly had come to encompass just about everything.

During this twenty-year period, as the foregoing suggests, a massive, if not explosive, *expansion in eligible grant recipients* also occurred. From the overwhelmingly state focus of 1960, when only 8 percent of the federal-aid total went directly to localities (chiefly a comparatively small number of cities and some special districts), there emerged over the next twenty years a "pinwheel" pattern of direct federal-aid disbursements to all 18,856 cities, 3042 counties, and 16,822 towns; practically all of the 16,500 public school systems and four-fifths of the private ones; at least a third of the 26,140 special districts and an undetermined but sizable number of nonprofit organizations; as well as to the fifty states.

All told about 63,000 (or nearly 80 percent) of the nation's approximately 80,000 units of state and local government were directly receiving federal-aid funds by 1980.[22] Between 25 and 30 percent of all such aid (depending on the year) bypassed state governments in the late seventies, compared to 8 percent in 1960 and 12 percent in 1968, thanks to the fact that localities were directly eligible for over 60 percent of the five hundred authorized and funded grants.[23] Moreover, larger local jurisdictions typically "participated" in far more than one aid program. An ACIR-ICMA (International City Management Association) survey of 490 cities over 50,000 in size and 100 counties in the over 100,000 category in the mid-seventies revealed that the average number of federal grants received by cities rose from 4.1 in 1969 to 8.8 in 1974. For counties, the averages for the two years were 7.7 and 18.4, respectively.[24] These figures, if anything, understate the expanded rate of participation, since jurisdictions that did not receive any federal grant funds in 1969 were excluded from the comparison.

Various factors combined to produce this broadening pattern of bypassing the states. Creative Federalism's focus on cities and urban programs was significant initially, though this gave rise to only 12 percent of the federal-aid total going directly to local governments in 1968, as was noted above. General revenue sharing and the comprehensive employment and training (CETA) and community development (CDBG) block grants were just as significant during the Nixon years, since these were the first assistance programs, other than Title I of the Elementary and Secondary Education Act, to incorporate substate allocation formulas, and such formulas by their nature tend inevitably to disburse funds more widely, no matter how restrictive their eligibility provisions. Finally, the three countercyclical programs only continued this trend, with the bulk of the funds in each of them going to local jurisdictions.

Critical Changes

In addition to growing in various ways, federal aid *changed* during the current period. As the foregoing suggests, the *forms* of federal assistance experienced significant modification. The traditional grant type was the categorical with its four variations (discussed in chapter 3). During the sixties, the project type of categorical expanded rapidly, with about four-fifths of the 210-odd new enactments under Johnson falling within this group. By 1975, project grants and project grants subject to formula distribution accounted for three-quarters of the total of 442 grants, and three years later they constituted the same proportion of the 492 categoricals then authorized and funded.[25]

Block grants and general revenue sharing were added to the categoricals, beginning with the enactment of the Partnership for Health block grant in 1966. The passage of the Safe Streets Act in 1968, the Title XX social services program in 1972, CETA in 1973, and CDBG in 1974 brought the number of block grants to five by the mid-seventies, and the signing of the general-revenue-sharing measure by President Nixon in the fall of 1972 brought the first federal general support program into being. A tripartite aid system thus came into being between the mid-sixties and the mid-seventies—though it was one in which the paramount position of the categoricals was never really threatened (down to 75 percent in 1975, but up to 80 percent by 1980).

But what does this mean in operational terms? Four factors are critical to any attempt to make sense out of these terms, since they have acquired varied meanings both in principle and practice. One relates to the extent that recipient jurisdictions are permitted unrestricted, wide, or narrow program discretion—that is, whether or not funds received must be spent on programs at all, or in specific but broadly defined functional areas, or on carefully prescribed projects or services. A second factor is the degree to which the grantor stipulates tight, broad, or nominal program conditions (project or plan approval and review, administrative and reporting requirements, etc.) as a concomitant to receiving grant funds. A third is whether a statutorily based or dictated distributional formula or a basically discretionary allocational approach is adopted, while the fourth relates to recipient eligibility and focuses on whether a broad or a narrow range of potential recipients is recognized under the pertinent statutory provision. These four factors are not discrete and disconnected. They interact with one another and the manner in which they combine produces the various forms of intergovernmental fiscal transfer now in operation (see figure 6-2). None of the five blocks possessed all of the traits of the ideal form at the outset and over time all experienced significant mutations, largely in the direction of more conditions and greater centralization, thanks to the extreme difficulties of maintaining a judicious balance between attaining national purposes (conditions) and assuring significant recipient discretion (few conditions).[26]

The federal-aid system not only changed in form during the current era, it also *shifted significantly in its program emphasis.* Looking at the broad functional classifications used by the Office of Management and Budget to report on federal-aid spending over the years, commerce and transportation accounted for 36 percent of the outlays in 1960 and income security 38 percent. By 1979, the former had slipped to 13 percent and the latter to 18 percent of the aid total. Meanwhile, four other functional groupings— health; education, training, employment, and social services; general support; and natural resources, environment, and energy— soared, rising to 17 percent (from 5 percent in 1963), 27 percent (from 8 percent), 10 percent (from 2 percent), and 6 percent (from 1 percent), respectively. Put differently, only one program

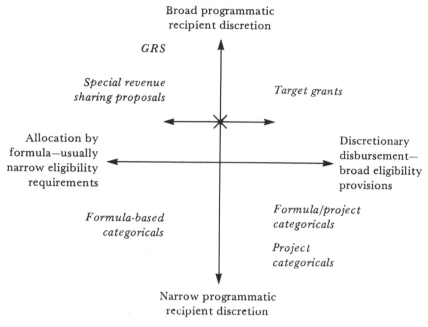

Figure 6-2   General Traits of Basic Forms of Intergovernmental Fiscal Transfers

area in 1960 (commerce and transportation) fell in the over $1 billion bracket, but by 1980 the number had grown to fifteen. The overall picture that emerges from these shifts and expansions within and among the major aid sectors clearly is one of greater breadth and diversity—as well as one wherein people-related and assistance programs (income security, education, training, employment, social services, and health) assumed a more dominant position (63 percent of the 1979 total, compared to 51 percent in 1963). Not revealed in this broad-brush presentation, of course, is the array of new, narrow, and subfunctional thrusts, noted earlier, that add still another dimension to this pattern of program diversity.

Still another basic change in the federal aid system has occurred with the *conditions attached to federal-aid programs.* Here the perennial congressional tendency to impose "strings" undercuts the ostensible arrival of a tripartite aid system. In the earlier era, grant conditions were almost wholly program specific, hence vertical, in their nature with institutional ("single state agency") and personnel (Hatch Act and merit-systems) requirements added to some (chiefly the public welfare and employment security areas). Today, all of these more traditional programmatic conditions still apply—obviously to the categoricals, which still dominate the grant scene, and increasingly to the block grants. Over time, the tendency among block grants is to acquire additional conditions within and, in some additional, functionally related categorical programs, without. Witness the much more conditional status of the Safe Streets, CETA, and CDBG programs now compared to their initial respective grant designs. Not to be overlooked here is that with the renewal in 1976 of general revenue sharing, this presumably least conditional of all federal-aid programs imposed requirements on its 38,000 recipients that ranged from citizen participation, audits of all funds expended, restrictions on debt retirement with GRS monies, and compliance with prevailing wages for construction projects to protection against discrimination in recruitment and employment of various population groups, in the provision of public services, in the selection of facilities to be financed out of federal funds, and by subcontractors.

Perhaps the most significant development in this era of "creeping conditionalism" was the piecemeal, yet persistent proliferation of conditions that applied generally or selectively to all or most of the federal assistance programs. Most of these sixty-one national policy requirements cluster under ten broad separate goals (see table 6–3). All but six of these requirements emerged during these two decades, and thirty-eight were enacted or promulgated during the seventies.

Most of these crosscutting conditions take the form of a single congressional enactment, but some take the form of multiple, not always identical, enactments in various grant programs (as with the 150-odd citizen participation requirements) and still others include a general requirement along with differing, more stringent enactments in the same topical area for certain aid programs (as with civil rights). Not all of the sixty-one are "intrusive." In fact, some are intended to facilitate the grants management role of recipient governments (i.e., several of the general and more specific administrative and procedural requirements cited in table 6–3). Yet about three-fourths of the total clearly are of a quasi-regulatory nature

Table 6-3   Major Sources of Federal National Policy Objectives Applicable to Grant Programs

Nondiscrimination

Age Discrimination Act of 1974
Architectural Barriers Act of 1968
Civil Rights Act of 1964, Title VI, VII; Executive Order 11764 delegates implementation responsibility to the Attorney General
Civil Rights Act of 1968, Title VIII
Comprehensive Alcohol Abuse and Alcoholism Prevention, Treatment and Rehabilitation Act of 1970
Drug Abuse Office and Treatment Act of 1972
Education Amendments of 1972, Title IX
Education for All Handicapped Children Act of 1975
Equal Pay Act of 1963
Nondiscrimination in Employment by Government Contractors and Subcontractors, Executive Orders 11141 (1963) and 11246 (1965)
Rehabilitation Services Act of 1973, Section 504; Executive Order 11914, delegates coordination to Department of Health, Education, and Welfare
State and Local Fiscal Assistance Act of 1972
Urban Mass Transportation Act of 1964, as amended 1970, Section 16

Environmental Protection

Archaeological and Historic Preservation Act, May 24, 1974
Clean Air Act of 1970, Section 306 and amendments of 1977
Coastal Zone Management Act of 1972, Sections 307 (c) and (d), as amended
Endangered Species Act of 1973
Federal Water Pollution Control Act, Section 508, 1970
Fish and Wildlife Coordination Act of 1934
Flood Disaster Protection Act of 1973 and Floodplain Management, Executive Order 11988, 1977
National Environmental Policy Act (NEPA), 1969
National Historic Preservation Act of 1966, as amended in 1970, 1973, 1976, and 1978
Procedures for the Protection of Historic and Cultural Properties
Protection and Enhancement of the Cultural Environment, Executive Order 11593, 1971
Protection of Wetlands, Executive Order 11990, 1977
Wild and Scenic Rivers Act of 1968, as amended

Table 6-3   (continued)

Health, Welfare, and Safety

Animal Welfare Act of 1966
Lead-Based Paint Poisoning Prohibition
National Research Act, Section 474, Protection of Human Subjects of Biomedical and Behavioral Research
Safe Drinking Water Act of 1974

Labor and Procurement Standards

Anti-Kickback (Copeland) *Act* (1934, 1946, 1960)
Contract Work Hours and Safety Standards Act
Davis-Bacon Act (1931, as incorporated into individual grants when enacted)
Office of Federal Procurement Policy Act, 1974
Urban Mass Transportation Act of 1964, as amended, Section 13c
Work Hours Act of 1962

Public Employee Standards

Hatch Act (1939, 1940, 1942, 1944, 1946, 1962)
Intergovernmental Personnel Act of 1970, as amended by Title VI of the *Civil Service Reform Act of 1978*

Access to Government Information and Decision Processes

Citizen Participation (numerous grant programs in the past two decades)
Family Educational Rights and Privacy Act of 1974 (Buckley Amendment)
Freedom of Information Act, 1974

Protection and Advancement of Economy

Cargo Preference Act
International Air Transportation Fair Competitive Practices Act of 1974, Use of U.S. Flag Air Carriers
Placement of Procurement and Facilities in Labor Surplus Areas

General Administrative and Procedural Requirements

Claims Collection Act of 1966
Department of Commerce Directives for the Conduct of Federal Statistical Activities, May 1978
Federal Grant and Cooperative Agreement Act of 1977
FMC 74-8, *Guidelines for Agency Implementation of the Uniform Relocation Assistance and Real Property Acquisition Policies of 1970, Public Law 91-646, October 4, 1976*

Table 6-3 (continued)

Improving Government Regulations, Executive Order 12044, March 23, 1978

OMB Circular No. A-40, *Management of Federal Reporting Requirements*

OMB Circular No. A-95, *Evaluation, Review, and Coordination of Federal and Federally-Assisted Programs and Projects, Revised, January 13, 1976,* based in part on *Demonstration Cities and Metropolitan Development Act of 1966,* Section 204 and the *Intergovernmental Cooperation Act of 1968,* Title IV

OMB Circular No. A-111, *Jointly Funded Assistance to State and Local Governments and Nonprofit Organizations—Policies and Procedures, July 6, 1976*

Treasury Circular No. 1082, *Notification to States of Grant-in-Aid Information,* August 8, 1973

Treasury Circular No. 1075, *Regulation Governing the Withdrawal of Cash from Treasury for Advance Payments under Federal Grant and Other Programs,* December 14, 1947

Uniform Relocation Assistance and Real Property Acquisition Policies Act of 1970

Nonprofit Recipient-Related Administrative and Fiscal Requirements

FMC 73-3, *Cost Sharing on Federal Research,* December 4, 1973

FMC 73-7, *Administration of College and University Research Grants,* December 4, 1973

OMB Circular No. A-21, *Cost Principles for Educational Institutions,* March 6, 1979

OMB Circular No. A-110, *Grants and Agreements with Institutions of Higher Education, Hospitals and Other Nonprofit Organizations—Uniform Administrative Requirements,* July 30, 1976

State and/or Local Government-Related
Administrative and Fiscal Requirements

FMC 74-4, "Cost Principles Applicable to Grants and Contracts with State and Local Governments," July 18, 1974

OMB Circular No. A-90, "Cooperating with State and Local Governments to Coordinate and Improve Information Systems," September 21, 1968

OMB Circular No. A-102, "Uniform Administrative Requirements for Grants-in-Aid to State and Local Governments, Revised," August 4, 1977

OMB Circular No. A-73, Audit of Federal Operations and Programs, March 15, 1978

Sources: ACIR, *Categorical Grants,* op. cit., table VII-1, p. 235, and Office of Management and Budget, *Managing Federal Assistance in the 1980's* (Washington, D.C.: Office of Management and Budget, March 1980), pp. 20-26.

and reflect a new thrust in federal conditions attached to grants—conditions that depart significantly from the older, largely program-specific type.

During the past two decades, then, federal regulatory efforts moved beyond the traditional direct approach largely directed at the private sector and into the intergovernmental fiscal transfer realm. While the individual purposes of each of these crosscutting conditions may be commendable, their cumulative impact can be questioned. Moreover, no authoritative analysis of their impact has been made by Congress or the executive branch. Yet random reports and certain case studies suggest that additional paperwork and overhead administrative costs as well as greater federal intrusion and litigation have been some of their by-products at the recipient level.

Another cluster of critical changes in the federal-aid system is reflected in those conditions, of both crosscutting and program-specific nature, that amount to federal efforts to *launch new processes and erect new institutions at the substate regional level.* Beginning with the enactment of the Demonstration City and Metropolitan Development Act of 1966, a process was mandated that required all applications for federal grants and loans in certain urban programs (now more than 240) to be reviewed and commented on by a representative areawide body before being processed by the relevant federal agency. This was extended by the Intergovernmental Cooperation Act of 1968 to nonurban and state level clearinghouses designated by the governor. Out of this process (subsumed since 1969 under OMB Circular A-95) has come a remarkable expansion of councils of governments (or regional councils) from roughly 20 to 25 in the early sixties to well over 650 now. Not all of the 550-odd designated metropolitan and nonmetropolitan clearinghouses that now are part of the A-95 processes are councils of governments, but the overwhelming majority of them are.

Meanwhile, during roughly the same fifteen-year period, more than a score of specific aid programs were enacted that included provisions encouraging or mandating the establishment at the substate regional level of a functional planning process or instrumentality.[27] Thus, in aided programs as diverse as aging, health planning, urban transportation, economic development, coastal zone management, water quality control, solid waste disposal, air pollution control, and a dozen others, multicounty planning units came into being. All told, approximately two thousand such units have emerged since the mid-sixties.

In some regions, the generalist-dominated, multipurpose COG received the functional planning, coordinative management, technical assistance, and occasional quasi-regulatory roles stipulated in these programs. But in others, as the two-thousand figure signifies, separate bodies usually dominated by program professionals were instituted—giving rise, in effect, to a new breed of "special district." Put differently, the COGs operationally have benefited only about half the time from the emergence of these categorical and block grant regional program thrusts. Moreover, during the seventies the federal regional program thrusts in three areas (urban transportation, water quality control, and solid waste disposal) moved beyond the functional planning and voluntary coordinative management goals of the other substate regional efforts. In these three, Congress mandated a regional review of implementing project proposals and their concurrence with plans developed by the designated areawide units (in most instances, regional councils).

In effect, then, and despite efforts like part IV of the A-95 circular, the federal government in its attachment of procedural and institutional strings to grant programs has pursued both a generalist and general-government-favoring as well as a specialist and specialized-unit-favoring strategy at the substate regional level. In neither of these approaches, however, has it encouraged the creation of regional institutions that are authoritative, legally or politically, since all of the federally encouraged mechanisms are not governments and follow a basically confederative format.[28]

Still another marked change in the character of federal aid is in the area of *matching, maintenance of effort, and "nonsupplanting" requirements.* In this realm of recipient fiscal responsibilities, a basic trend toward reducing the dollar match and a corresponding trend toward increasing the number of maintenance of effort or "nonsupplanting" of recipient funds conditions can be observed.

As table 6-4 indicates, the proportion of aid programs having low or fifty-fifty federal matching declined from 32.6 percent of the 1960 total to 13.7 percent of its 1976 counterpart. Concomi-

Table 6-4   Matching Ratios, By Number of Programs for 1960 and 1976

Federal participation	1960		1976	
Less than 50%	8	(5.9%)	2	(0.4%)
50%	36	(26.7%)	59	(13.3%)
50-100%	17	(12.6%)	145	(32.8%)
Some Cost Sharing[1]	10	(7.4%)	42	(9.5%)
100%	58	(42.9%)	170	(38.4%)
Other[2]	6	(4.4%)	25	(5.6%)
Total	135	(100.0%)	442	(100.0%)

1. Some nominal or negotiable recipient contribution is required.
2. Undeterminable.
Source: ACIR, *Categorical Grants: Their Role and Design* (A-52) (Washington, D.C.: U.S. Government Printing Office, 1978), adaptations of tables V-3 and V-4, pp. 162 and 164.

tantly, the proportion of grants calling for high or total federal fiscal participation rose from 63 percent to over four-fifths of the 442 programs funded and operational in 1976, even though the sector represented by the full-federal-funding group declined slightly in proportionate though not in absolute terms.

To bar the substitution of federal grant funds for recipient resources, maintenance of a certain degree of nonfederal effort or a nonsubstitution provision sometimes is made a condition of grant receipt. Such requirements usually stipulate that a recipient government match the federal grant with an amount at least equal to its previous expenditure for the aided activity, thus making it a function of earlier effort, not of the cost of the program.[29] Without such a condition, a fully federal funded grant could lead to a reduction in the participating government's outlays for the aided function. With the increase in the number of 100 percent federally funded grants, the number of such requirements has risen. As of 1976, at least one-fifth of all the categorical grants then funded contained statutory nonsupplant or maintenance-of-effort requirements.[30] In the case of formula grants, the figure rose to over 40 percent. In practice, however, it frequently is difficult to monitor and enforce such "strings," which suggests that the increase in low and no-match requirements is more significant than the parallel trend of more nonsupplant and maintenance-of-effort conditions.

A final group of significant changes in the federal aid system is highlighted in the various *ways in which the flow of assistance dollars shifted* over the two decades. At the most aggregative level, this is reflected in the 54/46 split in 1961 of federal-aid funds between nonurban and urban areas (which, of course, did not correspond with the population division of the time) and the roughly 30/70 split in any recent fiscal year (which does reflect population patterns more closely).

On the thorny front of fiscal equalization, other not unrelated changes occurred. Using per capita personal income as an indicator of state fiscal capacity, high-income states as a group received the lowest average grants in 1960 and the low-income states the highest average in relation to their respective populations, while the average for the middle-income states was just above the national norm.[31] This last group dropped below the national average by 1962 and below the high-income states' average by 1968 and has remained there ever since. Moreover, by the mid-seventies the high-income cluster overtook the low-income group, reducing the latter to a second-rank position for the remainder of the decade.

This development relates in part to the ascendancy of highways in the 1960 grant package, whose allocation formula(s) favored low population density states (which then frequently had low per capita incomes). The subsequent shifts were in part a product of the greater grant focus on urban areas and programs and the expansion of public assistance programs (AFDC and Medicaid). With the urban thrusts, comparatively well-off urban states (and their less well-off local jurisdictions) benefited; while with public assistance and despite the equalization factors built into its cost-sharing formulas, high rates of participation pushed several high-income states into the largest per capita assistance class, along with some in the lowest per capita income category.[32] It was these trends that produced the situation in the seventies where the high-income group ranked first and the lowest-income cluster second in their respective per capita assistance receipt rates.

Not to be overlooked in this brief description of the interstate equalization effects of federal aid is the fact that income redistribu-

188 Toward a Functioning Federalism

tion was and is not the prime goal of the overwhelming majority of the aid programs.[33] None of the five block grants contain a fiscal capacity factor in their allocational formulas and only GRS and about twenty-five categoricals rely in some measure on the ability of a recipient jurisdiction to finance public services as a factor in allocating aid funds.[34]

It has been the shifts in the program composition of the federal grant package that largely explain the distributional shifts, along with its focus on four allocational principles, not one: political fairness (with its emphasis on population or jurisdictional equality), program need (with its reliance on sometimes doubtful proxies in their formulas), recipient program effort (which involves some variation of the cost-sharing approach), and fiscal capacity or equalization (which even when emphasized usually conflicts with one or more of the above factors). The growing emphasis on more urban and more social welfare grants, then, along with the shifting interactions among the four allocational factors, produced the seemingly random shifts in interstate distributions of federal assistance since 1960.

A final facet of the changed allocational patterns of federal assistance is the degree to which local jurisdictions, especially some of the more hard-pressed central cities in the Northeast and Midwest, have come to depend in the seventies on federal financial aid (see table 1–4). While there is still some disagreement about the extent to which federal aid has been or can be "targeted" to local jurisdictions encountering a range of economic, social, and fiscal challenges, the figures indicate a growing reliance on direct federal aid (from a range of grant sources) by several central cities, with some of the most "pressured" having the highest "reliance" rates. The one major caveat to be noted here is that the higher percentages for FY 1978 are explained partially in terms of funds flowing from the three countercyclical programs and that only one of these (CETA) was reauthorized and is still operational. In general, then, the post-1978 figures were lower, reflecting the more stabilized condition of federal aid during this most recent period.[35] Yet larger central cities still fared better than medium-sized and small municipalities. Finally, all categories indicated far higher receipt rates than prevailed in the early seventies,[36] and the same generalization can be made aggregatively for counties, cities, and towns (see table 6–5).

Table 6-5   Federal Aid as a Percentage of Local Governmental Taxes and Own Source General Revenues, by Jurisdictional Category, 1957 and 1978

| | 1957 | | 1978 | |
	General revenue Own source	Taxes	General revenue Own source	Taxes
Counties	1.2%	1.5%	19.2%	27.7%
Cities	1.4	1.8	25.0	36.8
Towns	0.5	0.5	13.1	14.9
School districts	2.3	2.6	3.7	4.2
Special districts	8.9	26.1	34.0	150.0
All local	1.9	2.4	17.5	24.1

To sum up, the many dimensions of the growth of and changes in federal aid underscore and symbolize the emergence of the heavily intergovernmentalized system that now prevails. This is not to say that federal regulatory promotional activities have not been important. They clearly have, as the subsequent chapter will indicate. But the many contrasts highlighted above between the aid system of 1960 and that of 1980 provide the paramount basis for claiming that a new one has, in fact, evolved. Moreover, the functional, administrative, and political implications of this dramatic development signal the end of cooperative federalism as it was understood and practiced two decades ago and heralds the advent of a cooptive, as well as dysfunctional, federalism, whose problems and paradoxes rank among the top items on the nation's agenda of unfinished business.

NOTES TO CHAPTER 6

1. See *Special Analysis, Budget of the United States Government, FY 1981* (Washington, D.C.: U.S. Government Printing Office, 1980), p. 118.
   2. See ibid., pp. 48-49.
   3. Alaska scrapped its income tax in 1980.
   4. Advisory Commission on Intergovernmental Relations, *Significant Features of Fiscal Federalism, 1978-79 Edition* (M-115) (Washington, D.C.: U.S. Government Printing Office, 1979), p. 54.
   5. Ibid.

6. Only Arizona took action previously.

7. ACIR, *Significant Features of Fiscal Federalism 1976-77 Edition* (M-110) (Washington, D.C.: U.S. Government Printing Office, 1977), pp. 188-89.

8. See John Shannon, "Tax Revolt—Its Effects on Local Finances," unpublished remarks before the Office of Management and Budget National Conference on Improving A-95, Washington, D.C., November 1979.

9. See ACIR, *Significant Features of Fiscal Federalism, 1978-79 Edition* (Report M-115), op. cit., pp. 34-35.

10. See ibid., pp. 38 and 39.

11. See ibid., pp. 64-68.

12. Ibid., pp. 38-39.

13. See ibid., pp. 5, 38, 39.

14. ACIR, *Trends in Metropolitan America* (M-108) (Washington, D.C.: U.S. Government Printing Office, 1977), pp. 7, 8, 58-62.

15. Within the fifty states, of course, there was and is considerable variation in the extent of the "pass-through," given their varying servicing/funding patterns. See ACIR, *The State and Intergovernmental Aids* (A-59) (Washington, D.C.: U.S. Government Printing Office, 1977), pp. 14-23 and *Recent Trends in Federal and State Aid to Local Governments* (M-118) (Washington, D.C., July 1980), pp. 27-28; and G. Ross Stephens and Gerald W. Olson, *Pass-Through Federal Aid and Interlevel Finance in the American Federal System, 1957-77*, vol. 1, a report to the National Science Foundation, NSA/APR 77000348, University of Missouri-Kansas City, 1 August 1979, pp. 31-56.

16. See ACIR, *Recent Trends in Federal and State Aid to Local Governments*, op. cit., p. 9.

17. In 1977, school districts received 49.2 percent of all state aid; counties, 23.7 percent; cities, 23.6 percent; towns and special districts, 4.5 percent. The cities figure, it is to be remembered, includes New York and certain others, which perform various state-aided county functions. Cities were the prime beneficiaries in only one of the aid types: general support payments.

18. See Robert M. Stein, "The Allocation of State-Local Aid: An Examination of Between State Variance," unpublished paper presented at the Conference on State Resource Targeting to Urban Areas, University of Maryland, College Park, 15 May 1980, p. 31.

19. ACIR, *Central City-Suburban Fiscal Disparity: City Distress* (Washington, D.C.: U.S. Government Printing Office, Fall 1980), table A-17.

20. ACIR, *Categorical Grants: Their Role and Design* (A-52) (Washington, D.C.: U.S. Government Printing Office, 1978), pp. 26-28.

21. See James L. Sundquist and David W. Davis, *Making Federalism Work: A Study of Program Coordination at the Community Level* (Washington, D. C.: The Brookings Institution, 1969), pp. 3-5.

22. ACIR, *The Crisis of Confidence and Competence*, vol. 1 in the series *The Federal Role in the Federal System: The Dynamics of Growth* (Washington, D.C.: U.S. Government Printing Office, July 1980), chap. 2.

23. See ACIR, *A Catalog of Federal Grant-in-Aid Programs to State and Local Governments: Grants Funded FY 1978* (A–72) (Washington, D.C.: U.S. Government Printing Office, 1979), p. 3.

24. ACIR, *The Intergovernmental System as Seen by Local, State, and Federal Officials* (A–54) (Washington, D.C.: U.S. Government Printing Office, 1977), pp. 11–12.

25. ACIR, *A Catalog of Federal Grant-in-Aid Programs to State and Local Governments*, op. cit., p. 1.

26. See ACIR, *Summary and Concluding Observations, The Intergovernmental Grant System: An Assessment and Proposed Policies* (A–62) (Washington, D.C.: U.S. Government Printing Office, June 1978), pp. 8–12.

27. Overall, some thirty-two federal aid programs, as of 1976, contained a substate regional organizational or procedural focus, six more than in 1972; see ACIR, *Regionalism Revisited: Recent Areawide and Local Responses* (A–66) (Washington, D.C.: U.S. Government Printing Office, 1977), pp. 12–17.

28. Two-thirds of the COGs now, however, operate under some variation of a weighted voting formula.

29. ACIR, *Categorical Grants*, op. cit., pp. 173–74.

30. Ibid., p. 174.

31. Sophie R. Dales, "Federal Grants to State and Local Governments, Fiscal Year 1975: A Quarter Century Review," *Social Security Bulletin*, September 1976, pp. 30–31.

32. Ibid., p. 30.

33. See Rudolph G. Penner, "Reforming the Grants System," *Fiscal Federalism and Grants-in-Aid*, ed. Peter Mieszkowski and William H. Oakland (Washington, D.C.: The Urban Institute, 1979), p. 114.

34. See ACIR, *Categorical Grants*, op. cit., pp. 217–18.

35. See Subcommittee on the City, House Committee on Banking, Finance, and Urban Affairs, *City Need and the Responsiveness of Federal Grant Programs* (Washington, D.C.: U.S. Government Printing Office, August 1978).

36. Subcommittee on Fiscal and Intergovernmental Policy, Joint Economic Committee, *Trends in the Fiscal Condition of Cities: 1978–1980* (Washington, D.C.: U.S. Government Printing Office, 20 April 1980), pp. 19–20.

7

An Overloaded Servicing System

Since 1960, the sphere of national authority has expanded even more massively than it did during and after the New Deal. The roles carved out by the Depression, World War II, and the postwar years of the national government as regulator, reformer, and promoter of the economy were fleshed out even more fully under the galvanizing pressures of social reform, Vietnam, environmental concerns, inflation, recessions, and energy crises. Moreover, and to a far greater degree than in the earlier era, the national government assumed a vastly more assertive role as regulator, reformer, and promoter of social and environmental goals—as much of the preceding judicial and grant-in-aid analyses has suggested. To these two roles must be added that of senior partner in the intergovernmental fiscal transfer field.

Meanwhile, the states were assuming a far more assertive stance in revenue raising, their aid programs to local governments, direct assumption of new and sometimes hitherto local functions, and mandates and regulatory initiatives affecting their localities. These actions, when combined with those of the federal government, have given rise to an overloaded system—wherein the national government provides few direct services and the bulk of the services performed by subnational governments is conditioned by the funding, the regulations, and the conditions of higher levels, thus raising serious questions regarding efficiency, effectiveness, equity, and especially accountability. It is this convoluted and overburdened condition of contemporary servicing arrangements with which this chapter deals.

SOME DIMENSIONS OF THE GROWTH IN FEDERAL ACTIVISM

The expansion of the federal role over the past score of years has more than a grant facet to it. Witness the following *developments in the regulatory realm* alone:

——The total number of federal mandates of the direct ordering type on state and local governments rose from 10 in 1960 to 224 by 1978, while those imposed as conditions of federal aid soared from four in 1960 to 1,034 eighteen years later.[1]

——The number of pages in the *Federal Register* in which new or revised regulations appear grew from 14,479 in 1960, to 20,037 in 1970, up to 71,191 in 1979.

—— Fourteen new federal regulatory agencies were created between 1960 and 1980, compared to twelve for the previous 30-year period; of these fourteen, only one dealt with economic concerns, while six involved health and safety, and seven, social and citizens' protection concerns.[2]

——The funding for all federal regulatory units rose rapidly during the last decade.[3]

——More than fifty federal laws were enacted between 1965 and 1980 that superseded state enactments. These fell in six categories: health and safety, environmental protection and conservation, consumer protection, agricultural standards, civil rights, and miscellaneous.[4]

——With some of the above, federal preemption was total, which is to say it occupied the whole field and left no room for state or local variances or additions (as with the Flammable Fabrics Act, the United States Grain Standards Act, and the Radiation Control for Health and Safety Act of 1968); with others higher or comparable state standards, alternative approaches, or shared administration were and are permitted (as with the Gun Control Act of 1968, the Drug Abuse Control Amendments of 1965, the Federal Rail and Safety Act of 1970, the Safe Drinking Water Act, the Wholesome Meat Act, the Poultry Products

Inspection Act, and the Occupational Safety and Health Act of 1970).[5]

In addition to these many signs of expanding, federal regulation of more private-sector as well as of state and local governmental, *federal promotional activities* also increased. One crucial dimension of this phase of growing federal activity is the range of programs subsumed under the heading of federal credit assistance. This consists in part of direct-loan programs to individuals and organizations by regular federal agencies and by independent federal corporations whose operations may or may not be included in the regular budget. It also includes federally guaranteed loans that are transacted in private-sector money markets.

New federal commitments under these various credit assistance programs came to over $126 billion in FY 1979, compared to less than $50 billion in 1970 and $26 billion in 1960.[6] Most of these federally advanced funds in American credit markets are disbursed by thirty-two agencies, and the lion's share in 1979 was accounted for by guaranteed loans ($74.7 billion) and government-sponsored enterprise loans ($17.5 billion),[7] which are not subject to the federal budgetary processes. Overall, outstanding federal and federally assisted credit soared from nearly $100 billion in 1961 to over $190 billion by 1970, thence to more than $528 billion in 1979.

While most of these efforts benefit individuals, businesses, and other groups in the private sector, subnational governments are by no means excluded. Witness the loan and loan guarantee programs of Commerce's Economic Development Administration and National Oceanic and Atmospheric Administration, of HHS's health programs, of HUD's housing and community development units, of various transportation agencies, and of Treasury insofar as they deal with New York City and the District of Columbia.

Another basic form of federal promotionalism is found in the complex but crucial area of tax expenditures. Such outlays, in effect, are losses to the U.S. Treasury caused by provisions of the federal tax laws that allow a "special exclusion, exemption, a preferential rate of tax, or a deferral of tax liability."[8] Tax expenditure goals range from promoting various economic activities, to enhancing environmental protection, to reducing the income tax liabilities of taxpayers in special circumstances.

Both the dollar volume and number of "expenditure programs" have grown appreciably since 1967 (comparable data are unavailable for the early sixties). The former rose from $36.6 billion in 1967 to over $181 billion by 1980, while the latter nearly doubled during the same period, reaching 121 in 1980.[9] Commerce and housing credit, income security, health, and general purpose aid to state and local governments were the top four in estimated dollar amounts in 1967, 1972, and 1980.

The figures for the thirteen functional and numerous subfunctional areas under which "expenditure items" are classified suggest a roughly one-eighth public-sector as against a seven-eighths private-sector division of benefits in 1980. This is not to say that public policies (hiring welfare recipients, historic preservation, and residential energy credits, to cite three random examples) or past connections with public-sector efforts (veterans) are not assisted or promoted by some of those that appear to have a wholly private-sector orientation.

This expansion in the tax expenditure and credit assistance activities of the federal government clearly indicates that the subsidy-promotional role that was assumed in the earlier era in no way diminished during the past twenty years. Moreover, many of the earlier federal regulatory and grant programs, which served a private- as well as a public-sector purpose, continued and in some cases expanded during this period (notably economic development, mass transit, manpower training, health and social services, and energy resources development in the grant area and communications, consumer product safety, and fair trade practices in the regulatory realm). At the same time, not all of the specific subsidies or protective forms of regulation that prevailed in 1960 continued unabated. Farm subsidies declined significantly and airlines, natural gas, and trucking experienced varying degrees of deregulation. There were shifts then in promotional/protective points of attention, but also an overall increase of federal efforts in this key area of interventionism.

Given the expansionist, centralizing, and increasing intergovernmental character of these regulatory and promotional efforts, *where did they leave the states and their localities*—the presumed prime partners in a cooperative federal setup? The answer is: partially benefiting, partially bulldozed, partially partners, and partially unaffected. To the limited degree (compared to the private sector) that they participate in the loan and loan guarantee programs cited earlier, they benefited somewhat. To a far greater degree, they were and are aided by such tax expenditure programs as the exclusion of interest on state and local industrial development and housing bonds (an estimated $485 million in 1980), the deductibility of nonbusiness state and local taxes—other than on owner-occupied homes and gasoline ($147 billion), the exclusion of interest on general-purpose state and local debt ($2.4 billion), and the deductibility of local property taxes on owner-occupied dwellings ($7.7 billion)—to cite the four most obvious ones.

In the regulatory realm, the "partially bulldozed" response is more accurate. Unlike the earlier era, the expansion of federal regulatory efforts since 1960 has had a significant impact on state and local governments as well as on the private sector. The new thrusts in the environmental, energy, health, job safety and other working conditions, agricultural standards, and equal opportunity and access areas have had as pronounced an effect on state and local governments as on the nongovernmental sector. While federal preemption was total in some of these, in others states could institute higher standards or share collaboratively in the implementation.

Not to be overlooked here is that the federal courts have *not* given carte blanche to federal efforts in this area. The states' police power and the Tenth Amendment as well as the Fourteenth still sanction their authority to incorporate businesses, to regulate insurance companies and within-state public utilities, to audit state-chartered banks, to regulate a significant range of intrastate transportation endeavors, to establish higher standards of due process and equal protection than the national government, and to legislate in a way that establishes a more or less favorable "climate for business" and economic growth. For these somewhat conflicting reasons, then, the "partially bulldozed" response is apt, but not the "wholly preempted" judgment.

As some of the foregoing suggests, the states and localities have assumed a "partial partnership" role in some regulatory and promotional spheres. In those loan and loan-guarantee programs in which they participate and in those regulatory areas (gun control, drug abuse, rail and safety, safe drinking, wholesome meat and other agricultural-standards legislation, etc.) wherein higher state standards and/or shared administration are called for, this clearly is the case. Moreover, where states themselves have instituted parallel promotional programs, a kind of de facto partnership emerges. With the forty-two states as of 1979 that operated home ownership programs, with the twenty-seven that funded housing rehabilitation efforts, and with the twenty-four that had enacted tax incentives (credits, abatements, exemptions, and deferrals) for home improvement, this clearly was and is the case in the housing field.[10] The twenty-two states having loan and loan-guarantee programs for expanding commercial and industrial firms provide another example in the economic development area.[11]

Fifty independent sources of varying promotional and regulatory initiatives clearly still exist. Where the political will exists, then independent state action is still possible and legally permissible in some regulatory areas and in a wide range of promotional undertakings.

While the expanded federal regulatory efforts had a significant effect on state/local police power-based activities and while accelerating promotional programs had an increasing impact on subnational governments, *the multiple developments in the federal assistance area* clearly constituted the most significant single source—other than federal court decisions—of federal influence on state and local service delivery systems. Here there is the specter, if not the reality, of the national government assuming more policy and fiscal responsibilities for an ever-expanding range of governmental services and activities, including many that in 1960 were deemed to be wholly a state, local, or even a private concern. But there also was and is a steady, unyielding determination at the national level *not* to use its own instrumentalities to implement directly hardly any of these proliferating national program responsibilities. Hence the heavy reliance on grants-in-aid; hence, the fundamental reason for the overloaded system of intergovernmental relations that now prevails.

To be more specific, *the servicing assignments and delivery systems of the states and localities have been heavily affected by four fundamental trends in federal assistance over the past twenty years:*
—— the ever-widening spread of direct federal relationships with more and more state agencies along with nearly four-fifths of the nation's 80,000 localities;

——the emergence of a tripartite assistance package composed of categoricals, block grants, and GRS;

——the rapid expansion in the number of aided program areas ranging from some obviously national, to clearly intergovernmental, to several that in the fifties were local or private in character; and

——the many facets of "creeping conditionalism," which combine to suggest a concept of intergovernmental administration wherein a range of national objectives—social, environmental, programmatic—are to be promoted through the grant system with national administrators ostensibly being responsible for their implementation.

Each of these aid developments was not really "planned," and certainly the consequences of each and of the four interacting with one another were not anticipated. Yet this feature of contemporary American federalism, more than any other, has fostered the dysfunctional traits so prominent in today's intergovernmental relations.

The servicing impact of these four developments can be traced by exploring four questions:

——What jurisdictions are deemed by federal policymakers to be able and/or willing to perform a function?

——What impact has federal aid had on the service expenditures of recipient governments?

——What servicing assumptions and shifts have been prompted by federal assistance?

——What effect has federal aid and its conditions had on recipient service delivery systems?

The first issue leads directly to the "explosion of the eligibles" phenomenon, discussed earlier. But in the functional assignment context, this dramatic departure from the near-monolithic position the states enjoyed in 1960 as eligible recipients of federal grant funds becomes a question of what subnational governments the federal government considers to be appropriate providers of aided services. The current answer as reflected in the eligibility provisions of nearly five hundred aid statutes is: many jurisdictions are the appropriate providers of many programs. Witness the following:

——Of the 492 categorical grants that were funded and operational
in FY 1978, the states were exclusively eligible for 38 percent
and the localities for 6 percent, while states, localities, and
nonprofits were eligible for 43 percent.

——Among the thirty-one broad budget subfunctional aid categories under which these 492 categoricals as well as the block
grants and GRS are subsumed, the states were solely eligible in
only three (water transportation, other transportation except
mass transit, and hospitals and medical care for veterans),
while the localities were not designated as the sole recipient
governments under any of the thirty-one.

——As table 6-5 highlighted, all categories of local government experienced a significant increase in their receipt of direct federal
aid between 1957 and 1978, especially cities, counties, and
special districts.

In a formal sense, this increasingly more open approach to pro
gram eligibility and the resulting spreading out of aid funds arc explained by two seemingly conflicting developments: the growing
reliance in the seventies on formulas as a means of allocating funds
and of curbing federal administrators' discretion, and the acceler-
ated growth throughout the period in the number of project grants
with their focus on deciding competitively who best can do a job.

The first development is illustrated by GRS and some of the
block grants. Both of these newer forms of federal assistance rely
on statutory formulas to distribute all or most of their funds, so
their eligibility provisions should have been precise. But politics
and precise definitions rarely go together. Hence, while GRS
sought to distribute its funds solely to general governments, this
highly expansive distributional goal became even more so because
the term "general" was defined in census-based, legal terms. All
told, about eleven thousand ostensibly "general governments"
regularly receive GRS checks, even though their servicing role in
1977 was so minimal that none of them reported having any full-
time employees.[12]

The block grants too have tended to "spread out" grant funds
among eligible recipients, some of whom had little or no prior servicing experience with the aided function. One effect of the eligibility provisions in the community development block grant, for

example, was to extend funds to cities and counties who had not participated in any of the seven HUD categoricals that were merged to form the CDBG program. Among the recipient cities in 1977, nearly 300 of the 620 total fell in this category.[13] With counties, not much more than a dozen were deemed initially by most observers to possess the legal powers called for in the act's definition of eligible metropolitan counties. In CDBG's first year, the figure rose to over seventy and at present is above eighty. With CETA, the dominant role accorded to cities and counties (214 of the 399 prime sponsors) and to consortia composed of both (134) in its eligibility provision meant that manpower training funds would (and do) go to jurisdictions with little or no experience prior to 1973 with the program. Nonprofit organizations and in some cases industries were the chief recipients of the funds disbursed under the array of more than a score of categoricals that were consolidated under two titles of CETA, and some of these, it should be noted, still "implement" the program locally under contract with the local "generalist" prime sponsor.

The other basic formal (or grant design) reason for this "spreading out" effect of federal aid lies with the roughly one-quarter of total grant funds (one-third in the sixties) that currently are distributed on a competitive project grant basis. Project grants, it is to be remembered, typically have nearly wide-open eligibility provisions, given the ostensible demonstration, research, or pilot-project purposes of this grant type. Such provisions have been of special benefit to special districts and private nonprofit organizations, some of them with questionable servicing records and/or capacities. An educated guess would put the proportion of private recipients of DHHS's programs at the 70 percent mark and those of the Community Services Administration's grants at about 90 percent. Moreover, in the special district group, probably about 15,000 of the nearly 26,000 received federal aid in 1977 and over 6400 of these were units that lacked even one full-time employee.[14]

These findings regarding both project and formula grants indicate that the "explosion in the eligibles" over the past decade and a half had a dispersive servicing impact wherein non- or meager functioning substate governments as well as clearly broadly servicing units were aided. They also suggest that despite the presumed

federal bias in allocating aid funds to general governments, enunciated in Section 402 of the *Intergovernmental Cooperation Act
of 1968* (P.L. 90–577), special districts and private nonprofit units
have suffered no noticeable diminution of aid flows as a result.
Finally, they show that some subnational units assumed new or
almost new servicing roles as a result of eligibility provisions within
some of the block and categorical grants.

Aside from these formal, grant-design reasons for this "spreading out" effect, political factors also played a crucial role. The
growing urban orientation of aid programs during the sixties and
the concomitant tendency to "bypass" states were reflective of
the city concerns of the Democratic administrations and Congress
of the period. The increasing role accorded to counties was in part
a by-product of growing suburban strength in Congress after the
1970 census and the assumption of the Nixon administration that
metropolitan counties were fertile ground for Republican votes.
Not to be overlooked was the aggressive lobbying by the national
associations of subnational governmental officials, both generalist
and functionalist.

A second area wherein the impact of federal aid on state-local
functions can be discerned is the fiscal. Services obviously are
affected if federal aid affects recipient outlays for them—one way
or another. Certainly one of the programmatic assumptions implicit in the theory of categorical grants is that they should exert a
stimulative effect, and a probe of the entire package of categoricals
operational in FY 1975 found that for nearly three-quarters of
them this was the congressional intent, either wholly or in part.[15]
Hence the perennial charge that federal aid skews recipient budgets
and program priorities. In surveys of local officials, overwhelming
majorities (two-thirds in the case of city officials and four-fifths
with their county counterparts, according to one conducted in the
mid-seventies) have indicated that federal categoricals and block
grants, to a far lesser extent, distorted their respective local decisionmaking processes, both fiscally and programmatically.[16]

The design features of a grant then would appear to have some
effect on the extent to which recipient funding and programmatic
actions are constrained in the aided function, and some studies
have confirmed this hypothesis. An ACIR-Syracuse report on the
effects of federal grants found that all such aid tended to generate

additional state-local own-source expenditures in 1972, but that this applied with greater force for some types of grants than for others.[17] Stimulation was somewhat greater with project grants than with the formula-based type, for example, suggesting that the greater degree of recipient initiative required with the former is more likely to produce a greater conformance with recipient program/outlay preferences.[18] Moreover, differentiated stimulus rates were found to be related to grants with high, low, or no state/local matching requirements, with the greatest stimulus being associated—not unexpectedly—with high matching grants.[19]

Other analyses have concluded that still other factors help determine whether a specific grant program is stimulative or substitutive. The determining conditioner, according to one probe, is the recipient government's preference for the aided function compared to its preferences for other services requiring its own source funding.[20] In addition, the servicing scope and size of the recipient government, the number and variety of aid programs in which it participates, a grant's fiscal requirements, and the availability and size of the grant relative to the recipient's own ongoing spending (or nonspending) for the aided service are other factors to be considered here.[21]

These various findings suggest some uncertainty regarding the real spending effects of federal aid, aggregatively, specifically, and over time. Recipient servicing preferences, their range, and the extent of participation in the grant system seem to be as significant as the type, size, and other design features of a grant. Moreover, these indigenous factors form a cluster of variables with which computers cannot really cope, since they act and react with one another and with the external factors in a distinctive way in each of the thousands of subnational governments that receive federal aid.

Despite these uncertainties and caveats, it still may be stated tentatively that substitution (or fungibility[22]) is more likely to arise in jurisdictions that partake of a large number of aid programs (regardless of their form), that have access to several separate revenue sources, and that offer a broad range of public services.[23] When this generalization is linked to one made earlier regarding the increased rate of participation by more and more units within each of the subnational governmental groupings, a probable paradox emerges: As the number of federal aid programs, their recipients, and their dollar amounts increase, their stimulative effects decline, even though the ostensible purpose of at least three-fifths of these grants is stimulative. The lingering question, of course, is: Will a period of retrenchment force a confrontation of the problematical effects of federal aid suggested by this paradoxical by-product of proliferating aid programs? If, for example, national decisionmakers determined that all conditional aid funds become fungible over time, would they or could they face the obvious policy conclusion that general support payments (GRS expanded) would be the most logical, inexpensive, and equitable way to provide future federal assistance?

Closely related to this complicated issue of the fiscal effects of federal aid on service outlays is the equally complex one of what effect federal aid has had on the assumption and transfer of specific functions within subnational governments. Nearly all of the studies of the subject agree that federal aid has had at least an indirect impact on the assignment of functional responsibilities through its interaction with various state and local influences.

A recent probe of how federal assistance interrelates with one or more state/local level factors in altering municipal service systems found that:[24]

—— Federal aid between 1967 and 1977 exerted an increasingly more pronounced influence on the assignment of servicing responsibilities, and that the influence of state or local determinants declined;

—— Specific functions or groups of functions that clearly were stimulated included housing, corrections, social welfare, and local school services;[25]

—— A decline in federal aid received by a city tended to be associated with the transfer upward of at least one function; and

—— Overall, federal aid exerted a strong and positive influence on net servicing changes within the 845 municipalities analyzed, but was not as significant an influence generally on the assumption of new functional assignments as state or local determinants.

Looking back over the past fifteen years at specific aid programs, it is clear that federal grants promoted an expanded state servicing role in welfare and payments for medical services to the needy; a growing school district concern with special educational programs; a greater special district involvement, at least in part, with water and sewerage; a new role on the part of some counties in providing community development, manpower, and social services; and more broadly shared city involvement in manpower, community development, and the four other program areas cited above.[26]

The 208 federal programmatic mandates (of the total of 1260) that have been imposed directly on subnational governments or as a condition of federal aid chiefly during the seventies obviously cannot be overlooked here.[27] These subdivide into three groups: new program or activity mandates (125) having no quantity or quality specifications (i.e., directly ordering general-purpose governments to increase accessibility of public buildings to the handicapped or requiring GRS recipients to establish an affirmative action program in hiring their personnel); program quality mandates (71) wherein the characteristics or conditions of public services and goods or of recipients of such are prescribed (i.e., the nutritional requirements of meals in the school lunch program and specifying components of the training under the job corps program); and program quality mandates (12) that call for or imply the number of times a service is to be rendered or produced or the number of recipients that are to benefit from a service (i.e., the requirement in the day care program that recipient agencies must give priority in the provision of services to members of low-income groups and the stipulation under the mass transit program that grant recipients shall assure that rates charged elderly and handicapped persons during nonpeak hours will not exceed one-half of the generally applicable rates).[28]

To sum up, federal aid has become a significant determinant of changes in the servicing assignment roles of state and local governments, but not to the exclusion of indigenous factors within each of the fifty state/local systems.

A final fundamental area of federal grant impact is on the ways in which aided services and activities are delivered or carried on. Here the array of procedural conditions both crosscutting (horizontal) and program specific (vertical) come into play. According to the Lovell study, 82 percent (1032) of all the federal mandates are of the procedural type and these fall under six sub-headings: reporting (158); performance (463); fiscal (157); personnel (120); planning and evaluation (77); and record keeping (57).[29] All but 28 of the 1032 were established since 1960.[30] A mandate, it is to be remembered, is a "responsibility, action, procedure, or anything else that is imposed by constitutional, legislative, administrative, or judicial action as a direct order or that is required as a condition of aid," and the overwhelming majority of all the federal mandates (82 percent) take the form of compelling conditions of aid.[31] Among these, of course, are the crosscutting national purpose conditions, analyzed in the previous chapter.

But what effect have federally imposed conditions had on state and local service delivery systems? Based on its in-depth analysis of their impact on five counties and cities in five states, the Lovell study concluded that federal mandates, not unexpectedly, have a differentiated impact on local jurisdictions, in that their number varied from jurisdiction to jurisdiction (reflecting in part their varying rates of participation in grant programs). The local general fund paid at least some of the costs for 30 percent of the federal direct orders and 45 percent of the grant mandates. Federal horizontal mandates of both the procedural and program type were least likely to be assisted by federal financial assistance and with 57 percent of the direct orders and 51 percent of the grant conditions, the mandated activity had not been performed prior to its imposition and by a nearly two-to-one margin the procedural outranked the programmatic in terms of launching new activities.[32]

When viewed separately or in combination, these findings suggest that federal requirements have prompted numerous changes in how local services are rendered and some changes in what services are performed. They also indicate a growing federal presence at the local level, though not as strong in some instances as that of the states (as will be discussed later).

Other evidence of the impact of federal conditions on the operations of local recipients is provided by a 1979 survey of 1011 municipalities conducted by the National League of Cities. Among its many findings, the poll discovered that the greatest source of municipal difficulties with federal programs stemmed from procedural and across-the-board requirements, with 65 percent singling

out application, administrative, and financial reporting requirements, 64 percent citing eligibility requirements, and 45 percent
selecting Davis-Bacon labor standards.[33]

State operations also have been affected by federal-aid conditions and direct mandates. Despite the fact that overall federal aid
to the states stayed pretty well within 25–30 percent of state
general revenue, its impact and penetration became greater during
the seventies. Witness the findings of Deil Wright's most recent
survey of state administrators, wherein 74 percent reported that
their agencies received federal aid in 1978, compared to 64 percent in the 1974 poll, and 53 and 34 percent in 1968 and 1964,
respectively.[34] The proportion of agency heads that called for an
expansion of their programs declined from 66 percent to 54 percent during this same time span, but there was no change in the
high proportion (75 percent) in both years that felt federal aid led
to "national interference in affairs that are the appropriate domain
of the states." Moreover, there was a significant increase in the
seventies in the percentage of state administrators who felt that
federal funds would be allocated quite differently if grant conditions were not present (70 percent in 1978 versus 52 percent and
56 percent for 1964 and 1968, respectively).

To conclude, the spreading out of federal aid, its fiscal impact
on state/local servicing outlays, its evolving role as a significant
conditioner of servicing assignments at the subnational government
levels, and the effects of its conditions (as well as of direct mandates) on service delivery highlight some of the major manifestations of the servicing system's overload.

THE FIFTY STATE-LOCAL SERVICING SYSTEMS

The delivery of domestic services, however, traditionally has been
and still is predominantly a state-local function. As table 7–1
clearly indicates, the direct general expenditure responsibility for
twenty program areas, which of course includes intergovernmental
fiscal transfers and outlays from own-source revenues, leaves the
prime servicing role with the states and their localities in all but
four instances ("other education," natural resources, air transportation, and water transport and terminals). Even with the many

signs of expanding federal activity since the mid-sixties, the figures here indicate only a marginal (2 percent) increase in the federal government's direct servicing role in these functional areas between 1967 and 1977.

Within specific functional areas, however, some shifts did occur.[35] The most dramatic at the federal level, of course, was the increase in direct outlays for public welfare caused by the federal assumption in 1972 (and operationally in 1974) of most of the fiscal and all of the administrative responsibility for the "adult categories" (aid to aged, blind, and disabled). The significant reduction in the federal share of health expenditures between 1967 and 1972 is explained more by major hikes in state and local outlays for these functions than by any reduction in federal health expenditures, with the federal share standing at 41 percent for both 1972 and 1977. Similarly, the federal proportion of the direct outlays for water transport and terminals declined by 16 percent during this ten-year period and for housing and urban renewal by 10 percent between 1972 and 1977.

At the state level, the biggest shift was in the "other public welfare" sector, with the state share rising from 40 percent in 1967 to 54 percent in 1972 and 1977. Much of this shift was due to the expanded state outlays for social services, which were funded partially by federal grants. In public higher education, there was some decline in the state share, suggesting the growth in community colleges. Similarly, there was a drop in the states' proportion of highway expenditures, with a local, not federal, pickup of the difference.

At the local level, sewerage and other sanitation, local fire protection, local parks and recreation, and parking facilities remained wholly in local hands throughout the decade. Moreover, local education remained a 99 percent locally provided service throughout, with the centralized systems of Alaska and Hawaii accounting for the remaining 1 percent.

Performing services, however, is one thing; financing them increasingly is wholly another. The traditional "dual-federal" linking-up directly of most domestic services to their funding source within their assigned governmental jurisdictions no longer applies. At this point, the funding of a service is almost always a matter of intergovernmental fiscal transfers as well as of own source revenues. Yet, as was shown earlier, all federal aids now

Table 7-1 Percent of Direct General Expenditure Responsibility by Level of Government and Specific Function: 1966-67, 1971-72, 1976-77

Function	1976-77 Federal %	1976-77 State %	1976-77 Local %	1971-72 Federal %	1971-72 State %	1971-72 Local %	1966-67 Federal %	1966-67 State %	1966-67 Local %
Education: local	...	1	99	...	1	99	...	1	99
higher	...	81	19	...	84	16	...	88	12
other	60	40	...	61	39	...	63	37	...
Highways	1	59	40	2	66	32	1	67	32
Public welfare: cash	39	31	30	1	50	49	1	49	50
other	25	54	21	19	54	28	27	40	33
Total	(30)	(46)	(24)	(11)	(52)	(37)	(14)	(45)	(41)
Hospitals	18	41	41	19	39	43	20	41	39
Health	41	28	30	41	25	33	57	20	24
Police	11	13	75	8	14	78	8	13	78
Local fire protection	...	...	100	...	...	100	...	...	100

Sewerage	...	...	100	...	...	100	...	...	100
Other sanitation	...	...	100	...	...	100	...	...	100
Local parks and recreation	...	...	100	...	...	100	...	...	100
Natural resources	79	17	4	78	17	5	77	18	5
Housing and urban renewal	39	3	57	49	1	51	38	1	61
Air transportation	60	5	34	68	4	28	65	5	30
Water transport and terminals	67	11	22	77	7	16	83	6	11
Parking facilities	...	...	100	...	...	100	...	...	100
Correction	5	60	35	5	59	36	5	62	33
Libraries	...	8	92	...	8	92	...	9	91
Other and unallocable	51	20	29	58	15	27	64	14	22
Total direct	30	27	43	27	27	46	28	26	45

Source: ACIR, The Roles of State and Local Governments: Adapting Form to Function (Washington, D.C.: U.S. Government Printing Office, 1981), table 2–1; compiled from U.S. Bureau of the Census, Governmental Finances, 1966–67, 1971–72, and 1976–77 (Washington, D.C.: U.S. Government Printing Office, 1968, 1973, 1978), table 7 (1967, 1972), table 11 (1977).

come with some, if not many, conditions and state aid is still 90 percent conditional in character. These conditions, in effect, divide authority for the performance of an aided function between the granting and recipient governments, producing one of the major by-products of incessant intergovernmentalization: an administration situation where accountability is frequently impossible to assign.

By comparing over time the net total of direct and intergovernmental outlays for a function by governmental level with the direct expenditures alone, some of the most basic shifts in the pattern of shared funding and shared administration in seven key functional areas are highlighted:[36]

——The predominant local role in funding and directly administering primary and secondary education in 1962 was modified greatly by the increased financing responsibilities assumed by the states and the federal government during the seventies.
——The servicing responsibilities for highways shifted slightly toward the localities, but the heavily intergovernmental pattern of funding of 1962 experienced no change over the next fifteen years.
——Welfare experienced a steep increase in federal funding and in federal direct servicing as well as a major decline in the earlier counterpart local roles.
——With health and hospitals, natural resources, and air transportation, some comparatively minor shifts in both the servicing and funding areas occurred, but the roughly equal roles in 1962 of all three levels in health and hospitals persisted through 1977, while the predominant 1962 federal role in the remaining two functions declined somewhat over the next decade and a half.
——By way of contrast, the housing and urban renewal function experienced a sharp rise in the federal financial role and some increase in its servicing role, but localities continued to dominate the latter.
——For the seven as a whole, the localities dominated the servicing realm (47 percent) for the entire period, while the federal government assumed an expanding financial but declining

direct servicing role, leaving the states in an expanding servicing and static financial position.

Turning to the nationwide servicing roles of the various units of local governments, in 1977 cities led in expenditures (and the direct servicing role) for police, highways, fire protection, sewage, other sanitation, parks and recreation, housing and urban renewal, air transportation, libraries, and parking facilities—just as they had a decade earlier. There was some proportional city decline during this period in fire protection, parks, sewage, and other sanitation, however, and these reductions were largely reflected in larger county percentages in these areas. Moreover, counties were the dominant local providers of public welfare, hospital, health, correction, and natural resources services, and this continued the 1967 assignment pattern save for modest percentage increases in all of these functions except welfare.

Not unexpectedly, independent school districts dominated the local educational expenditure field, but the dependent school systems of cities and counties accounted for one-fifth of the outlays in both years. With townships, a very minor servicing role was reflected in the overall expenditure figures for nineteen local functions. This is explained by the fact that only twenty states have them. Within the eleven "strong township" states, a more prominent servicing role emerges; where they accounted in 1977 for 32 percent of total highway outlays, 20 percent of those for parks and recreation, 18 percent of the libraries and sanitation (other than sewerage) expenditures, and fairly significant shares of those for police and fire protection. By way of contrast, townships in the remaining nine states accounted for over 5 percent of the total expenditures in only two functions: police and highways. Finally, special districts assumed a significant servicing role in water transport (65 percent), natural resources (44 percent), housing and urban renewal (43 percent), hospitals (26 percent), and sewerage (25 percent), and these proportions only varied by a margin of four percentage points or less from their 1967 counterparts— except for hospitals, where the special district share of total direct local outlays grew by 8 percent.

Comparisons of local jurisdictional outlays in metropolitan

and nonmetropolitan areas reveal that the metropolitan pattern clearly resembles the national one depicted above, while the non-metropolitan assigns a greater servicing role to counties and a lesser one to cities.[37] Moreover, special districts assumed a greater role in housing and urban renewal and in natural resources in nonmetropolitan areas.

Looking at the states' overall role in the state-local servicing system, they were the "senior servicing partner" (accounting for 55 percent or more of the total of state-local direct expenditures for a function) in highways, hospitals, health, public welfare, natural resources, and corrections.[38] They were a close second to the municipalities in providing water transport and terminal facilities. The major general shift for them between 1967 and 1977 was the growing direct state servicing role in welfare.

Other shifts occurred, however, when the states and the five types of local government are viewed as part of one servicing system.[39] In addition to the welfare shift, hospital services moved from a state, county, or municipally dominated function in 1967 to a status in 1977 of having "more than one provider" in state after state. Similarly, police and sewage lost their former munici-pally dominated classification in several states, with the "more than one provider" servicing arrangement generally gaining. Not as many states in 1977 had their municipalities serving as the prime urban renewal/public housing provider as in 1967.

Overall, there was a sharp increase in the "dominant provider" roles of counties and some increase in those of cities between 1967 and 1972. The following five years, however, witnessed a drop in the county "dominant provider" count to a point where it was actually less in 1977 than it was a decade earlier, and with the cities the slippage was even greater. Again, the "more than one provider" arrangement was the principal beneficiary of these shifts, thus highlighting the increase in servicing reassignments that occurred during this period.

Regional servicing patterns, however, did not always parallel the national one.[40] In New England, the states, cities, and towns were the dominant providers, with the states having a greater role than in any other region and the counties having a much lesser one.[41] With the Middle Atlantic states, no single class of providers dominated many functions and the "more than one provider" scored high in various service areas. In the Southeast, cities ranked high in several services, but so did the twelve states and the counties in others. Cities also had a relatively high number of dominant provider roles in the Great Lakes and Plains states, with counties having far fewer in the former and hardly any in the latter. To a greater degree than in any other region, cities were the dominant service providers in the Southwest. The Rocky Mountain states showed no distinctive regional pattern, but in the Pacific Coast states the counties assumed a servicing role unmatched in any other region.

Analysis of the fifty systems over time, and especially during the past twenty years, indicates a general trend away from local dominance and toward state seniority in service funding terms, the gradual emergence of a more balanced state-local sharing of service delivery responsibilities, and a continuing local superiority in terms of the size of its work force.[42] When a composite index of degrees of centralization are fashioned from these three factors, the number of heavily and moderately decentralized state-local systems slips from twenty-one to four and the number of moderately and heavily centralized jumps from nine to twenty-one between 1957 and 1977.[43]

Despite this general trend toward a greater state role within the fifty state-local servicing and funding systems, the traditional diversity of the servicing systems by no means disappeared. Witness the fact that in 1977, there still were four tending toward a decentralized system and twenty-five that were balanced, along with the twenty-one that were centralized or tending in that direction. Similarly, when the state financing share of state-local revenues, its expenditure proportion of total state-local outlays, and state-local per capita expenditures are used as differentiating measures, a typology emerges that reflects wide variations in the state-local division of funding and servicing responsibilities as well as in the cost of the total package of services that each of these systems delivers.[44]

At one extreme, there were those characterized by state government ascendancy in both the expenditures and origin of financing areas and in 1977 these included ten state systems, which in turn subdivided into three groupings based on the varying per capita cost of their servicing packages (see table 7-2). At the other,

Table 7-2 Classification of State-Local Fiscal Systems: Total Expenditures of State and Local Governments: 1977

	High state expenditure responsibility	*Moderate state expenditure responsibility*	*Low state expenditure responsibility*
High state financing responsibility			
High expenditure per capita	Alaska Delaware Hawaii		
Moderate expenditure per capita	North Dakota Rhode Island	Maine New Mexico	
Low expenditure per capita	Alabama Arkansas Kentucky South Carolina West Virginia	Mississippi North Carolina Oklahoma	
Moderate state financing responsibility			
High expenditure per capita		Washington Wyoming	Maryland Minnesota Wisconsin
Moderate expenditure per capita	Louisiana Utah Vermont	Connecticut Idaho Illinios Iowa Kansas Pennsylvania	Arizona Michigan
Low expenditure per capita		Tennessee Texas Virginia	Indiana
Low state financing responsibility			
High expenditure per capita		Massachusetts Montana Oregon	California Colorado Nevada New York
Moderate expenditure per capita	New Hampshire South Dakota		Nebraska New Jersey Ohio
Low expenditure per capita		Georgia	Florida Missouri

Source: ACIR staff computation, based on data supplied by Syracuse University's School of Citizenship and Public Affairs ACIR, *The Role of State and Local Governments: Adapting Form to Function* (Washington, D.C.: U.S. Government Printing Office, 1981), table 2-15.

there were the locally dominated systems wherein state financing and direct servicing responsibilities are comparatively low, and nine fell under this classification. This group, in turn, also broke down into a high, medium, and low cluster according to their differing per capita outlays for services. Ranging between these extremes were six other groups with a total of twelve subdivisions within them. These findings suggest that the general trend toward a significantly greater funding role and somewhat greater servicing responsibilities of the states is by no means uniform, and that the interaction of the funding and direct servicing factors along with the equally significant cost item is a distinctive process within each of the fifty, producing a highly variegated pattern of state-local functional relationships.

Still another dimension of this diversity is found in the states' varying approaches to local mandates. The Lovell study found that such actions had increased greatly since 1960 in the five states surveyed, with 84 percent of the 2811 total being instituted since 1960 and 59 percent since 1970.[45] At the same time, differences were found in the extent to which the five engaged in mandating, though only minor variations emerged regarding type of mandates adopted.[46] A mid-seventies survey of all the states, however, produced a somewhat different picture of state mandating.[47] Compared to those in other regions, southern states were found generally to mandate less and decentralized states (where local governments contributed more than half of the state-local revenues) showed a greater tendency to have more mandates. Moreover, of the seventy-seven potential mandating areas surveyed, fourteen were found to be heavy action areas (where thirty-five or more states had mandated), including mandates governing three types of local personnel matters, four public safety areas, solid waste disposal in the environmental protection field, and six educational issues, while minimal mandating (action by fifteen states or fewer) was found in three other local personnel, nine other public safety, and three other environmental protection areas, as well as in nine social service and other fields.

These findings combine to suggest considerable differences among the states in the extent and thrusts of their mandating activities. To the degree that it is heavy, however, there can be no doubt that the administration, delivery, and scope of local services are significantly affected.[48]

Finally, the varying roles of the different categories of local government within each of the fifty systems must be reckoned with. As the earlier examination of regional servicing implied, there is considerable variation in the servicing role of the jurisdictions within each of the local governmental groupings. This variation is very much a product of the distinctive funding, functional, legal, and historical features of each of the fifty systems, not to mention other obvious factors like population size, diversity, and geographic location.

One fundamental indicator of the servicing variations within each of the five traditional local governmental groupings is the extent to which a jurisdiction requires full-time employees. As table 7–3 indicates, 23 percent of the cities, 35 percent of the special districts, and 43 percent of the towns and townships had no need for even one full-time employee in 1977. These accounted for 26 percent of the total of all local governments, and this figure did not include 308 nonoperating school districts.

The diversity of the various local governments' servicing roles and the resulting complexity of state-local systems generally is perhaps best highlighted by a brief recapitulation of the functional variations within each of the five census groups.

——Cities are the most multipurpose of all units of local government, yet the scope of a municipality's services varies greatly according to its size, social heterogeneity, and presence or absence of an overlying servicing county—to cite only the more obvious conditional factors.

——With the counties, they are significant or very significant service providers in nine states (462), moderately significant in thirty-three (2538), insignificant or minor in six (132), and nonexistent in two (which formerly had 14).[49]

——Towns and townships, as was suggested earlier, divide into those in weak township (largely midwestern) states and those in strong town or township (largely northeastern) states; in the former, they are minor civil subdivisions with very limited functional authority, while in the latter they are "minimunicipalities," usually performing a range of services.[50]

——School districts, while less diverse than counties and towns, divide nonetheless into four basic groupings: a state-run system (Hawaii), a dependent system in which the state is the super-

vising general government (Alaska), eight dependent systems, in
which the schools are a dependent service provided by cities,
counties, or towns (four New England and four southern
states), and forty systems in which primary and secondary
education is provided by independent school districts (15,260).
——Special districts almost defy generalization, since their use,
purposes, and significance vary greatly from state to state.
They are nonexistent or insignificant functionally in eight
states (Alaska, Hawaii, Iowa, Vermont, New Mexico, South
Dakota, Kentucky, and Michigan), but they are quite important service providers in seven others (Texas, California, Illinois, Arizona, Georgia, Washington, and Nebraska), and of
moderate significance in the remaining thirty-five states. All
but 1720 of the 25,962 total in 1977 were single functional,
all but 6552 overlapped local governmental boundaries,[51] and
903 "giants" (3.4 percent of the total) accounted for over
four-fifths (81.4 percent) of their total expenditures.

From these brief descriptions of the five local-governmental
groupings, a complex, if not confusing, picture of local service providers emerges. And this is as it should be. The American system
of local governance is more complicated than that of any other
system, federal or unitary. Moreover, when it is remembered that
the variations in state roles are an integral part as well as a funda-

Table 7-3   Types of Local Governments by Numbers of FTE Employees,
1977

Local governments	Zero	One	2-5	6+	Totals
Counties	N.A.	N.A.	N.A.	N.A.	3,042
Municipalities	4,420	1,211	2,773	10,452	18,856
Towns/townships	7,267	1,300	1,113	7,142	16,822
Special districts	9,204	1,304	1,248	14,384	26,140
School districts	N.A.	N.A.	N.A.	N.A.	15,260
Totals	(20,891)	(3,815)	(5,134)	N.A.	80,120

Number of local governments by number of FTE employees, 1977

Source: Preliminary Data from the 1977 Census of Governments obtained by the ACIR.

mental conditioner of this perplexing local pattern, one can only conclude somewhat ambiguously that different levels (state and local) and different local governments are responsible for funding and delivering sometimes similar and sometimes dissimilar public services in different states.[52]

What Generalizations Can Be Drawn From These Various Servicing Developments Within the Fifty State-Local Systems?

From one cluster of nationwide-based findings emerges the conclusion that most (but not all) of the systems have experienced some similar changes. Among these shared shifts, of course, is the emergence in a large majority of cases of a dominant state role in financing the combined state-local package of services, a growing state role in the direct provision of services, and the continued ascendance of local governments in rendering a majority of the services in the overall package. In addition, the recent increase in most systems in the number of local functions that are performed by more than one class of local governmental provider, and the growth in the number of mandates imposed by the states on their respective localities, must be noted. These five fairly commonly shared trends combine to provide yet another major manifestation of the intergovernmentalizing process, with local government operations more dependent on state aid and subject to more state-imposed conditions and direct mandates as well as to more servicing shifts. Moreover, even with the moderate countertrend of growing direct state servicing responsibilities, the entangling effects of federal aid, its conditions, and mandates in these functional areas are not avoided.

Somewhat ironically, the differences among the fifty systems provide no real basis for assuming there is a strong countervailing voice in their diversity that is capable of resisting or rationalizing the steady thrust toward a greater overloading. Federal intergovernmental efforts, after all, now affect nearly all fifty systems. In its grant enactments, related conditions, and mandates, the national government rarely has taken note of the varying pattern of direct state servicing responsibilities; the varying costs of the fifty separate state-local packages of services; the varying degree to which the states have imposed their own different conditions and mandates; and the varying servicing roles of cities, counties, and towns and townships among state systems, not to mention frequently within them.

The federal failure generally (though not totally) to recognize these elementary differentiating facts of state-local servicing operations and funding is reflected in its cavalier approach to "bypassing," to program eligibility, to accepting census classifications of subnational governments, to mandating, and to enacting grant programs that deal with multifaceted social and economic concerns and that assume that potential recipient substate governments possess the legal authority, the range of services, and the geographic scope to deal with these concerns. This lack of federal sensitivity to differing state/local functional relationships and capacities, among other things, has produced a propping up of nonviable local governments; the assumption of entirely novel functions by some subnational governments; the application of the same horizontal mandates to all recipient subnational governments, regardless of size, scope of services, and setting; a frequent duplication of state efforts in the same regulatory areas; a cluster of disincentives to greater state exertions in the financing and expenditure areas; and, above all perhaps, the questionable implementation record of many of its own aid programs.

In effect, the pinwheel pattern of federal interaction with all of the categories of subnational governments clashes with the varying servicing and financing interrelationships that these categories have with one another in their fifty different systems. The result, of course, is that with centralizing tendencies in both systems, the localities of America are exposed to the compound effects of both the federal and state governments being involved in different and sometimes similar ways in the funding, delivery, and scope of the services they deliver—services that still constitute the bulk of domestic governmental functions. Moreover, even as the states contribute to this trend, they also suffer from it, given their reliance on federal aid and their exposure to federal conditions and mandates.

CONCLUSION

To sum up, contemporary domestic servicing arrangements and their proliferating network of intergovernmental relationships reflect an increasing inability to function effectively, efficiently, or responsibly. In broadly systemic terms, this has arisen because of the ever-expanding role of the national government in regulatory, promotional, and aided program undertakings of both a major and minor nature, because subnational governments and other intermediate instrumentalities are relied upon to implement many of the national government's regulatory policies and practically all of its service-related programs; and because, despite this apparent centralization of policymaking, fifty different state-local servicing, financing, and political systems still function—not only as recipients of federal grants and implementation of federal policies, but also as quasi-independent sources of varying program, fiscal, and administrative policies and regulations in a range of crucial domestic governmental areas.

This separation at the national level of expansionist policymaking from actual policy execution, the growing separation at all levels of revenue raising from direct service expenditures, and the growing gap between national policy goals and those emerging from the political processes of state and local governments are the chief reasons for this dysfunctional federalism. They suggest, after all, that we have forgotten that federalism, if it means anything, means a rough but real division of labor. Hence the current confusion at all levels as to their respective functional role; hence the congestion at the center and at the peripheries; hence the system's increasing dysfunctionality.

In practical administrative terms, it is reflected in the spectacle of a comparatively small band of federal administrators attempting to supervise, monitor, and assess some five hundred assistance programs even as about four-fifths of subnational governments are involved with one and usually more of them. It is reflected in the activities of most of the twelve million full-time state and local employees—employees who are under differing administrative and personnel systems and who now are engaged generally in furthering national policies and state and/or local program goals as well.

It is mirrored in the multiple fiscal and administrative difficulties generated by the emergence of three-score overcutting national policy conditions alongside the numerous program specific ones. It is seen in the countless situations wherein line administrators at all levels are placed in the unenviable, if not impossible, situation of attempting to carry out several frequently conflicting assignments, only one of which is the furtherance of his or her program's basic mission.

It can be sensed when the labyrinth of geometrically expanding vertical, diagonal, and horizontal linkages within current intergovernmental relations is encountered, and it can be roughly understood when an attempt is made to depict in graphic or organizational chart terms the formal, not to mention the informal, intergovernmental connections now required in a single program area. In the most elemental administrative sense, perhaps, it is reflected in the massive fragmentation of administrative responsibility among programs, agencies, and governmental levels that these recent trends have produced. All of these and other signs of administrative ineffectiveness, it should be remembered, were neither envisioned in the theory nor found in the practice of the cooperative federalism of 1960.

In fiscal terms, these recent intergovernmental developments have not produced the savings that national policymakers thought would result from relying on other than the federal bureaucracy to implement most of their domestic policies and programs, and state and local decisionmakers have discovered that intergovernmental fiscal transfers are not always right answers to their own fiscal questions. From the national vantage point, the duplication in aid programs, the general inability to target them, the presence among them of more than four hundred puny (in dollar terms) and generally parochial (in program focus) grants, the "bypassing" of states, the emerging phenomenon of "fungibility," recipient tendencies to treat grant funds as "funny money" (especially in the no-match variety), and especially the interest-group pressures that seek the continuance and expansion of grants all add up to a fiscally inefficient system. From the recipient's vantage point, the continued ascendancy of categoricals, their increasingly intrusive and costly conditions, their skewing of budget priorities, their overtime stimulative effect, and their induced interest-group pressures combine to form another cluster of forces undercutting economic efficiency at the subnational levels.

These, then, are some of the administrative and fiscal dimensions of the system's dysfunctionality. But, in large measure, they are a product of recent political changes—the subject of the next chapter.

NOTES TO CHAPTER 7

1. Katherine Lovell, et al., *Federal and State Mandating to Local Government: Impact and Issues* (Riverside, CA: University of California, 1979 draft), p. 71.

2. See Office of the Federal Register, *1977/78 U.S. Government Manual* (Washington, D.C.: U.S. Government Printing Office), and Louis M. Kohlmeier, *The Regulators* (New York: Harper & Row, 1969), appendix pp. 307–12.

3. See Subcommittee on Economic Growth and Stabilization of the Joint Economic Committee, Congress of the United States, *The Cost of Governmental Regulation* (Washington, D.C.: U.S. Government Printing Office, 1 April 1978), pp. 57–59.

4. See James B. Croy, "Federal Supersession: The Road to Domination," *State Government*, Winter 1975, 35.

5. See Joseph Zimmerman, "Partial Federal Preemption and Changing Intergovernmental Relations," paper prepared for the 1979 Annual Meeting of the American Political Science Association, 3 August–3 September 1979.

6. U.S. Office of Management and Budget, *Special Analyses, Budget of the United States Government, Fiscal Year 1981 and Fiscal Year 1980* (Washington, D.C.: U.S. Government Printing Office, 1980), pp. 144 and 54, respectively and Congressional Budget Office, *Federal Credit Activities: An Analysis of the President's Credit Budget for 1981* (Washington, D.C.: U.S. Government Printing Office, February 1980), p. 3.

7. U.S. Office of Management and Budget, *Special Analyses, Budget of the United States Government, Fiscal Year 1981*, op. cit.

8. Ibid.

9. Committee on Ways and Means, U.S. House of Representatives, *Estimates of Federal Tax Expenditures* (Washington, D.C.: U.S. Government Printing Office, 1 June 1973), pp. 8 and 9; and U.S. Office of Management and Budget, *Special Analyses, Budget of the United States Government, Fiscal Year 1981*, op. cit., pp. 230–34.

10. National Academy of Public Administration and the U.S. Advisory Commission on Intergovernmental Relations, *The States and Distressed Communities: Indicators of Significant Actions*, a report to the Office of Community Planning and Development (Washington, D.C.: U.S. Department of Housing and Urban Development, September 1979), pp. 8–12.

11. Ibid., p. 18.

12. See G. Ross Stephens and Gerald W. Olson, "The Redistributive Function of Federal and State Governments," paper delivered at Resource Targeting to Urban Areas Conference, University of Maryland, College Park, Maryland, 15 May 1980.

13. See Thomas J. Anton, "Outlay Data and the Analysis of Federal Policy Input," unpublished paper presented at the Urban Impacts Conference, Washington, D.C., 8-9 February 1979, p. 31.

14. Stephens and Olson, op. cit., p. 3.

15. Advisory Commission on Intergovernmental Relations, *Categorical Grants: Their Role and Design* (A-52) (Washington, D.C.: U.S. Government Printing Office, 1978), chapter 5.

16. ACIR, *The Intergovernmental Grant System as Seen by Local, State, and Federal Officials* (Report A-54) (Washington, D.C.: U.S. Government Printing Office, 1977), p. 24.

17. ACIR, *Federal Grants: Their Effects on State-Local Expenditures, Employment Levels, and Wage Rates* (Report A-61) (Washington, D.C.: U.S. Government Printing Office, 1977), pp. 5-8.

18. Ibid., p. 7.

19. Ibid., pp. 7, 8.

20. ACIR, *Categorical Grants*, op. cit., pp. 177-83.

21. See ibid., chapter 6, and Richard P. Nathan, Charles F. Adams, Jr., and Associates, *Revenue Sharing: The Second Round* (Washington, D.C.: The Brookings Institution, 1977), p. 78.

22. Fungibility signifies the difficulty of tracing the real fiscal and program effects of aid, given its multiple displacement effects; hence, it sometimes is used as a synonym for substitution.

23. ACIR, *Summary and Concluding Observations* (Report A-62) (Washington, D.C.: U.S. Government Printing Office, 1978), p. 42.

24. ACIR, *The Dynamics of Municipal Functional Assignment: A Cross-Level Analysis* (Washington, D.C.: U.S. Government Printing Office, forthcoming).

25. Since the available data were not disaggregated to the point where specific federal grants could be identified, no doubt other, more specialized services were assumed as a consequence of aid.

26. ACIR, *Governmental Functions and Processes: Local and Areawide* (Report A-45) (Washington, D.C.: U.S. Government Printing Office, 1974), p. 67.

27. Lovell, et al., op. cit., p. 67.

28. Ibid., pp. 35-38.

29. Ibid., p. 67.

30. Ibid., p. 72.

31. Ibid., pp. 32, 67.

32. Ibid., pp. 160-96.

33. *Problems, Programs, and Needs*, a Report on the National League of Cities' Survey of Municipal Officials (Washington, D.C.: U.S. Government Printing Office, January 1980), p. 14.

34. ACIR, *State Administrators' Opinions on Administration Change, Federal Aid, Federal Relations* (M-120), prepared by Deil S. Wright at the University of North Carolina (Washington, D.C.: U.S. Government Printing Office, December 1980).

35. ACIR, *The Role of the States in Local Governments: Adapting Form to Function* (Washington, D.C.: U.S. Government Printing Office, 1981), chap. 2.

36. Ibid.

37. Ibid.

38. Ibid.

39. Ibid.

40. Ibid.

41. Counties, of course, only exist in a formal, servicing sense in four of the six: Maine, Massachusetts, New Hampshire, and Vermont.

42. Stephens and Olson, op. cit., pp. 57-72.

43. Ibid., pp. 62-63.

44. ACIR, *The Roles of State and Local Governments: Adapting Form to Function* (Washington, D.C.: U.S. Government Printing Office, 1981), table 2-15.

45. Lovell, et al., op. cit., p. 71.

46. Ibid., pp. 68-70.

47. ACIR, *State Mandating of Local Expenditures* (Report A-67) (Washington, D.C.: U.S. Government Printing Office, 1978), pp. 40-43.

48. See Lovell, et al., op. cit., pp. 161-96.

49. Stephens and Olson, op. cit., p. 81.

50. A further refinement of this dualistic division would produce the following breakdown: seven states with the strong New England type of town (the six in the region plus New Jersey); three with a mix of New England and midwestern types (Pennsylvania, New York, and Wisconsin); two with classified towns, most of which resemble the midwestern type but with a few having municipal authority (Michigan and Minnesota); and eight with solely the midwestern variety (Illinois, Indiana, Kansas, Missouri, Nebraska, North Dakota, Ohio, and South Dakota). See ibid., p. 82.

51. U.S. Bureau of the Census, *1977 Census of Governments, Volume I, Governmental Organization* (Washington, D.C.: U.S. Government Printing Office, July 1978), p. 70.

52. ACIR, *Governmental Functions and Processes,* op. cit., pp. 2-11.

8

Political
Dynamics

INTRODUCTION

In the previous four chapters, some fairly drastic changes in the conceptual, judicial, fiscal, and servicing areas of recent intergovernmental relations have been documented. When combined, they suggest neither a dual nor a cooperative operational theory of federalism, but rather an increasingly overburdened and dysfunctional federalism wherein intergovernmental relations have become more pervasive, more expansive, less manageable, less effective, and above all less accountable. But why did this occur in the recent period? The answer, of course, is found in the realm of political ideas, attitudes, the mode and extent of political participation, and the political process itself.

To stress the political here is not to denigrate the judicial and fiscal. The Court, as chapter 5 demonstrated, exerted considerable influence on the growth in federal authority and activity. Yet the Court's flashing green-light signal to the political branches of the national government has been on since 1937 in the regulatory area and since the twenties with the conditional spending power, though the real expansion of what is protected by the Fourteenth Amendment began in the sixties—at a point when political constraints had begun to erode rapidly.

With the financial factor, the national government started the sixties with a much stronger revenue system than that of the states and their localities and with a strong political sense of prudence regarding budget size and especially deficits. Enhancing the federal fiscal capacity were its broad-based income tax, the responsiveness of this levy to conditions of growth (even when stimulated by tax cuts) and of inflation, the separately financed social security system, the ability to shift funds from defense to the domestic sector, and, above all perhaps, a growing tolerance for deficit spending. All of those combined to create the image of a federal cornucopia in the sixties and early seventies, a cornucopia to be tapped by those with the requisite mind, mouth, and political muscle. Only in the late seventies did some sense of fiscal constraint return to Washington, and with some fanfare, which suggests how extraordinary the earlier fiscal behavior of national decisionmakers had been.

Developments in both the judicial and financial sectors, then, point to the political, since it was the combination of major change and some significant standpattism in this crucial area that coincided with basic shifts in budgetary behavior and with a new, mutually reinforcing relationship between the federal courts and the political branches. So it is to politics we must turn to fathom the fundamental reasons for the collapse of cooperative federalism and the substitution of a dangerously dysfunctional version in its place.

The Legacy of Political Ideas and Practice

Before turning to the more obvious and contemporary dimensions of political change and continuity, it is necessary to touch briefly on some central questions raised by the legacy of the New Deal and the postwar cooperative federalism concept as it stood in 1960. Our political past is no modest molder of our contemporary public thinking and practice. This legacy, after all, contained the taproots of today's theory and practice of intergovernmental relations and of the national government's activist role. Moreover, the ambiguities within it partially explain our current difficulty in understanding and coping with the confusing changes, the collapse of constraints, and the continuities in the realm of recent political developments.

Functionally, the federal domestic role had expanded greatly since 1930 into a range of regulatory, promotional, direct servicing, and financial assistance undertakings. Yet its chief focus in 1960 was primarily on economic, not social, concerns, hence on private-sector, not state and local, actions.

Conceptually, this expansion in the federal role began with a murky, though contested, theory of an activist national government that was rooted in the New Deal's "relief, regulation, and reform." This concept became broadly accepted by the fifties and was defended in terms of cooperation, a "concert of interests," and consensus. It also acquired "cooperative federalism" as one of its labels.

The rough outlines, then, of a new nationalist public philosophy had emerged by 1960, but the old public philosophy, or at least its laissez-faire governmental component, was never really displaced. It simply acquired an ideological competitor, and to compound the intellectual confusion, both claimed they were derived from Jefferson's concepts of individual liberty and equality.

Meanwhile, a pattern of interdependence between the federal government and the subnational units had emerged and the "cooperative federal" theorists talked of practically all domestic functions as shared ones. Yet the level of interpenetration actually was quite limited, focusing more on promotional and distributive political goals than on social democratic or redistributive ones and leaving whole sectors of subnational governmental programs and activities untouched. Moreover, while cooperative federalism had become the dominant intergovernmental concept politically, dual federalism, as the foregoing suggests, was by no means eclipsed by it in the practical and political areas of governmental operations and services.

Politically, some observers of the system in the fifties and early sixties found that Madison's pluralistic governmental and interest-group-based system was still very much intact. Others, however, felt it had collapsed under the pressure of positive national governmental actions based on the "concert of interests" approach to pressure group politics and on the noninterventionist role of the Court after 1937. In fact, while Madison's interest-group pluralism had acquired a real positive policy dimension, it still retained enough of its constraining and negating traits to limit federal action as much as it allowed action. This made the system appear simultaneously traditional and somehow untraditional.

Hence, while the formal authority of the federal government appeared preeminent after 1937, this was reflected primarily in its expanded regulatory and promotional activities, not in the crucial area of providing governmental services or even in its grant programs.

Such were the ambivalence and continuing tensions in the political ideals and practices of 1960. Yet the public was sanguine about the system in the Eisenhower and Kennedy years, both governmentally and politically.[1] As a people, we have been described as exhibiting a "striking number of inconsistencies and contradictions among . . . commonly held and widely different ideas."[2] The inconsistencies and contradictions that emerged from the earlier era, while crucial, were not all that glaring to the public-at-large in 1960. After all, the federal role, though expanded, was modest by current standards, and the federal system, though slightly "marbleized," clearly was functioning. And these may well have contributed to the optimistic popular consensus that had been reached by the late fifties. It was and is the current generation that was forced, ultimately, to confront some of these incongruities; and in the process, the optimism of the fifties gave way to the pessimism of the late sixties and the seventies.

A CONSTRAINED OR UNRESTRAINED SYSTEM?

If national politics, its processes, and its institutions were deemed a short two decades ago to be fairly severely constrained, what has transpired to convey the impression, if not the reality, of a system out of control?[3] If the limits of Madison's interest-group pluralism are still operational, why have three-fifths of the states called for constitutional curbs on Congress's spending power? If our traditional noncentralized party system is the ultimate and sure guarantee that federal-grant-related actions, whether by elected national officeholders or by appointed officials, will not be inimical to recipient government interests (as the cooperative federalists promised), then why is federal intrusion now a top agenda item among the governors, state legislators, county officials, and mayors?

Clearly, some basic political changes have occurred since 1960.

But how extensive have they been and how much do they depart from the past?

Political Transformation

Some argue that a fundamental political transformation has occurred in the system since the mid-sixties, and this is the real reason for the collapse of earlier constraints. They point to the massive legislative breakthroughs of the sixties—in civil rights, Medicare and Medicaid, aid to education, the war on poverty, and environmental and consumer protection, to cite only the most obvious— and the shunting aside of "veto groups and Congressional blocks that," as Wilson has described them, "were thought to stand astride each checkpoint in the legislative process, letting nothing pass without first extracting every necessary concession."[4] They single out the decline of the southern hierarchs, the liberalization of the Senate's cloture rule, the chipping away at the seniority principle, the strengthening of the caucus, and the growing assertiveness of junior members (and of Congress itself) as further evidence of the collapse of the old internal constraints that served— sometimes formally, but more frequently informally—to check simple majority action.

They emphasize that most of these trends have continued in the seventies and have in fact been strengthened. In support of the latter interpretation, they note the dramatic changes in congressional politics that occurred in the past decade (the further decline of local party organizations, the parallel emergence of solely candidate-oriented campaign units, the rash of retirements, and the advent of a Congress where a majority are freshmen or sophomores—undergraduates, that is).

They cite the unusually heavy outpouring of legislative enactments and reenactments in this period of presumed relative normalcy. They underscore the dramatic program departures that many of these enactments constituted (as in the environmental, educational, manpower, disabled, and fire protection areas). They go out of their way to stress the heavily regulatory thrust of numerous recent congressional statutes, including the increase in across-the-board requirements attached to federal aid programs, the incidence of unreimbursed federal mandating (pure drinking

water and the educationally handicapped), and the growth in federal enactments that supersede state laws. They rarely forget to
tick off the figures that dramatize the escalation of federal aid,
overall budget outlays, and deficits. Above all, perhaps, they warn
that many of these developments, which would have been deemed
highly controversial in the early sixties, occurred in a period of
divided government—of Republican presidents and Democratic
Congresses—where endless deliberations and accommodations,
along with deadlocks and a dearth of innovative policy departures,
are the usual results.

For this group, then, the system has experienced more than a
dramatic change over the past decade and a half; it has undergone
a fundamental transformation, a quiet revolution of sorts. And the
direction of this transformation, they caution us, has been toward
greater majoritarianism, greater federal activism (if not intrusion),
fewer real constraints within Congress, and fewer viable external
constraints on Congress in the form of the presidency, the courts,
or anti-governmental-growth interest groups. This view of recent
national political developments, then, serves as the primary systemic explanation for the recent call for a constitutional curb on
Congress's overall spending decisions and for other curbs on federal
activism.

No Systemic Change

An opposing group of analysts views the recent past differently.
For them, there has been change but nowhere near as dramatic or
debilitating as the previous "out-of-control" school of thought
claims. Most in this group usually concede that there was a burst
of legislative activity in the sixties, but as Wilson notes, they attrib-
ute this more to the consequences of Senator Goldwater's 1964
defeat than to any profound changes in the system.[5] The Johnson
sweep brought in more than two score freshman House Democrats.
Hence, the 89th Congresses reflected a rare combination of northern Democratic numerical ascendancy and strong presidential
leadership. The voluminous statutory results are history, but not
continuing history, these observers claim.

With the seventies, "normalcy returned," in their view, "and
with it (depending on one's political convictions) stagnation or

prudence."[6] The congressional battles over energy, tax code revision, campaign finance, deregulation, welfare reform, national health insurance, Humphrey-Hawkins, and national land use planning, they insist, all point to a continuation of the veto politics of Madison's interest-group pluralism. Successful or unsuccessful coalition-building and "logrolling" efforts, they contend, characterized all of these legislative campaigns of the seventies, not simple majorities, accepted presidential leadership, and the absence of constraints.

This "not-much-change" group also argues that many of the congressional reforms have had a more cosmetic than concrete effect, have been more apparent than real. The reform of Senate Rule XXII (cloture) in no way curbed the near-endless debates over energy and the Panama Canal treaty. Only a handful of committee chairmen have been sacked as a consequence of the presumed reform of the seniority rule. Continued heavy Senate reliance on the unanimous-consent device as a means of conducting its business and continued House adherence to its difficult discharge petition and "suspension of the rules" procedures suggest no great departure from Congress's traditional loyalty to certain practices that protect minorities. All these signs of the seventies, this group believes, indicate that there have been no basic changes in the operational features of the national political/governmental system. It is not, for them, quite as it was in the days of Harry S. Truman, but it resembles the system under Truman far more than that under Lyndon B. Johnson.

The Need for a Synthesis

Little political change, or near total transformation? Continuing crucial constraints or a new era of minimum constraints and easy majorities? Madison still triumphant or Jefferson newly triumphant? The contrasting interpretations of the recent past presented above do little to provide clear-cut answers to these three interrelated questions. And how could they? Neither is wholly correct nor wholly incorrect, as Wilson has observed. But how can this be so?

The basic explanation is found in the fact that old-style veto-group politics still apply with certain issues and under certain circumstances, and that a new-style coalition-building politics operates with still other issues and under other circumstances. Hence the judgment that both interpretations are partially correct. Moreover, the continuance of traditional interest-group politics, albeit in restricted areas, helped to conceal the magnitude as well as the nature of many of the changes since the mid-sixties.

To arrive at a better understanding of how this complex, confusing, if not schizophrenic (to borrow a Wilson description) condition arose, other recent developments—sometimes hinted at, oftener ignored in the two earlier assessments—need probing. In the areas of political ideas and issues, organized interests and even disorganized interest groups, representation and representatives, the legislative process and its product, and policy implementation are found to be the fundamental reasons for our present state of political discontent and systemic dysfunctionality.

THE DYNAMICS BEHIND RECENT DEVELOPMENTS

Attitudes and Issues

Perhaps the most dramatic of the recent developments have occurred in the realm of political ideas and issues. Over the past decade and a half, most of the older lines of demarcation between what is a private or purely societal concern and what is a public issue have eroded badly—to the point where some would say they have been erased completely. Hardly any facet of the multiple concerns of and relationships involved with our society's primary unit, the family, have escaped public scrutiny, debate, legislative enactments, and court cases. Other social institutions have experienced a similar fate. Witness the politicized position in which private institutions of higher education, our religious bodies, the great foundations, and even some of our fraternal and athletic associations now find themselves. How much this trend is a product of the progressive weakening of many of these institutions and how much it hinges on radically transformed concepts of individual rights and of the "police power" of governments is open to debate. But it is unarguable that the orbit of what is political and public has expanded massively since the mid-sixties.

All Issues Are National

Paralleling this proliferating politicization of heretofore private-sector concerns and issues has been the steady erosion of any real distinctions between what is a state and local issue and what is a federal concern. The last genuine efforts to debate and define national purposes and aid programs in a constitutional context took place in the fifties and early sixties. The 1964 presidential contest was the last in which such questions were raised prominently in a national campaign, and the outcome of that election did much to end the need to defend, rationalize, or attack new federal-assistance efforts with any specific reference to the expressed (or implied) powers stipulated in Article I, Section 8 of the U.S. Constitution.[7]

Part of that election's result, of course, was the enactment of a wide range of aid programs by the 89th and 90th congresses, several of which involved wholly new departures for the national government and some of which were novel to any government. While many of these were relatively direct in their program thrusts and limited in their scope and appropriations, the "legitimacy barrier," to use Wilson's phrase, had fallen. Hence, subsequent actions in these program areas, while frequently more expansive, intrusive, and specialized—really quite novel and presumably controversial—were not viewed as major departures from the largely collaborative and simple purposes of the initial legislation. They were treated largely as mere extensions of the original enactments. Witness the extraordinary evolution of the federal role in primary and secondary education, rehabilitation, fire protection, and the environment (to cite only a few of the most obvious program areas) since the mid-sixties.

In terms of federal activities, this led, in the seventies, to a steady expansion of grant enactments (more than 150 new grants), to plunges into more subfunctional (and even sub-subfunctional) program areas, to new regulatory thrusts via the grant device, to sustained efforts to stimulate greater state and local program and personnel endeavors, and to greater efforts to achieve greater supervisory authority. In terms of roles, it produced a situation wherein a reading of even a few issues of the *Congressional Record* would highlight a range of items that would span those of a neighborhood, municipal, or county council to those of a state legislature and the U.N. General Assembly—with the concerns of a national legislative body occasionally sandwiched in. From potholes to national health insurance, these were and are the bounds of the national government's current domestic agenda.

A New Interest-Group Politics

Not unrelated to these latitudinarian changes in the scope of what is "public" and what is "national" are equally pronounced shifts in the interest-group basis of American politics. From Madison and Calhoun to Drucker and Fisher (and among political scientists from Arthur Bentley in the first decade of this century to Earl Latham and David Truman in the fifties and sixties), the primary role of interest groups as the crucial conditioner of the American political system has been emphasized, analyzed, sometimes criticized, and sometimes idealized. But all that was written on the topic before the mid-sixties now seems dated, if not dubious.

But why? Certainly, there has been no decline in the paramount role of pressure-group politics. The answer, of course, is that the bases and nature of this special (and traditional) brand of politics recently have undergone such extreme alterations that the contemporary politics of pressure groups bears only a faint resemblance to its predecessor of less than a generation ago. In the earlier period, only those interests that were large, organized, and relatively well financed were able to pay the price of participating in national politics, and this meant that those representing basic economic forces (i.e., business, labor, agriculture, and medicine) tended to dominate this scene. Today, all this has changed. There has been, as economic historian Douglas C. North has phrased it, "a drastic reduction in the cost of using the political process," and all manner of groups have taken advantage of the cheaper price.[8]

The new arrivals may not occupy the spacious quarters that house the traditionals. But they can usually muster enough support to rent a modest suite or perhaps only a single office, which frequently is all that is needed operationally to mount an effective campaign. This, of course, does not hold for groups whose interests and areas of action are multiple, but for the new breed of largely-single-issue pressure group, such accommodations can be perfectly adequate.

It is the advent, then, of this newer type of pressure group concerned with largely social, moral, and environmental topics along with the growing proliferation of programmatic groups (paralleling the enactment of more and more excessively specific categoricals), and the final arrival of all the generalist intergovernmental groups (including the towns and townships)—that has created the impression (and the reality) of contemporary Washington awash with specialized interests. It is this development that produced more than one hundred pages of fine print in a recent *Congressional Record* listing registered lobbyists.

What has propelled them to that small enclave on the Potomac? The national politicization of nearly all issues (cited earlier) is one basic factor. Another, of course, is the ever-present lure of federal money, especially during the earlier period of rapidly escalating federal outlays to states and localities and to nonprofit bodies. Yet another is the easier access to and greater responsiveness of congressional members and the relatively easy access to courts (thanks to class-action suits and fee-splitting as well as to the activism of the judiciary itself). The need to deal with and help shape accelerating administrative actions—whether of a regulatory, rule-making, programmatic, or fiscal character—also must be numbered among Washington's magnetic points. For some, it is because Washington beckoned, that is, created a program or regulation that gave them a job and a policy to protect and defend. In short, with the national government's assumption of the roles of basic policy-maker, first (if not last) resort funder, master regulator, chief arbiter, and prime mouthpiece for our civic morality, all groups having a concern in any of these areas will come. And nearly all have, as the office building boom in Washington (not to mention the telephone directory) attests.

This pulverizingly pluralistic, highly variegated pattern of interest-group politics clearly is in marked contrast to the older pattern. So are its goals and mode of operation. The old interest-group goals of subsidies, favorable regulations and court decisions, preferential tax programs, as well as program (typically categorical) enactments and expanded reenactments (as well as earmarks) have not disappeared. They merely are shared by a greater number of more diverse groups. Many of the later arrivals, however, have still other objectives, including the advancement of certain social objectives by conditions attached to grant programs and to procurement, the establishment of executive branch agencies and units based on demographic—not economic—characteristics of our population, the promotion of procedures in governmental and intergovernmental bureaucracies that ostensibly will sensitize them to one or more pet concerns of pressure groups, the promotion of greater public visibility, and the achieving of better access to new funding sources as well as to the national media.

The near eclipse of the party mechanisms in and out of Congress; the frequently fluctuating, yet steadily issue-oriented mood of the electorate; along with the easier access to the presidency, bureaucracy, Congress, and the courts (when compared to the closed-door, or partially so, conditions of a generation ago) combined to provide expanded opportunities for pressure-group campaigns of either the single- or multi-issue variety. Above all, perhaps, hardly any of these groups now can be discounted as irrelevant, unimportant, or irresponsible, since practically all of them (even if their formal membership base is narrow to nonexistent) can claim fairly accurately (thanks to the polls) that some portion of public opinion supports their particular position. Few Washington politicians in this age of freshman and sophomore senators, congressmen, and department heads are willing openly to controvert their respective claims.

The current interest-group scene in Washington is a not-too-cloudy mirror image of the profuse specialized pluralism of the nation as a whole. For some, this is as it should be, in that countervailing forces have been established to negate the actions of the traditional establishment interests. For others, the national government has become not an object of interest-group politics, with party and presidents serving as mediators and brokers, but the interest-group state, with no force capable of transcending or curbing the pressure groups.

Representation and Representatives

Representation, as a principle of American federalism, and our national representatives, as the people's delegates in Washington, also have experienced major changes since the early sixties, as some of the foregoing analysis suggests. These changes form a third political dynamic that needs some explanation.

Perhaps the most important shift in the representational concept is the growing popular habit of rejecting the legitimacy of the very process by which representatives are selected. Despite populist-oriented efforts to democratize these processes in both the presidential and congressional arenas, the low voter turnouts and the growing awareness of the influence of appointed national officials and of intermediate interest groups have combined to cast a long shadow of doubt over the significance and representativeness of these electoral contests. Hence, the greater aggressiveness of interest-group activity, the ill-concealed contempt on the part of some (as well as of the public-at-large) for Congress, the increasingly skeptical view of the president's role as tribune of the people, and the much steadier focus by nearly all on the administrative process and access to it.

Elections, of course, are not ignored, but they now are only one facet of any group's effort to influence the national government. Some would say this has been the case at least since the thirties. The progressive erosion in the past decade of the electoral processes, others would emphasize, has undermined the authoritativeness and legitimacy of both of the national government's political branches and the efficacy of the representational principle in our federative republican system. This recent trend, they stress, has helped encourage the kind of interest-group intrusion described above and generated the current tendency (seemingly on the part of everyone—save the administrators) to blame the federal bureaucrats for just about everything that is bungled, burdensome, or blatantly unresponsive (from the perspective of the various critics) in the system. In short, for these observers, all interests in Washington lay claim to being "representative" of some group and the formal, duly elected representatives of the people are having increasing difficulty in asserting a superior, more legitimate claim to that designation.

The changed behavior of members of Congress, these critics stress, illustrates this leveling development in detail. The rapid escalation in retirements (caused as much by the decline in psychic rewards as by the hike in pensions), the increasingly important but overloaded ombudsman role of all members vis-à-vis the bureaucracy and especially the maze of grant programs, the decline of the apprenticeship norm and the growing habit of more and more members assuming positions on a wide and frequently eclectic range of public issues, the steady advance of legislative staff influence, and the easier rise to media prominence on the part of many very junior members—these are but a few of the recent signs of a marked shift in the behavior of individual members.

Some analysts now find a greater degree of ideological voting on the part of senators and congressmen, who are generally much more coherently issue oriented than their rank-and-file constituents. But other observers note the easy pragmatism of many members reflected in the new ways and means of helping to assure reelection (i.e., the new ombudsman role; the personal platform that covers an array of social, moral, and economic concerns; the avoidance of depth and the eagerness for breadth in issue coverage; as well as the now favorite habit of running against the institution that they collectively form—the Congress). For these students of national affairs, then, there is a wide gap between some of the campaign rhetoric and floor speeches and votes, which appear to be more issue conditioned, and other more pragmatic campaign efforts and floor actions, as well as day-to-day activities. This gap, they believe, reveals some basic flaws in the theory that congressional members have become more cohesively issue oriented, hence more responsible and presumably more representative of the real concerns of their constituents.

In a very real sense, the members probably are as representative of their constituents as their predecessors of a generation ago, but not because they adhere to a more coherent ideological course. Instead, it is the very welter of diverse issues that cuts across the ideological spectrum that is the raw ideational material with which they must cope. Widely conflicting interest group and constituency pressures now are brought to bear on them. Hence the widely perceived image of growing member independency, of balky freshmen, of few sure votes, of more and more informal caucuses with overlapping membership, and of the growing difficulties of the congressional leadership despite the presence of very able leaders. Hence the decline on grant reauthorization votes of wide margins of difference between Republicans and Democrats.[9]

The people's formal representatives in the Congress today clearly have an infinitely more complicated task in discharging their representational function than their predecessors in the fifties or early sixties. Their constituencies are larger and much more heterogeneous; today's issues are much more panoramic and cross-cutting; Washington-based interest groups are much more numerous and assertive; and the formal and informal (party) changes in Congress along with the relative lack of tenure on the part of a majority of the members have left most of them in an embarrassingly exposed position. And all this in an era that questions some of the basic assumptions of the representational principle itself.

Changes in Lawmaking

A fourth fundamental shift since the mid-sixties is reflected in the process and product of current national decisionmaking. The process, of course, is one that has become heavily overburdened. The expanding concerns of the national government, the volume of reauthorizations along with the near-habitual tendency now to add specialized subfunctional programs and to dictate administration and sometimes regulations, not to mention the need to consider legislation in entirely new areas, have combined to form a legislative process that gives only a hint of keeping up with the dynamics now built into it.

Complaints abound in the cloakrooms regarding not knowing what is involved in a vote, the pace of legislative activity, and the excessive demands on a member's time and private life. Abbreviated debates, and sometimes no real debate at all, on what a generation ago would have triggered a filibuster in the Senate or resorting to "dilatory actions" in the House are now a familiar part of the deliberations of both bodies. Despite greater staff, legislative oversight over the past decade generally has been sporadic, if not specious, with only a handful of subcommittees taking seriously their responsibilities in this crucial area.

What is more, the process, in effect, now involves two contrasting approaches, as was suggested earlier. The first involves consideration of entirely new public issues. Here, ideology, questions of the appropriate federal role, veto-group politics, minoritarian procedural protections, and delay still come into play.

The second approach involves renewals and reauthorizations. Here, those pressure groups actually or potentially caught up with the program (or its general functional area), affected administrators and recipients, and the range of interests on the substantive and funding committees (or subcommittees) and sometimes a president and a secretary are at work. Questions of legitimacy, overall direction, and impact rarely are raised. Instead, the size of outlays, to whom, under what conditions, and, above all, what more is needed to establish a solid coalition for reenactment—these are the issues that dominate this now major portion of national lawmaking.

The politics of cooption, then, are paramount in this renewal phase of the process. Hardly a specialized interest or particularistic issue subsumed under the functional area affected by a reauthorization is ignored, and final votes on the typically omnibus measure usually exceed the two-thirds mark with little evidence of partisanship, ideology, or mere issue-orientation reflected in its passage. Instead, the numerous titles, the mandated procedures and conditions, and the new range of specialized and general beneficiaries of the multifaceted measure are such that even the most myopic can discern the cooptive process at work therein. Old-style veto-group politics in these instances have been replaced with a new-style (but not totally unfamiliar) brand of logrolling. Recent enactments in the primary and secondary education, vocational rehabilitation, and public health areas are but a few of the case studies that can be cited that dramatically demonstrate the distinctly cooptive and congressionally dominated traits of second- and third-generation domestic policymaking at the national level.

What product results from this process? In a word, *hyperlexis,* to borrow Manning's term.[10] What has resulted is a "pathological condition caused by an overactive lawmaking gland," as Manning defines it, and nowhere is this condition more acute than at the national level. The fundamental changes in political ideas and issues, in the interest-group basis of contemporary national politics, in our understanding of the representational principle, in the behavior of our representatives, and in the national legislative process provide a set of causal explanations as to how this condition emerged.

The immediate effects of this transformed process have been a clogging of our court dockets, sometimes an expansion of administrative discretion beyond any recognizable statutory parameters, and sometimes such a severe constraining of administrators as to make them not much more than recording secretaries of the Congress. They generally have led to assigning near impossible implementation tasks (frequently merging program execution, regulation, and quasi-adjudicatory roles in one mandate) to federal executives, while rarely authorizing adequate personnel to carry out all of the mandates. Intergovernmentally, they have confounded the roles, interrelationships, and varying servicing systems of the states, their localities, and the private sector, thanks to the growing popularity of "pinwheel federalism"[11] in Washington and among substate governments.

The politics of posturing has replaced the politics of fair play and common sense, and this raises continually the specter of a huge promise-performance gap that far exceeds the ones that allegedly existed in the late sixties. Functionally, at the national level this hyperlexis has produced grant statutes that deal with practically every aspect of what used to be deemed wholly state or local (or even private) program concerns, with nearly every activity of domestic American government burdensomely intergovernmentalized as a result. Fiscally, it has generated, in this decade, rapid increases in direct federal expenditures and in assistance outlays that have surpassed the rate of growth of the Johnson years with a stimulative—not a substitutive or mere supportive—effect on state and local expenditures and personnel at least through 1972 and an unfathomable effect since then. Above all, perhaps, the political fallout from this phenomenon has produced congestion in the political and administrative processes of the national government as well as those at the state and local levels.

The Implementation Issue: An Area of Continuities

Even with these major changes in political ideas and attitudes, in interest-group politics, in representation and congressional behavior, and in the policymaking, fiscal, and political areas, the dysfunctional traits of contemporary American federalism would not be as widespread and as worrisome if some strands of stand-pattism also were not present. Where then have there been *no* basic changes since 1960? The critical cluster of static attitudes and practices are found in the area of national policy implementation. They include:

——no real expansion in the size of the federal bureaucracy and any shift in the presidential and congressional desires (regardless of political orientation) to keep it comparatively small,

even though an enormous number of new assignments have
been mandated to it;

——no real change in the relying almost exclusively on grants-in-
aid as about the only instrumentality for carrying out the national government's prime domestic servicing responsibilities;[12]

——no shift in the congressional and presidential view that using
state and local governments and administrators to carry out
even the most "national" of programs is cheap, convenient,
clever, and a curb on the federal bureaucracy;

——no real erosion of the dominance of the old public administration approach to federal grant administration, which held that
with proper conditions and adequate sanctions state and local
administrators can be included in a "chain of command"
whose pyramidal peaks are in the federal departments and
agencies (if not in Congress);

——no shift in the belief of liberals that with the right formula
and/or the right administrator, equity can be promoted and
targeting achieved; and

——no essential change in the difficulty of most conservatives to
comprehend and to criticize effectively this overloaded system.

These standpat attitudes and approaches to program implementation stand in stark contrast to the dynamic expansion in national
public agenda items, in the pluralistic base of pressure-group politics, in representation and national representativeness, and in the
legislative process. Panoramic, pulverized, pondering, and prodi-
gious are but a few of the adjectives that have described each of
the latter but not the continuing attitudes regarding implementation. Here, caution, constraint, and a kind of conservatism come
into play.

Yet the combination of the traditional approach to program
implementation and the dynamically different ones in the more
overtly political areas provides another fundamental reason for the
dysfunctional condition of today's system. For it is the combination of an endlessly proliferating national policy agenda and an
interest-group-dominated enactment process, with the steady reliance in nearly all cases on subnational instrumentalities for the
program implementation, that provides the basic reason for the
serious questions regarding administrative effectiveness, economic

efficacy, equity, and political accountability now being raised about the system's operations.

THE CURRENT DILEMMA

There is a growing popular reaction to these negative results, however. As the dynamics of recent change have manifested themselves more clearly and as the questionable results of a dysfunctional federal system have become more apparent, opinion polls have recorded soaring popular dissatisfaction with the federal income tax, with the effectiveness of the national government's program efforts, and with the trustworthiness of its leaders (and Watergate by no means explains these continuing trends).[13] In very real terms, the electorate has sensed intuitively that the system is "out of hand," that there is no one at the throttle, that seemingly there is no throttle.

In a broad sense, Proposition 13 and its offspring elsewhere are one manifestation of this pervasive sentiment. Another, of course, is the drive for a balanced federal budget through constitutional or statutory means. Still another is the battle to reduce federal revenues as means of forcing expenditure reductions. The continuing campaign for "sunset" legislation, more austere presidential budgets, and the greater seriousness with which many members now view and participate in the congressional budget process provide additional evidence of Washington's awareness of this popular criticism.

Embedded in all of these approaches (save for "sunset") is the assumption that greater fiscal constraint will restore popular confidence in the national government's sensibility and self-control. Their advocates, however, divide basically into two camps on ways of achieving this end. One group, of course, deems the constitutional amendment approach the only reliable method of instilling discipline in what they feel to be an undisciplined, easy majority decisionmaking process. In support of their argument, this band of *constitutional fiscal revisionists* enunciates a new version of Calhoun's concurrent majoritarianism, arguing that the greater power today of special interests, the hyperresponsiveness of Congress, and the breakdown of the old system of internal constraints necessitate a constitutional solution to what they consider a major systemic defect. Statutory and procedural alternatives are rejected on grounds that the political forces and the easy-to-build simple majority coalitions that have produced the repelling record of budget deficits will undo any such minor reforms at the first opportune moment (i.e., once popular pressure relaxes). With a required two-thirds vote for an unbalanced federal budget, old-style veto-group politics would reappear, they contend. Hence, a formal constitutional resolution is needed to restore the concurrent majoritarian political principle to its former operational vigor.

The other group of fiscal conservatives rejects the amendment remedy as being too drastic, too rigid, and too oblivious of real world corrective forces that already are at work in the system. This group of *incremental fiscal critics* condemns the constitutional approach as being radical and risky: radical in the sense that an amendment should not be used as a means of correcting an essentially political problem that already is on the way to being solved; and risky in that—in the case of the constitutional convention approach—our basic charter in its entirety would be up for potential revision.[14] They also attack the rigidity of the proposed remedy, stressing its potentially disastrous effects in times of recession and of crisis (even though some of the proposed amendments afford special opportunities to surmount such difficulties).

Equally important, many in this group emphasize, is that political and procedural factors already are at work that negate the need for any careless (and costly in terms of the national interest) tinkering with the Constitution. In effect, they find in some of the political dynamics, which the constitutional amendment advocates condemn, the means of achieving greater fiscal responsibility. Washington's greater responsiveness, the greater ease in establishing an interest-group base there, and the new-style pragmatism and eclectic voting behavior of many representatives and senators have become, for this group, the practical bases for effectuating incremental, yet important, ways of reducing the deficits and curbing growth.

President Carter's recent "no growth" (in terms of inflation) budgets, the 1980 congressional debates on expanding the debt and especially on the first budget resolution, the fiscal conservatism of many of the junior members (regardless of their ideological or party label), the recently acquired retrenchment belief of some of the seniors, the renewed aggressiveness of existing and recently arrived new economy-minded groups, and even the tenor of some of the campaign oratory in 1980 are cited to support the contention that the system still is restrained, responsive, and responsible. Some in this group also stress that the votes on the budget resolutions force a new kind of riveted congressional attention to overall fiscal actions and these help to undercut the spendthrift ethic that seemingly (if not actually) dominates the reauthorization process. Countervailing forces of fiscal constraint, then, are emerging, so their basic argument runs, and reasonable, nondisruptive remedies to the dilemma of deficits will be forthcoming. For these incremental fiscal reformers, then, the system is still constrained, cooptive politics is not pervasive or paramount, and the informal, not the rigidly formal, Calhoun is still the ideal gentleman with whom to associate.

Apart from these two schools of reformist opinion, however, stands a third—one that believes that the others are dealing largely with symptoms, not the real sickness. Most in this group, including this writer, concede that heavy federal outlays and deficits are important national issues, but they warn that an exclusive preoccupation with them in no way addresses the malady of an overloaded system. For them, recent political developments have helped produce a new, feebly functioning, poorly programmed, badly managed, inadequately accountable nonsystem of intergovernmental relations, which also happens to be expensive. They point out that today's nonsystem represents the national government's primary efforts in the domestic arena and that budget cutting is only one of many weapons that must be utilized if some semblance of management, some hint of cost effectiveness, and some signs of political accountability in it are to be regained.

Budget cuts, they point out, need not involve a sorting out of the effective from the ineffective programs. They need not engender a debate or a decision over what is genuinely a national concern. They need not enforce a greater discipline on cooptive politics and on interest groups that have the habit of always seeking more. They need not involve anything more than across-the-board proportional cuts with no reassessment of national priorities, no gauging of the real impact of programs, and no weighing of the actual (and potential) fiscal/servicing positions of the states, their localities, and the private sector.

These critics of the current federal role in the federal system clearly focus as much on critical managerial, programmatic, structural, political, and basic attitudinal concerns as they do on money matters. If the running debate over deficits generates some grant consolidations, helps eliminate doubtful, if not debilitating, programs, restrains the tendency to run amok with regulations, and restores the capacity to deny funds to the fanciful, the foolish, and the freeloaders, then for them, some real reforms will have been achieved. Put differently, if the debate triggers a sober sorting out of what managerially, fiscally, and ethically is within the reasonable and realistic reach of the national government, then, in their view, some of the most enervating effects of recent political developments will have been checked.

Will the emerging countervailing forces of constraint be powerful enough and penetrating enough to go beyond the basics of budgets to rebuilding the system itself? This is the key question these *antidysfunctional federalists* pose. If these deeper issues are avoided, they fear, it makes little difference which of the fiscal alternatives prevails.

Yet the present climate of discontent is a good one in which to raise the systemic questions. The issue, after all, is partly a money matter, but it is more than this. The system itself is in question. Its traditional and much vaunted traits of functionality and flexibility are at stake. Whether a national-interest state can be substituted for the special-interest state hangs heavily on whether the American people, their parties, and their leaders can achieve a shift in attitudes and approaches to national agenda issues, to the role of elected national officials, and to program enactments and executions as dramatic as, but different from, those that evolved over the past decade and a half. Out of this might emerge a new consensus, a new public philosophy that will provide the "social glue" that now seems to be the chief political function of grants-in-aid and many regulations.

NOTES TO CHAPTER 8

1. See Angus Campbell, et al., *The American Voter, An Abridgement* (New York: John Wiley and Sons, 1964).

2. Austin Ranney and Willmoore Kendall, *Democracy and the American Party System* (New York: Harcourt, Brace & World, 1956), p. 471.

3. Much of the following analysis appeared in the author's "Constitutional Revision, Incremental Retrenchment or Real Reform: An Analysis of Current Efforts to Curb Federal Growth," *The Bureaucrat* 9, no. 1 (Spring 1980): 35-47.

4. James Q. Wilson, "American Politics, Then and Now," *Commentary* 67, no. 2 (February 1979): 40.

5. Ibid., p. 40.

6. Ibid.

7. The 1980 contest produced a few replays of the earlier one, but non-intergovernmental issues tended to obscure them.

8. Quoted in ibid., p. 41.

9. See Advisory Commission on Intergovernmental Relations, *The Condition of Contemporary Federalism: Conflicting Theories and Collapsing Constraints* (Report A-78) (Washington, D.C.: U.S. Government Printing Office, 1981), chap. 3.

10. Bayless Manning, "Hyperlexis: Our National Disease," appearing in the *Congressional Record*, 16 March 1978, pp. S3948-52.

11. This metaphor arises from the emergence of direct federal links to practically all subnational governments and the tendency to accord equal treatment to all public interest groups, regardless of their functional and jurisdictional positions within the fifty state-local fiscal/servicing systems.

12. Medicare and the SSI program are the only basic exceptions to this generalization.

13. *Public Opinion* 3, no. 4 (August/September 1980): 8-40.

14. Efforts to flesh out this option provided in Article V of the U.S. Constitution and to regularize as well as to restrict the resulting process date back to 1967 and the pioneering work of former senator Sam Ervin. Bills now pending that would achieve these goals include S. 3 and H.R. 1664 (96th Congress).

9

Epilogue

This has been a chronicle of the collapse of key constraints in the system, the continuing strength of certain political attitudes and intergovernmental approaches, and the concomitant evolution from a dual, to a cooperative, thence to the overloaded, dysfunctional, federalism of the present. Eight kinds of "overload" have been identified and probed.

THE OVERLOADS

There is a *judicial overload* involving the state-local as well as the federal courts, stemming from judicial activism, the full emergence of the courts as attractive arenas for "lobbying," changes in judicial rules that encourage such efforts, and the multiplication of loosely drawn, conflicting, and frequently regulating congressional grant enactments—to cite the more obvious reasons for the clogged condition of courts' dockets.

There is a *fiscal overload* that is reflected in the steady increase in the combined tax burden imposed on families by federal-state-local levies, in the rising outlays for federal programs whose potential costs were rarely gauged initially, in the rise in the number of entitlement enactments and of popular demands for more services, in the overly sanguine assumptions about the productivity and health of the American economy and of the federal income tax, and in the reliance on governmental, especially grant-in-aid, solutions to social and governmental problems for

251

which more difficult and politically more unpopular responses would have been (and are) more appropriate and, in some cases, less costly.

There is a *servicing overload* symbolized by the mushrooming federal-assistance package wherein a narrow band of clearly national programs, a larger group of uncontestably intergovernmental, and a wide range of formerly and narrowly state-local and private undertakings now are included. The extent to which the budgets of most governments at all levels now include large intergovernmentally funded sectors is merely the most obvious fiscal manifestation of this. Moreover, as frequently as not, federal-aid programs blithely ignore the varying functional assignment patterns within the fifty systems and some of the federal-local grants wrongly assume that most cities, most counties, and most towns perform the same kind of functions and that they rarely interact with one another fiscally or functionally. And these, too, have contributed to burdening state and local servicing systems.

There is an *administrative overload*. Witness the attempt by the national government to "supervise" various of the undertakings of sixty-three thousand subnational governments. Witness the effort of eight to nine hundred thousand federal administrators and employees to run "programs" that are actually administered by about twelve million state and local civil servants under separate personnel, pay, and administrative systems. Witness the continuing, and increasingly futile, incremental efforts by presidents to improve grants' management by relying on reorganizations, new budgeting techniques, and administrative circulars. Witness the perennial federal tendency to ignore the stark administrative fact that five hundred programs are involved here, that their peculiar requirements are largely a product of congressional dictates, and that nobody but a thin and ever-bending band of generalists—both elected and appointive—is really interested in across-the-board grants' management reforms. Witness the dilemma of state elected officials, who are expected to and are attempting to "coordinate" and "plan" big, largely intergovernmentally funded (both from federal and their own sources) programs when specialists and their agencies are strengthened by most federal grant conditions. Witness the federal-aid encouragement of special districts and of single-purpose regional planning units. And witness the separatist impact of aid programs on the already heavily fragmented jurisdictional pattern of local government and most of their internal structures.

There also is a *regulatory overload*, with both the federal and state governments enacting direct mandates on lower levels of government, with both relying on conditional grants as the overwhelmingly predominant means of achieving intergovernmental fiscal transfers, and with some three score crosscutting conditions now appended to most federal-aid programs. A new era of regulation thus has emerged—one that evolved in a piecemeal, unpremeditated fashion and that seeks to achieve national and state purposes by dictating the behavior of lower-level units of government—unlike earlier efforts, which focused chiefly on the private sector and utilized the independent regulatory commission device, not grants-in-aid, to achieve their policy goals.

There clearly is a *political overload*. Parties have become pale replicas of their not-so-authoritative former selves; procedural reforms within Congress and the conventions, while ostensibly geared to achieving greater responsiveness, better representation, and real accountability, have further segmented the parties and encouraged greater interest-group activity. Functional, social, and moralistic pressure groups as well as economic have grown in strength and numbers, and they have helped to create more programs and regulations, while some have been created by them.

Most of these groups have joined to help frustrate basic grant reform (consolidations and devolution), to thwart the generalists in the system, and to convert the national government itself into a conglomerate of special interests. The political branches of the national government—symbolized by a demythologized presidency with meager managerial powers in fact, but with a clear capacity to utilize the federal grant, regulatory, and promotional undertakings for political purposes and by a Congress that is hyperresponsive to and a creator of organized interests—no longer appear to possess the capacity or the procedures to transcend these specialized pressures, thus ignoring Madison's admonition as to the basic role of the national government.

An old-style, but vastly invigorated veto-group politics dominates consideration of major new policy initiatives, but a new style of cooptive politics (based on a contemporary adaptation of traditional logrolling) assures fairly easy renewals of earlier program enactments—renewals that frequently contain significant new departures, new regulations, and new functionally related programs. The interest-group basis of American politics, then, clearly has been expanded massively—to the point where the territorial representational strength of subnational governments has been nearly eclipsed despite the strong supportive efforts of the generalist intergovernmental lobby. The political branches of the national government, the political processes that fill the elective positions within them, the policies that emanate from them, and their intergovernmental implementation have been nearly overwhelmed by technocratic, programmatic, and single-purpose forces. And this constitutes a form of political overload that the system never encountered before.

There undeniably is an *intellectual overload* of the electorate and of elected officials, and both are brighter than their predecessors of a generation ago. A federative republic that is rooted in democratic principles by its very nature cannot be a simple, easily comprehended system. But the bewildering complexity, confusion, and incessant changes in the contemporary system baffle most significant policymakers in Washington almost as greatly as they do the citizenry-at-large. And when a system that is largely incomprehensible—even in its most basic operations—to the electorate also is becoming more demanding of tax revenues, more dysfunctional, and more unaccountable, that system is in trouble. Hence the low public esteem for politicians, politics, and parties and the meager confidence in government (especially the federal government), its programs, and the political processes that are supposed to legitimize both.

Finally, there is a *philosophic overload* that undergirds the attitudinal and nearly all of the other more obvious manifestations of the system's overload. The public philosophy of the early sixties encompassed a cluster of conflicting concepts: the old Jeffersonian theory of the negative state and the new liberal idea of the positive state, the traditional doctrine of dual federalism and the recently enunciated theory of cooperative federalism, the primacy of the individual as well as the predominant role of intermediary groups in society, the economy, and politics, and government by limited majority rule as well as government by supermajorities. These many conflicting dimensions of the public philosophy of 1960 suggest that an intellectual overloading already had occurred by then, but the several inconsistencies were not all that burdensome or bewildering. There was after all a social ethic, shared by most of the citizenry, that provided the necessary bond of societal, if not systemic, cohesion—an ethic that stressed opportunity, endeavor, achievement, and practicality.

During the past two decades, the inconsistencies in the earlier public philosophy have become much more apparent—especially with the eager scrapping of most of the arguments for and lingering manifestations of the old negative state concept, with the nearly total erosion of dual federalism as an operational principle, and with the simultaneous and totally conflicting strengthening of the individualistic as well as of the interest-group impulses. Moreover, the conventional civic ethic of the early sixties was rent asunder during the late sixties and early seventies, with all of the traditional social values being debated, rejected by some, and reformulated by others.

The lack of any coherent public philosophy and the shattering of the traditional and widely shared social ethic have generated the greatest overload of both the system and the electorate. It has helped give rise, after all, to the current political climate wherein moderation has been succeeded by intemperate approaches to issues, individuals, and interests; where accommodation has given way to interpersonal, intergroup, and interlevel confrontation; where restraint has been replaced with unrestrained individual and factional assertiveness; and where the earlier brand of pragmatism that linked workability to institutional and social results has acquired a much stronger competitor in the form of a pragmatism that emphasizes short-term, narrowly political, positive results and ignores long-term societal and systemic consequences. These shifts in political attitudes, ideas, style, and goals have not only generated their own very special kind of intellectual and methodological overload, they also have provided the raw materials out of which most of the other systemic overloads were fashioned.

REVISITING MUNCIE

In the final analysis, however, it is necessary to return to communities like Muncie to gauge the impact of these overloads. Huge amounts of federal dollars flowed into Muncie in the last decade, four times more than the city's fathers realized when confronted with the figures. With this flood of federal aid and transfer payments came a city budget—a majority of whose revenues come from intergovernmental sources (68 percent of which was federal in 1975)—a rise in local grantsmanship efforts, a decline in the role of traditional local politicians, a skewing of local budget priorities, an increase in local agency autonomy and in the number of "paragovernments" within and around the city's formal governmental structure, a recognition that noncompliance with grant regulations need not produce much more than a minor reprimand, and a personal dependency that few would have envisioned in the late thirties.[1]

The intergovernmentalizing of Muncie, then, has produced:

——a decline in fiscal autonomy and a concomitant decline in the discretion of local policymakers;
——an increase in agency proliferation and in agency autonomy as well;
——an expansion in vertical programmatic linkages and in vertical lines of ostensible bureaucratic accountability;
——a decline in old-style community-based (or territorial) politics and in local political accountability; and
——above all, perhaps, a rapid growth in resentment against government generally and Washington in particular on the part of nearly all Munsonians, regardless of socioeconomic background, even as their individual and collective reliance on outside assistance also increased.

One way or another, all of these manifestations of the intergovernmentalization of nearly all aspects of Muncie's public life suggest the triumph of vertical functional (and regulatory) forces over the traditional horizontal and territorial. And to compound the dilemma, the ideal of government within the minds and hearts of most Munsonians still is that of the old negative state and of a dual-federalist system, just as it was for their forebears in the twenties and the late thirties. Here, then, is one of the ultimate ironies of the failure of national activist and cooperative federalist thinkers to develop and gain popular acceptance of a principled, not just a pragmatic, basis for governmental and intergovernmental interventionism. For as both concepts triumphed operationally, they still are rejected attitudinally and philosophically.

IS A FUNCTIONAL FEDERALISM FEASIBLE?

Muncie may not be wholly typical of the electorate-at-large, especially in the extent of its devotion to the old public philosophy. Yet the yawning gap between governmental theory and practice in Muncie exists in much of the nation as well. And this chasm is the ultimate manifestation of systemic overload and the most dependable index of dysfunctionality in a democratic system.

As was noted in the previous chapter, inconsistencies and ambiguities have been a famous, if not fortuitous, feature of our political tradition and system. But when they reach the point of a near total separation of ideality from reality, as they have presently, then the system and its citizens are in deep trouble.

The cure, of course, is to narrow the gap between theory and practice by modifying one or the other, or preferably both. Actual practice suggests that:

1. The federal government is the prime promotional, regulating, banking, and brokering agent in the system.
2. The states, partly through their own efforts and partly because of what has been thrust upon them from above and below, are now the prime middleman supervisors, coordinators, and partial bankers of large, chiefly intergovernmentally funded programs, but they also are resilient though differentiated representatives of fifty varying political systems—systems that are more accountable, accessible, and competitive than they ever have been, thanks ironically to federal judicial actions on reapportionment and congressional actions on voting rights.
3. The localities, despite a recent flurry of functional transfers upward, are still the prime direct service providers in the system, though they are increasingly constrained by higher-level dictates and grant conditions, due in part to their growing dependence on federal and state aid.

These are the functional roles that the traditional levels of government actually have assumed within the system. Collectively, they suggest the need for more humility and less pretense at "running" things on the federal part, a greater recognition of what now is expected fiscally and managerially of the states, and a resolution of the quandary in which most localities now find themselves—as direct implementors of federally instigated, of state-mandated and -nurtured, and of traditional local services, with little to no capacity to figure out what their basic role should entail.

Reality involves more than the discovering "who is doing what"; it also covers "who is paying for what." And the growing gap between the actual performers (the localities and the states), on the one hand, and the real funders and regulators (the federal government and increasingly the states), on the other, is, of course, the chief reason that the rough, but nonetheless functional, division of labor outlined above is not easily recognized or accepted. The financiers, after all, are unwilling to forego the pleasure of directing things, even though they are ill equipped to do it. This growing separation of governmental funding from governmental servicing is symbolized by the excessive use of conditional grants. Efforts on the part of disbursing governments to bridge this gap are reflected in mandates, conditions, and more grants and on the part of many recipient governments and agencies by launching a lobbying operation in Washington, with the program people, not the elected officials, usually being the more successful. Both the center and the extremities thus are "stimulated" programmatically and fiscally and are overloaded managerially and politically. Everyone in this elliptical process appears to be concerned with everyone else's business, and this basically is why the system is becoming more and more dysfunctional.

The obvious cure, of course, is a fiscal, programmatic, and political strategy of decongestion of and some disengagement within the intergovernmental system. A much reduced reliance on intergovernmental fiscal transfers (through grant consolidations and eliminations, and through devolutions and some full program centralizations); a real curb on the unrestrained regulatory and direct mandating activities of the federal and state governments; and a clear confrontation of the negative fiscal and functional results of local government jurisdictional fragmentation are three essential components of such a strategy. But will any of these broad approaches to reform be adopted?

In light of most of the prior analyses, the response presumably should be "not likely." But certain current political trends and certain facets of our political tradition indicate that a more considered judgment of "possibly" would be just as appropriate.

In the rugged realm of politics, the widespread distrust of and disillusionment with government suggest that an attitudinal climate exists wherein restructuring proposals can at least be advanced. Moreover, the domestic fiscal retrenchment drive is not likely to diminish and this could lead to the setting of some basic fiscal and program priorities at the national level and the sloughing off of the petty, the parochial, and the patently nonnational concerns that clutter the congressional agenda.

Furthermore, there is a strong strand of doctrine in our political tradition that has not been totally submerged by recent developments and that might even gain renewed vitality as our constitutional bicentennial approaches. This, of course, involves a return to Madison and his nearly two-centuries-old counsel that the paramount task of a free government is to regulate, not be dominated by, factions; that the structure and processes of a "compound republic" must provide the institutional and political means of performing this fundamental assignment; and that narrow, aggressively assertive actions of specialized interest groups, if unchecked, will destroy the very basis of individual and group freedom.

Madison's formula for frustrating the ill effects of factions (interest groups) obviously is as relevant today as when he penned it. His is still the answer for those who would deal with interest-group politics, but seek to deny by a combination of external and internal systemic constraints the possibility and certainly the legitimacy of an "interest-group state."

Finally, the politics of domestic retrenchment and a growing awareness of our Madisonian heritage could well bring us to the point of articulating a theory of federalism that is both prescriptive for and descriptive of the system. Realism suggests that interdependencies are a fact of the latter-day twentieth century; hence, the old doctrine of dual federalism is simply that, an outdated doctrine. Pragmatism, however, suggests that the dysfunctional federalism of today, while an accurate description of current intergovernmental relations, certainly is unacceptable as a norm, since it signifies a system that does not work very well and whose dynamics will produce an even more impossible operational situation in the future.

A new functional theory obviously is needed to provide the conceptual means of narrowing the gap between intergovernmental practice and principles. Hence, it would focus on the functions of government, their funding, the functionality of the system, the sharing of some (but not all) servicing obligations, parity of the partners, the need for strong territorial representation in Washington, and the significance of constraining legislative and party procedures and processes—just as cooperative federalism did either in theory or in practice. At the same time, it would emphasize that there are necessary limits to sharing, to the extent of intergovernmental penetration, to ignoring structural and constitutional issues, and to assuming that the generalists and general governments in the system can take care of themselves and that specialists, single-issue interests, and single-purpose administrative and governmental units are no threat. The actual practice of cooperative federalism in the fifties and early sixties as well as the intergovernmental actions generated by cooperative federalism's mostly illegitimate offspring—Creative Federalism, New Federalism, and Congressional Federalism—suggest the need for these constraints.

In short, a principled though still pragmatic concept of a functioning federalism would provide a healthy modification of old intergovernmental ideas, whether of the dual or of the theoretic cooperative variety.

Such a theory also would provide both the normative rationale and the empirical explanation for some indispensable systemic reforms, since it would be partially derived from intergovernmental practices. It would indicate in more than simply programmatic and administrative terms the need for several major grant consolidations. It would underscore the necessity for full federal assumption of the funding and administration of certain functions, like welfare and unemployment compensation, because of their undeniable national nature and the heavy erosion of both the equity and administrative efficiency norms as they are presently handled in the intergovernmental realm. It would demonstrate that an array of puny, particularistic, and nonnational (save in the eyes of their respective "functional triangles") grants need to be

devolved wholly to the state or local level. It would show that in several functional areas, one or two federal policy mechanisms, not several (grants, loans, subsidies, mandates, and court decisions), are appropriate and adequate. It would pinpoint the costs, the conflicts, and the corrosive effects on the public's respect for law of a federal regulating, requiring, and mandating process that is piecemeal, proliferating, and oblivious to its overall impact on institutions and individuals. Finally, it would dramatize the need for restructuring local governments as an alternative to relying on more intergovernmental fiscal transfers and as a means of strengthening them politically, administratively, and programmatically within the federal system as a whole and within the fifty state-local servicing and funding systems.

Whether the principles of a functional federal system and the tough prescriptions that flow from them prove to be persuasive and politically acceptable hinges in large measure on whether the present deep dissatisfaction with the functioning of the system can be converted into a powerful, positive coalition for change. Only time, the electorate's behavior, and the nature of political and judicial leadership at all levels will tell.

NOTES TO CHAPTER 9

1. See Penelope C. Austin, "The Federal Presence in Middletown," a paper presented at the Annual Meeting of the American Sociological Association, San Francisco, California, 5 September 1978.

Index

Advisory Commission on Intergovernmental Relations, 84,
 118, 125
Articles of Confederation, 20,
 21, 24-26, 27, 38, 65-66,
 90

Bill of Rights, 49, 137, 140,
 143-144, 152
Burger, Warren E., 135, 136,
 139-144, 147, 151-154

Calhoun, John C., 47-48, 234,
 243, 245
Citizen tax burdens, 166-167,
 168, 170
City servicing role, 211, 212,
 213, 216, 251
Civil liberties, 70, 71, 72, 135,
 136-137, 138, 139-140,
 143, 147, 151, 152
Civil rights, 55, 71, 72, 136-
 138, 139-141, 143-144,
 147, 151-154
Colonial influences on the
 Framers, 21, 22

Commission on Intergovernmental Relations, 83
Community development block
 grant, 6, 105, 110, 177,
 180, 200
Comprehensive Employment
 and Training Act (CETA),
 6, 8, 105, 109, 110, 177,
 180, 188, 200
Congressional federalism, 101,
 107-113, 118, 123, 124,
 260
Congressional politics, 229-234,
 236-241
Constitution of 1787, 21, 26-
 43
Constitutional convention. *See*:
 Constitution of 1787
Constitutional fiscal reformers,
 119, 170, 228, 230, 243-
 244
Cooperative federalism, 16, 53,
 60, 62, 65-67, 76, 78, 84,
 86-87, 90-91, 94-95, 100,
 101, 102, 128, 136, 149,
 151, 154, 189, 226, 227,
 228, 254, 256, 260

"Cooptive politics," 111–112,
231–232, 239–241
County servicing role, 211, 212,
213, 216, 253–254
Creative federalism (Lyndon B.
Johnson), 101, 102–104,
105, 106, 107, 108, 112,
113, 120, 123, 128, 174–
175, 176, 177, 229, 230,
260

Declaration of Independence,
23–24
Distributive politics, 91–95,
111–112
Dominion theory of empire,
22–23, 26–27, 39
Dual federalism, 42, 46–47, 48–
53, 54, 55, 56, 60, 64–65,
67–69, 70, 100, 135, 136,
207, 254, 255, 256
Dysfunctional federalism (overloaded system), 5–6, 100,
111–112, 135, 149–154,
167, 173–174, 189, 192,
197, 206, 218–221, 225,
226, 240–241, 242–243,
251–255, 257–258

Elazar, Daniel J., 41, 42, 66–67

Family Assistance Plan, 106
Federal administration, 51, 64,
93, 197, 220, 240–241
Federal aid
"across the board condi-
tions", 10, 110–111, 180–
184, 198, 205, 219, 220,
253

block grants, 6, 8, 103, 105,
106, 108, 109, 110, 171–
178, 179, 199–200
"bypassing", 6–8, 12, 81–82,
89–90, 102, 109, 111, 121,
123, 176–177, 188–189,
197, 198–201, 219
categorical grants, 9, 10, 60–
62, 78–84, 103–104, 105,
106, 108, 109–110, 111,
112, 121, 123, 126, 177–
178, 199
conditions, 9, 11, 61–62, 82–
84, 105, 110–111, 112, 117,
146, 147–148, 149–150,
154, 179–185, 204–206,
253
countercyclical programs, 6,
8, 11, 108–109, 175, 177,
188
fiscal effects of grants, 10–11,
185–189, 201–203, 221,
251–252
forms of grants, 9, 52, 61, 82–
83, 103, 105, 106, 108,
109–110, 112, 123, 177–
179, 199–200, 201–202
formula grants, 8–9, 10, 61–
62, 82, 176–178, 199–200
general revenue sharing, 6, 9,
105, 108–109, 177, 179,
199, 203, 204
impact on performing services,
203, 204–206
impact on recipients, 4–5, 9–
13, 81–82, 83–84, 102–103,
112, 174–177, 187–189
impact on servicing roles,
203–206
institutional conditions, 13,
184–185, 252–253
maintenance of effort requirements 11, 185–187

matching requirements, 61, 82, 185-186

number of programs, 6, 61-62, 81, 103, 104, 109-110, 174

outlays, 7, 8-9, 51-52, 62, 79-82, 174-175, 251

"pass-through funds", 171

program thrusts, 9, 61-62, 78-81, 103, 110, 120-122, 175-176, 229, 233-234, 250

project grants, 10, 82-83, 89, 103, 177, 179, 200

recipient discretion, 9-10, 202-203

recipient program preferences, 202

special revenue sharing, 105, 106, 108

target grants, 103

"targeting", 11, 12, 103, 111-112, 113, 114, 188

Federal commerce power, 49, 50, 56, 68, 69-70, 71, 141, 143, 144, 154, 225, 226-227

Federal conditional spending power, 62, 145-151, 154, 225

Federal credit activities, 194, 197

Federal debt, 160-161

Federal deficit spending, 160-161, 225-226

Federal direct servicing activities, 192, 197, 207-210, 214-242

Federal expenditures, 64, 73-74, 159-160

Federal grants management, 105-106, 107, 109, 112, 114-118, 123, 124, 125-128, 242, 252

Federal mandates, 193, 204-206

Federal policy implementation, 241-242, 252-254

Federal preemption, 10, 138, 141, 152, 193-194

Federal promotionalism, 93-94, 194-196

Federal regional councils, 105, 116-117

Federal regulation, 56, 63-64, 68-70, 71-72, 141, 143, 154, 179-184, 193-194, 196-197, 225, 227, 228, 253

Federal revenues, 51, 57-58, 73-74, 75, 160-161, 167, 225-226

Federal role, 51-53, 63, 64-65, 70, 72, 84-86, 91-94, 151-154, 192-196, 197-206, 206-211, 225-228, 241-243, 257

Federal social security taxes, 160-161, 166-167, 226

Federal tax expenditures, 194-195, 196

Federal taxing power, 57-58, 68-69, 145

Federative theory of empire, 22-23, 25, 26-27, 39

Fourteenth amendment, 55, 56, 137, 140-141, 142, 144, 147, 152, 196, 225

Functional federalism (a reform strategy), 245-246, 256-261

Grodzins, Martin, 41, 42, 66-67

Hamilton, Alexander, 22, 23, 36, 40, 41, 47, 138

Incremental fiscal reformers,
244–245
Inflation, impact of, 162, 167–
170, 226
Intent of the Founders, 36–43
Interest group impacts, 103,
111–112, 122, 149–150,
201, 227–228, 231–232,
234–236, 239–240, 253–
254
Intergovernmental relations,
concept of, 19–20

Jefferson, Thomas, 24, 47, 48,
227, 231, 254

Local expenditures, 73–74,
159–160
Local property tax relief efforts,
165–166
Local revenues, 58–59, 60, 75,
163–165
Local role, 207–212, 212–215,
216–218, 257

Madison, James, 29, 30, 32, 35,
36, 37, 38, 39–43, 47, 48,
53, 64, 66, 89–90, 227,
228, 231, 234, 253, 259
Marshall, John, 47, 48–50
McLean, Joseph, 67
Muncie, Indiana, 3–6, 13, 65,
255–256

National Legislation process,
111–112, 149–150, 176,
239–241
National Urban Policy (Jimmy
Carter), 102, 120–122

Nationalist theories of union,
47, 49–50
Nationalization of public issues,
135, 233–234
New Deal, 65, 68–69, 78–79,
85, 91–92, 93, 103–104,
145–146, 225, 226, 227
New federalism (Richard M.
Nixon), 101, 102, 104–107,
108, 112–113, 128, 175,
177, 260
New partnership federalism
(Jimmy Carter), 101, 102,
113–123

Overloaded system. See: Dysfunctional federalism

Partnership for Health Act, 103,
110
Picket fence (bureaucratic) federalism, 101, 102, 123–128
Popular attitudes, 228, 254,
259
Proposition 13, 162, 243

Regional servicing variations,
212–213
Representation, 21, 22–24, 27–
31, 236–239, 254
Revolutionary influences on the
Framers, 22–24

Safe Streets Act (1968), 103,
177, 180
Scheiber, Harry, N., 41
School district servicing role,
211, 216–217

School finance cases, 136, 142, 144, 152

Sherman, Roger, 29, 34, 37, 39

Social services: Title XX to the Social Security Act, 110, 177, 204

Special district servicing role, 211, 212, 217

State aid, 14, 60, 76-78, 170-173
  benefitting jurisdictions, 60, 76-77, 171, 172
  extent of equalization, 172-173
  forms of, 77, 172
  program focus, 171

State-centered theories of union, 21, 24-26, 47-48, 50

State expenditures, 73-74, 159-160, 167

State legislative reapportionment, 136-137, 142

State legislative reauthorization of federal grants funds, 142-143

State/local tax efforts, 163-165, 167, 170

State/local tax and expenditure curbs, 162, 163

State/local tax systems, regressivity of, 165-166, 167

State mandates, 65

State revenues, 58-59, 74-75, 161-162, 167

State role, 14-15, 52, 53, 56, 63-65, 86-88, 90, 136, 140-143, 144, 153, 192, 195-197, 207, 208-211, 212, 213-215, 218-219, 257

Substantive due process, 56

Taney, Roger, 50

Tenth amendment, 145, 146, 147, 148, 196

Town/township servicing role, 211, 212, 216

Transfers of functions, 203, 206-212

Varying state-local servicing systems, 213-215
  federal recognition of, 218-219, 252

Warren, Earl, 135-139, 140, 141, 143, 147, 151, 152

Wright, Deil, 20, 206